# Advanced Driving

## HOW TO FURTHER SKILL AND ENJOYMENT IN MOTORING

**John Lyon**

**Haynes Publishing**

# Contents

# Advanced Driving

First published in February 2012

British Library Cataloguing in Publication Data
A catalogue record for this book is available from the British Library

ISBN 978 0 85733 221 9

Published by Haynes Publishing, Sparkford, Yeovil, Somerset BA22 7JJ, UK
Tel: 01963 442030 Fax: 01963 440001
Int. tel: +44 1963 442030 Int. fax: +44 1963 440001
E-mail: sales@haynes.co.uk
Website: www.haynes.co.uk

Haynes North America Inc.
861 Lawrence Drive, Newbury Park,
California 91320, USA

Design by Donald Sommerville
Diagrams by Dominic Stickland

Printed and bound in the USA by Odcombe Press LP, 1299 Bridgestone Parkway, La Vergne, TN 37086

**Author's acknowledgements**
I wish to give thanks to Jacqueline Culver and Mark Hughes, without whom publication would not have happened, and to Porsche for the generous loan of a Cayman S for photography.

**Photograph credits**
All photographs featuring Porsche Cayman S and associated road scenes by John Colley. Library sources are The Brockbank Partnership at russellbrockbank.co.uk (page 15), Magic Car Pics (pages 55 and 116) and iStock (pages 19, 20 top, 24, 59, 89, 171, 194-9, 205-6, 208-10, 215-7 and 219). All other photographs from author's collection.

# Introduction
## 'How to further enjoyment and skill in motoring'

I can think of no greater motivation for writing *Advanced Driving* than to quote the above objective of the High Performance Course (HPC), with which I have been involved for most of my life.

I give my thanks to the late Tom Wisdom (journalist, racing and rally driver) whose enthusiasm and inspiration encouraged the British School of Motoring (BSM) to begin HPC all those years ago in 1962. HPC gave our clientele the opportunity to acquire 'safe driving for life'.

I make no apology for the occasional repetition of the important principles in order to pass on the skills of advanced driving to you, and I hope you find that some of the statements are thought-provoking and provide you with the inspiration to drive with skill and responsibility as an advanced motorist.

To be a co-driver with the HPC is undoubtedly a most enviable job, which includes the privilege of allowing me to take the wheel of some of the finest performance cars ever built. They range from the Jaguar lightweight E-type to the McLaren F1.

I have driven and, have been driven along Europe's finest roads, from the famous Nürburgring Nordschleife and Spa, to the Alps in Italy and Switzerland. My greatest joy of all has been meeting the people involved with the Gold Driving Club, who have become lifelong friends. I would be happy to hand over the keys to any one of these highly skilled advanced motorists, who inspire me to carry on my life's work for as long as I can. My gratitude is extended to each and everyone involved with HPC.

I hope you enjoy reading this book and I would be delighted to meet you, to try to contribute towards furthering your enjoyment and skill in motoring.

*John Lyon* ADI (fleet)

*Earlier days. Proudly wearing my HPC (High Performance Course) badge with my treasured Miller Minor, a tuned Morris Minor developed by David Miller of Downton Engineering. When tested by* Motor *magazine, the car achieved 0–60mph in 8.3 seconds and a top speed of 120mph!*

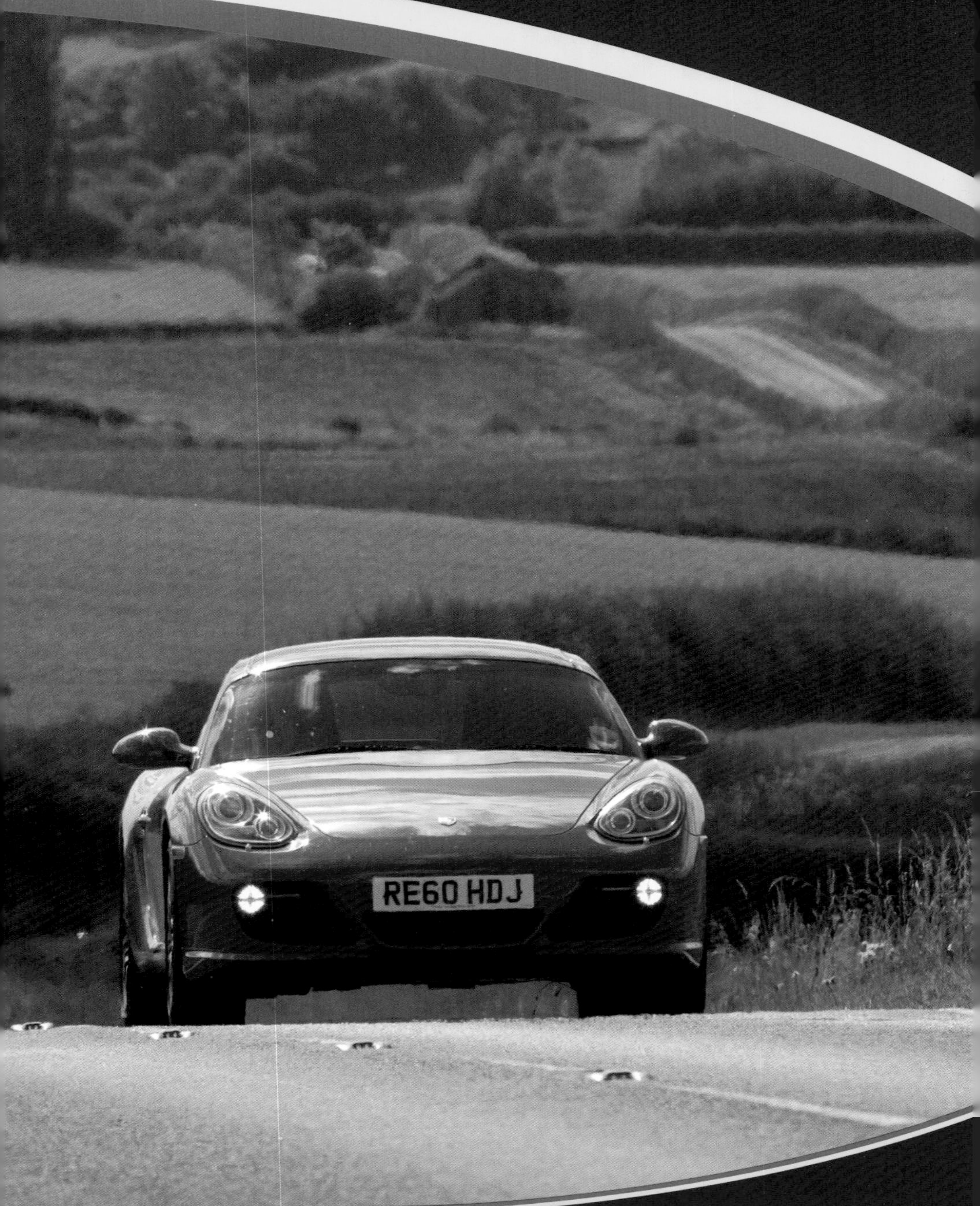
RE60 HDJ

# 1 The background

*The joy of driving – here in a Porsche Cayman S.*

**K**nowledge is the key to advanced driving, and I am sure this book will help you to find that knowledge. But you must also appreciate that knowledge is only a foundation and is no substitute for the right kind of driving experience. I hope you will forgive me if I express my more personal views about driving in order to highlight the facts with anecdotes based upon my own experience. And always remember that, whatever I say, you alone are responsible for your own driving behaviour when you take the wheel.

On-road tuition is essential if you are to become an advanced driver, and I hope that by reading this book you will be inspired to take practical coaching from a carefully chosen master of roadcraft. All paid driving instructors have to be approved by the Driving Standards Agency (DSA). Instructors are graded, with grade six being the highest standard. In my view, to give advice after the basic driving test, a driving coach should preferably be on the Fleet register run by the DSA. They should also have police advanced instructor training, to have acquired the skill and discipline required to coach and drive at their very high standard.

*Early days for the British School of Motoring's High Performance Course – on the skidpan at Brands Hatch with a Sunbeam Alpine.*

## Driver types

The Transport Research Laboratory (TRL) has conducted research to analyse driver attitude. They characterise drivers into four types:

- **Disassociated passive** This type of driver disassociates their mind from the activity of driving, for instance by chatting to passengers, using their mobile phone, or simply lounging in the car with an arm on the door, cruising along then being surprised by the occasional hazard and braking unnecessarily to avoid it. This driver is reluctant to pass and is often overtaken.

- **Disassociated active** Consistently distracted but driving excessively fast, this driver complains about everyone else on the road, cursing, swearing and blaming others when the cause is their own bad driving and lack of concentration. Overtaking is thoughtless.

- **Associated active** This driver generally has a relaxed concentration, blending their driving with the pace of the traffic. They keep to the spirit of the law and the principles of the *Highway Code* with occasional lapses. They are receptive to advice and can be coached to become advanced drivers.

- **Active and safe** Driving is measured, thoughtful and controlled with a sense of speed and pace, with the car always in the correct position, speed and gear. This type of driver displays the advanced skills that will be explained in the following chapters.

To these four types I would add one of my own: fast and dangerous.

This driver displays a dangerous attitude, driving with reckless abandon. Problems are invariably solved by violent handling and braking, and their driving is an accident waiting to happen.

Many such drivers are young men: evidence shows that one-fifth of death and serious injury on the road is caused by males between 17 and 25 years of age, particularly in their first year of driving.

An electronic 'spy in the cab' is not the answer to this problem in the long term, as it will not change a driver's attitude or teach them the appropriate skills.

There is no substitute for realistic training from an ex-police driving instructor, imposed with discipline. Both parents should sit in the back and learn as well, as that may be the root cause of the problem. Parents should always drive by example when they have impressionable young minds on board.

The advice contained in this book is built on my experience as a co-driver with the High Performance Course (HPC). BSM founded the Institute of Advanced Motorists (IAM) in 1956, followed by HPC in 1962, based on highly respected police driving techniques.

## Police driving

Better men than me formed this technique over many years and, although cars and motoring have changed profoundly in recent years, perhaps to the detriment of driver skills, 'Experientia docet' (experience teaches) is still the motto of the Metropolitan Police Driving School at Hendon. Their driving technique is just as appropriate and relevant today as it always has been.

In 1934 the police accident mileage rate was one accident for every 8,000 miles, which resulted in considerable adverse press comment. In response, the Police Driving School was formed at Hendon, along with other schools throughout the UK. In 1936, an advanced course of driving for the Flying Squad, Q-cars (unmarked patrol cars) and traffic patrol officers was introduced. Early in 1937 the Home Office appointed, as civilian advisor for the training of police drivers, one of the most famous racing drivers of the day, the Earl of Cottenham. His aim was to bring the technique of advanced driving to a new standard of perfection by personally training six specially selected instructors at each driving school to pass on his teaching.

Lord Cottenham's advice can best be judged by results. By 1938, police road traffic accidents had been reduced to one every 27,000 miles. His Lordship's advanced driving technique was the foundation of the High Performance Course in 1962.

All HPC co-drivers, myself included, were

# VOICE OF EXPERIENCE

## My Austin Seven Special

As a lad I built my own Austin Seven Special, with ash-framed aluminium body by Cambridge Engineering of Kew Green. Being so light it was quite quick, a real sports car and great fun to drive with a close-ratio crash gearbox and a 750 formula racing engine.

I passed my driving test in it on my 17th birthday! I didn't have a provisional licence for the lady examiner to complete the pink slip. 'Have you got five shillings?' she asked. 'Yes,' I said. 'Good, well go down the post office and get one. I've filled in the slip now and I can't cancel it!' I got my licence and my slip. I drove home happy in heart! I loved that car. It had a short chassis of 1931 vintage, Bowden front suspension, and Bowdenex cable brakes that I had to adjust once a week to prevent them pulling to one side, so I didn't use them at all if I could avoid it. Because the car was so light, it slowed rapidly by lifting off the accelerator.

I was young and stupid in those days and full of ideas of motorsport, although I had virtually no money (nothing's changed) and I could run it all week on five shillings (25p today). I had only an aeroscreen, with a tonneau cover for security in town and to prevent water ingress when parked; the heater was the engine! Then I acquired a girlfriend and, when winter came, she insisted I fitted a hood, windscreen and wipers – or sell the car. The hood had no doors and the side screens had a tiny zip allowing me to give only a virtually useless little hand signal. Being of 1931 vintage, it

was not required to have trafficators. With a six-volt battery, the more electrics it had, the more it was likely to run down the battery. It was the original 'Keep It Simple Stupid' car.

With no indicators, I would just give an arm signal, and blend and fit with London traffic; place the car, slowing down only when in position to turn. Experienced London drivers didn't mind at all, but you had to be decisive and signal early and clearly, if necessary. It required great skill to drive and, like Graham Hill and Willie Green who both drove Austin Sevens at that time, it taught me how to drive well, with virtually no brakes and poor vision out in the wet. It is not an experience I would recommend to anybody today and would be quite dangerous in the wrong hands.

I now own the successor to the Austin Seven, my Super Seven HPC, which is a light, simple sports car with fantastic performance for overtaking and fitting in with traffic. The brilliance of Herbert Austin was recognised by a genius, Colin Chapman, in his first Austin Seven Racing Special and he developed it into a Lotus Six, predecessor to the Lotus Seven. The car is so tactile and nimble, and being so light it has fantastic stopping power. Its ability to swerve provides primary safety, giving the ability to avoid the accident in the first place. Secondary safety is a full harness seat belt and roll-over bar. However, if I thought I was going to have an accident, I wouldn't get in the car in the first place (some people drive as though they are looking for one).

*Very early days – this is me on track in a Lotus Six, forerunner of the Lotus Seven and all later descendants built by Caterham Cars.*

selected and given three months of training by John Miles MBE, who had been an advanced instructor at Hendon. I felt I had to leave HPC in 1965 when the Government imposed 'temporary' national speed limits on us. I became a motor racing instructor with the Jim Russell school at Snetterton in Norfolk. In 1969 I returned to London, where I was selected to be a civilian instructor at Hendon. I met one of the founder members of the Metropolitan Police Driving School, Inspector O.V. 'Tommy' Thomas BEM, who put me through the instructors' course. Later, notwithstanding

that the 'temporary' national speed limit had apparently become permanent, I returned to HPC to manage the course for BSM and took it over to run as my own business from 1986 until the present day.

'Hendon-trained' is a standard of driving respected throughout the world. It is the standard met by members of the Gold Driving Club, and is achieved through many years of hard work and occasional coaching, rather than intensive training over a short period.

## Maintaining skills

When carrying out a familiar, everyday task such as driving, many people disassociate their minds from it and engage a kind of autopilot. This unthinking method of doing

**13**

something is not, in the light of more experience, the best way. It is for this reason that occasional coaching, throughout your motoring life, is essential to improve and develop your driving. As with all elements of education, those who have not been fortunate to receive it will often not appreciate its value. I hope that after reading this book you will understand the value of advanced driving.

## No easy answers

At this stage I should give warning that the technique advised in *Advanced Driving* is not the easy, thoughtless way. It becomes natural only after persistent coaching, experience and hard work. The key to success is

*Above left: Giving a demonstration drive in a 3-litre V6-engined Ford Capri – note my light touch on the steering wheel with hands at quarter to three. Left: The High Performance Course used some spectacular machinery – here I am at the wheel of a Ferrari Daytona.*

*Even the inimitable Brockbank, the best motoring cartoonist ever, was inspired by the British School of Motoring's High Performance Course. The caption stated: "My client reeks of pepper and is obsessed with what he calls 'getaway'."*

knowledge of all the elements applied with deep thought over many years. Remember that highway law alone in the UK requires you to know and obey three and a half thousand statutes!

You never finish learning, continually analysing your technique and asking the question, 'why?' The High Performance Course is the university of realistic driver education. However the course is only the beginning. There is no substitute for experience that will confirm and consolidate your skills as time goes by.

It is my profound wish that after reading this book, and taking advanced coaching, you will establish a foundation of technique that will assist you and help you to achieve 'safe driving for life'.

# 2 Preparing to drive

*Specialist tuition at Millbrook, the proving ground in Bedfordshire – this is me with daughter Antonia.*

**A**lways start at the beginning, by getting to know your car. If it is new to you, investigate the car and its specifications, so that you know what to expect before you drive.

Start with the engine, its valve and cylinder layout, cubic capacity, bore and stroke ratio, fuel metering, the power and torque outputs, and at what engine speeds they are delivered.

Look up the kerb weight of the car and its power-to-weight ratio, as well as the distribution of weight, front to rear. This will give you an idea of what acceleration to expect and the influence of weight balance upon handling. Not forgetting to note the maximum load permitted and towing weights allowed.

Look at the gear ratios and in particular the maximum speed in each gear. Don't allow yourself to be caught out by having to change gear alongside a vehicle when passing. Know the likely acceleration when laden and unladen between 40 to 60mph and 50 to 70mph when overtaking.

Is the car front-, rear- or four-wheel drive, and how will this affect acceleration and cornering?

What is the suspension design, and what influence will it have upon handling? What is the speed rating and condition of the tyres?

Consider also the brakes and steering specification, and look up the turning circle to judge the car's manoeuvrability.

Conclude with a subjective personal opinion of the overall character of the car.

## Essential documents

Next, you need to ensure your documents are up to date – tax, MOT and insurance. If you are travelling in Europe, obtain your free European Health Insurance Card (EHIC), which is valid for five years (www.ehic.org.uk). Also consider getting a Sanef 'liber-t' *péage* transponder (www.saneftolling.co.uk) to simplify paying French motorway tolls. Take your registration document and breakdown cover, all kept with your passport secure and on your person. Before you leave, look at the car's mileage and service schedule, often done nowadays by scrolling a menu on the instrument panel, to ensure a service does not become due while you are away.

Advanced driving is all about preparing yourself and your car. On most journeys, the driver already knows the road intimately and is aware of which route to take. However, if heading somewhere unfamiliar, prepare for the drive with forethought and planning.

## Car checks

Preparation for a long drive should be thorough. Even if the car is kept secure in a garage, fluids can leak away, so check them before leaving. The check is similar to a pilot doing a pre-flight and should include the following:

- Cooling fluid is levelled when cold. Radiator and hoses need to be examined for leaks and deterioration.
- On level ground, dip the oil to check it is on the high mark. Clear fresh oil, that is, not black. Rub the oil between your fingers to check the viscosity and condition.
- Inspect alternator belts for fraying and tension. Take a spare belt.
- Remove the tops of the brake and clutch reservoirs and check levels, allowing for a little expansion.
- Check the tyre pressures with an accurate gauge. Set them for load and speed, including the spare. Each tyre should be inspected to check it meets legal requirements. Run your hands around the tyres, not forgetting the insides, to check for cuts and bulges. My advice is not to run any tyre on less than 3mm anywhere across the tread. The four contact patches, each one the size of the palm of your hand, are your only contact with the road – yet only 1 in 25 drivers set all four tyres to the recommended pressures.

Above & right: *Two of the regular checks you need to make to your car – oil level and tyre pressure.*

⊖ A first aid kit and fire extinguisher should be carried. Check the expiry date on both. Remove and tilt the extinguisher to feel if it is full. Be sure that it is the correct specification.

⊖ Check the jack for serviceability and know how to use it. Undo wheel nuts and re-tension them to ensure they are not too tight, or too loose, with an upward pull on the wheel brace. Tighten the wheel nuts directly opposite each other in turn. Take a tube extension if you struggle to release them.

⊖ Inspect the tool kit to see that there is no tool missing from its slot. In addition, consider any useful tool for an emergency, including mole grips, a utility knife, and a length of insulated wire with a light bulb and crocodile clip to

Above: *A warning triangle (and high-visibility vest) is essential in case of emergency.* Right: *Checking windscreen wiper blades.*

track electrical circuits. I carry a throttle and clutch cable in my Caterham Seven, along with fuses, tie-wraps, insulating tape and rubber gloves. Consider packing a plastic sheet to lie on when working under the car.

- Carry a warning triangle for emergencies and a high-visibility vest to ensure you can be seen if you have to stop by the side of the road.
- Be sure your breakdown membership is up to date and the phone number is entered into your mobile phone.
- Check that all lights are working, including side, number plate, head, dip, main beam and brake lights, and that indicators are flashing at the correct speed.

- Carry spare bulbs, then if one goes out, you can replace it and will not be committing a mobile offence if stopped by a traffic officer, which could save you the indignity of a breathalyser check.
- Test the wipers (lift them off the screen first) and inspect the blades (you will find they have approximately the same life as a set of tyres).
- Check and if necessary top up the

washer bottle with anti-freeze liquid, and ensure the washers are free from blockage.

↻ Check the battery condition and top it up, if necessary, with distilled water just covering the plates.

↻ Tap the horn in the car park to make sure it is working.

↻ Inspect seat belts for fraying and clasps for operation.

↻ Load the car. Heavy luggage should be stowed low down and made secure. All loose items must be strapped down. Loose carpets and mats are potentially lethal if they become trapped under the pedals, and they work towards the pedals once they get loose.

↻ Top up the fuel tank and spare petrol can.

↻ Finally, a wash, leather and vacuum will complete your check.

## Interior checks

Always spend a short time checking the interior of an unfamiliar car. You should be able to locate all the controls without looking down and taking your eyes off of the road.

We have all seen the driver who moves straight off, then opens and shuts the door, adjusts seat and mirrors on the move, wipes the windscreen when they want to signal and tries the brakes for the first time on the approach to a pedestrian crossing. Don't be one of them.

Check the cockpit and controls with a consistent routine. The cockpit drill is simple. The routine is: doors, seat, seat belts, mirrors, handbrake, in neutral, start engine with clutch down.

Check gauges and warning lights, major and auxiliary controls, and their location. Carry out a static, and finally a running brake test.

Close the door properly on the second catch and listen to the way the passengers close theirs. Note that everyone is wearing seat belts. Their safety is your responsibility.

It will take 20 minutes to become part of the car. Only professional drivers settle down immediately and are able to handle a car on the limit of its ability straight away.

Modern cars have infinitely variable driving positions to suit all body shapes and sizes. For many years, British cars compromised the range of seat adjustments to give more passenger room in the back and to suit the rather shorter percentile size of the UK driver. German and American cars generally allow more room for the taller driver. Your comfort is so important that you should check carefully that a car suits you before you buy it. Good visibility is also vital; many supercars are woeful in this regard.

It is most important to feel part of the car, to have the best seat and driving position for comfort and accurate steering control. Do not tolerate any discomfort; it will nag you and cause fidgeting and bad habits. I have a Tillet competition seat with leather inset lining in my Super Seven HPC. I have set it mechanically for the ideal driving position

## VOICE OF EXPERIENCE

### Comfortable clothing

Comfortable clothing is important for driving. The famous long-distance aviator Sheila Scott took the BSM Grand Touring Course with me, and her advice was to have natural fibre cotton or woollen clothing that lets your body breathe. Clothing should be loose (no tie of course) and with light slip-on, non-slip shoes with heel protection and no welt to catch the side of the brake pedal. With the old-fashioned wooden steering wheel, I wear cycle racer's gloves with fingers missing for sensitivity. Polaroid sunglasses are essential in low winter sun. Take a reflective coat and a stout pair of boots in the winter, just in case your car 'fails to proceed'.

and is perfect for long hours at the wheel, as well as racing.

To give yourself the most efficient and comfortable driving position, first adjust the base of the seat for reach, then for height. Thighs should be in light contact with the base of the seat to provide the best stability for your body and feel of the car when cornering. You cannot drive 'by the seat of your pants' if you are sitting on the point of your backside, with knees flapping around, as many drivers do. Ask them why they sit like this, and they will reply: 'I have got to bottom the clutch.'

No, you do not have to do this, and if you do so on every gear change, it will stress and flex the diaphragm spring in the release mechanism. The clutch is only a 'make and break' between the engine and gearbox. To change gear you only have to clear the drive to free the gearbox, reconnecting it at the right time. Dab the clutch pedal over the point of clutch control. No more, no less.

It is good to be relaxed with the right ankle too. Crank your knee up with an acute bend and the ankle joint will lock, as when your hand bends back against the joint. If you sit too close, your foot may catch the side of the brake pedal. In an emergency, when a quick reaction is needed, it could be disastrous.

Next adjust the height of the seat, so that your eye line is through the centre of the windscreen. Don't sit with your head in the roof lining, or so low that you are looking through the steering wheel.

Now move the seat back, so that the rake is at the right angle for you. Then check the position of the head restraint, so that it is close to the back of the head and will support the centre of the head to prevent whiplash in the event of a rear-end collision. It is not a head rest!

Adjust the steering wheel to be reasonably low so that when placing your hands on the wheel at a quarter to three they are below the level of your heart, for comfortable driving over long distances. Make sure you can see the top of major instruments without dropping your head.

Adjust the distance of the wheel from your body by stretching both your arms forward so you are able to apply sufficient pressure with both hands at 12 o'clock on the wheel. With modern power steering, it is unnecessary to use great strength. Arms should be gently bent at a quarter to three, definitely not straight but relaxed, with a 120-degree bend to the elbow.

Many drivers who are tense and concerned about driving think they have better control and vision if they sit too close and too high at the wheel. It causes many bad habits, like crossing hands over the top of the steering wheel, or leading the driver to hold the gear lever or rest an arm on the window sill (an offence under construction and use regulation number 120).

Today, it is vital to consider the airbag. In the severe impact of a crash, the airbag will explode instantly into your chest at 180mph

## VOICE OF EXPERIENCE

### The value of a seat belt

While racing a saloon car in October 1972, I had a tyre burst when flat-out in the very fast old Russell bend at Snetterton. I careered into the bank at over 100mph, was launched 35ft into the air, turned over two and a half times, landed on top of the following car driven by Simon Kirby (who was unhurt) and slid upside-down on fire in the middle of the track.

I undid the harness while sliding along and I was out of the side window before it came to rest. It was hot in there! All I suffered was a stiff neck. I helped the marshals fight the fire. One said he felt sorry for the driver, not realising it was me! It was the last race of that season and nearly forever for me, if it were not for that seat belt. I have never understood why people are reluctant to wear one.

*The correct driving position – relaxed but alert.*

– potentially fatal if you are sitting too close to the wheel. If you have crossed your arms while steering, it will break them. (A surgeon once told me he had operated on someone who had 27 breaks in their arms caused by having them crossed while an airbag went off.) Any driver under five feet tall should consider disconnecting the airbag, if they are forced to sit too close to the wheel; a full harness may be better.

Next the seat belt is clicked on. A simple lap and diagonal is a legal requirement, unless there are exceptional circumstances. In a violent impact the belt will stretch. I prefer a full harness, with a lap strap tight to hold me down in the seat over bumps and slightly slack shoulder straps, particularly if the car has no airbags. You will soon get used to slipping in and out of a harness quickly.

While sitting correctly, adjust the mirrors. Look at the centre of the rear window in the rear-view mirror, place your fingers along the top of the mirror, thumb underneath (not on the glass), and adjust it as level as you can. A flick of the eyes without moving the head is usually enough to give a wide clear view, as long as you are not sitting too close to the wheel (if you follow someone who cannot do this, be warned, watch out!). Any movement in the mirror should be detected using peripheral vision, which again is not possible if you are too close and the mirror is too far to the side of your vision.

# VOICE OF EXPERIENCE

## Driving in France

I must say I particularly enjoy long-distance continental motoring, not on motorways but across country, along the great French D-roads. What a true motoring country! Vast distances, beautiful little villages, cafés for lunch and wonderful hotels, with fine food and wine (in the evening). From Calais to Monte Carlo and from Nantes to Mulhouse, every trip has provided me with extraordinary memories.

For the two door mirrors, you should be able to see both sides of the car and far back down the road. A double-angle (Dutch mirror) helps to see into a blind spot. A slight head turn to use peripheral vision to check the blind spot (this glance is termed the life-saver) is always vital when changing lanes.

Next, make sure the handbrake is on and the gearbox is in neutral, depress the clutch for extra safety and to take some load off the starter motor (ensure headlights are off also) and start the engine.

Immediately check that the ignition warning light is out, the oil pressure gauge is reading correctly and the ammeter, if fitted, settles down to a charge, after an initial loss.

Make sure there is sufficient fuel for your journey, noting how many miles are left before refuelling is needed. If you are still unfamiliar with the controls, investigate them all, starting from left to right. Practise operating them, without looking down.

When you have completed the interior checks, do a static brake test with the engine running before moving off. Press the brake lightly, then release the handbrake and note if the brake failure warning light goes out. Check for lost movement in the brake pedal; any more than one inch of free play before the brakes take up and you should be suspicious. Now press really hard and if the pedal feels spongy, not firm and solid, there may be air or water in the system. (If there is a fault with the seals in the slave or master cylinder, the pedal will sink slowly, perhaps to the floor.)

Only now consider moving off with precautionary all-round awareness and observation, both sides, front and rear.

It is true to say that I can tell an advanced motorist before the driver moves off. I will then feel at ease within the first 50 yards – otherwise I have no wish to be a passenger.

To test the brakes properly before arriving at any hazard, particularly if the car is unfamiliar, carry out a running brake test. To do so, the road must be perfectly clear both front and rear. At 30mph in top gear, place the ball of your foot squarely on the pedal, quickly take up any free movement and make rubbing contact with the pads on the discs. Initial pressure should be moderate to transfer weight progressively to the front of the car, then mash the pedal to the floor. See how the car reacts and responds in a simulated emergency. There should not be any effect on the steering or pull to the left or right.

ABS, if fitted, will kick in and keep the car stable. If you have not felt ABS before, do not think something is wrong if the brakes pulsate and make a corresponding noise. That's normal and correct. The car should pull up rapidly without drama, skidding or slewing about.

In a car without ABS, none of the wheels should lock up before the others do, but if the brake limiter to the rear brakes is not working as it should the back wheels will lock up first and the car will slew and skid down a camber. Always carry out this brake test in a straight line on a level and clean road.

Remember the limit of stopping at moderate speeds is not the brake performance, but tyre grip to the surface. Estimate that value at all times while you drive. Many do not. I am convinced that there would be less tailgating if drivers carried out running brake tests on varying surfaces when it is safe to do so.

According to the *Highway Code*, to assess the distance required to stop on a good dry firm surface, take your speed, multiply it by the first digit and divide it by two, and the answer is your braking distance in feet. In addition, thinking distance is one foot per mph. For example at 70mph, multiply by 7, then divide by 2 which equals 245ft, plus 70ft thinking distance, equals a total of 315ft to stop (96 metres).

For the actual figures for your car, check the relevant *Autocar* road test. Thinking distances depend on you and your ability to concentrate. But ultimately, how are you to know how the tyres will stop you in an emergency unless you try a running brake test?

These simple checks complete the preparation for a day's drive.

## Route planning

If you have a long journey to complete, try preparing the car and planning the route the evening before. Tuck the family into the car very early in the morning, so they go back to sleep, then get a good start, covering perhaps 200 miles on the motorway. Then stop for breakfast whilst everyone else is fighting to get to work. The rest of the journey can be an enjoyable and leisurely drive across country, on non-primary A- and B-roads, to enjoy the countryside with

# VOICE OF EXPERIENCE

## A tale about packing a car

One of the many HPC trips abroad which remains vivid in my memory is a run to the Ollon-Villars hillclimb in Switzerland for ice and snow driving practice during the winter of 1972/3.

HPC had two Ford Escort RS1600s and a couple of Mexicos. For the drive home I was in a Mexico with a roof rack of luggage packed on top. It felt awful, top heavy and sluggish, so I took everything out of the car and packed it again tightly inside. Heavy items went down in the footwells to keep the centre of gravity as low as possible and I strapped and secured all the loose items. I had nothing left to put on the roof rack, so I took it off. The difference was amazing. Cornering was more stable, I could keep up with the RS1600s quite easily, and I returned 25 per cent better fuel consumption than the other Mexico on the drive home.

*Enjoying myself with a Ford Escort RS1600 on a closed road at Ollon-Villars in Switzerland.*

frequent stops. With the wise use of maps, a journey need never be boring. There is always something interesting worth looking for.

Use 1:625,000 Ordnance Survey travel maps for long distance, then the 1:50,000 Landranger for detailed planning. Never read a map on the move. Instead write a strip route with place names, road numbers, distances and approximate travel times between towns; then tape it to the dash to read as you go. The average speed across country is 43mph, according to the Department of Transport, and 62mph on the motorways, if you are fortunate not to meet a jam. With an early start, that is less likely to occur.

Satellite navigation will take you either the shortest or quickest route unless you program, as you wish, for each section (not, of course, on the move: you must be stationary with the engine switched off to use sat-nav or a mobile phone).

Place the sat-nav windscreen holder so that

it does not block your view of the road. To make driving safer, use the safety preferences in the menu.

A sat-nav is only electronic assistance. Do not slavishly follow your sat-nav instructions. Be sensible and conform to the law and rules of the road.

To help you to plan your journey before you start:

- ◎ Confirm your route using www. transportdirect.info
- ◎ Check traffic conditions using www. highways.gov.uk/trafficinfo (or ring 08700 660115).
- ◎ Look at the weather forecast at www. metoffice.gov.uk

Try to relax a little when you first take the wheel. Getting into the right attitude is so important before you start to drive. On a long drive, aim to take a break every two hours – three or four hours if you are a very experienced driver. Do guard against fatigue. Stop for coffee and stretch your legs with a short stroll.

As a keen driver, driving for pleasure, you may not wish to use motorways or primary routes. Take the non-primary A- or B-roads marked on OS maps in red or yellow. As his lordship the Earl of Cottenham stated all those years ago, 'any competent driver should be able to average 50 miles to the hour'. Remember that was with a ten horsepower Hillman with mechanical Bendix brakes that tended to grab, lock up and pull violently to one side and then the other. He used to call out 'shimmy!' to a driver who did not recognise the motoring equivalent to the motorcyclist's uncontrollable steering 'tank slapper'. How motoring has changed.

In the isolated comfort of an air-conditioned modern car, protected by crumple zones, airbags and the electronic assistance of anti-lock brakes (ABS) and stability control (ESC), we may think ourselves invincible, flashing across highways at average speeds unimaginable only 60 years ago. It comes as a shock to experience a sudden unexpected stop, when you may find there is not enough distance left to be able to do so safely.

Perhaps it would good for us all to experience a vintage car, out in the open air, with mechanical brakes and a crash gearbox. The only modern equivalent, although far faster, more efficient and less challenging, is my own Super Seven HPC – named after the course I run. The Seven has over 450bhp per ton, providing effortless acceleration for easy overtaking. If you crash, secondary safety is a full harness and roll-over bar, whereas primary safety – the safest course of all – is simply to avoid the accident in the first place.

## And, finally, the driver

There are three situations in your driving when you are most vulnerable to a potential situation that can lead to an accident or, at least, a near miss:

- ◎ When you are ill, unwell or not fit to drive; and many do drive.
- ◎ When you are late for an appointment and under stress.
- ◎ When you are lost and temporarily cannot find your way.

It is when you are under stress that you need to be able to draw upon your knowledge, self-discipline and skill to apply the Driving Plan punctiliously and with decisive deliberation. Without roadcraft training it will be extremely difficult to perform the task of safe and advanced motoring. Pure experience is not sufficient.

On one hand, satellite navigation systems, with global positioning, have given us the precise ability to know our exact position and intended destination, but, on the other hand, skills of map reading, forward planning and long-range anticipation are consigned to the back seat. Again the lazy will take the easy way and avoid the challenge. You don't even have to know your route in advance, or your destination apart from the postcode. If using the phone or sat-nav, park safely and switch the engine off!

# 3 Handling skills

*A hallmark of good control: hands in a 'balanced' position with a light touch.*

**M**any motoring enthusiasts believe that the physical handling of a car is the most important driving skill. This is not surprising, considering the media interest in magazines, the internet and television about cars and motorsport. It takes long experience to realise that handling represents only a small part of the skill required to drive well.

Most of the keen drivers you will meet can impress you with their knowledge of the car they drive and their enthusiasm is to be admired. It is perhaps disappointing to realise that alongside this there is usually very little knowledge of advanced driving. They seem to consider it to be beneath them to talk of such, as though such techniques are known to everyone. To sit as a passenger with one of these drivers can be a frightening and shocking experience. Ignorance is bliss in many cases, and any advice will be spurned.

Even experienced drivers seem to think that if there is an incident on the public road, the cause of it is the other driver, never themselves.

## Self-discipline

Safe and efficient mastery in advanced driving is created by skill, discipline and hard work, some training and many years of experience of the right kind. In very rare cases you may come across a 'hand' – someone who has the flair to handle a car with supreme confidence, although this may be misplaced through lack of experience, creating an element of potential danger that may not be understood by the driver.

To be unselfish and well-mannered is so important in life, never more so than in advanced driving. One's attitude towards the safety of others is paramount. With many years of practice, I have found that the right mental approach to safe and efficient driving is created by discipline of the kind that comes from within your own enthusiasm, analysing and criticising every thought process.

Self-discipline provides the determination to concentrate sufficiently well to drive a car with complete mastery. Many can only concentrate for a short period, but all drivers can improve their ability by knowing the difference between right and wrong, good and bad, and safe and unsafe driving.

Expert roadcraft advice is a great help, as two brains are better than one. Listen to your mentor, watch, read and study. When you drive, pick out the good drivers. Watch them and learn, and you will see that the expert is swift and sure, safe and sound – a driver who proves by example that they are advanced, using their experience to help assist the flow of traffic through their following distance and sense of speed.

Ask any first-class athlete and they will tell you that skill and discipline are required to win and be the very best, alongside enthusiasm, dedication, concentration, and years of practice.

When you sit as a passenger beside a driver for the first time, it is reassuring to see them show evidence of responsibility towards yourself and others, by driving at a safe speed for comfort. To witness flair in handling the car with a sympathetic, smooth and flowing style, is what some may refer to as 'polish', the stock in trade of the professional. Someone who has the rare gift to be able to handle a car with supreme control, co-ordination and finesse. You can sense the intangible margin of safety that this driver possesses.

Concentration is vital 100% of the time, to the complete exclusion of anything irrelevant. Unconscious competence becomes so after years of thoughtful intelligence and persistent hard work. Success is achieved with speed sense, forward planning and observation of detail, to anticipate and foresee what you may reasonably expect to occur. To anticipate the unreasonable is more difficult, and it may seem uncanny to the inexperienced passenger when the advanced driver does so.

## ACCELERATION SENSE
### Without unnecessary braking

A diagrammatic illustration of acceleration sense in relation to vision. If you change gear unnecessarily ten times in one mile, that equals 100,000 gear changes in a year's motoring of 10,000 miles! In this one straight, early changing, with light acceleration and unnecessary braking, may also lead to a lack of concentration, forward planning and poor judgement of speed and distance. Instead accelerate for one-third of the distance, then decelerate for the remaining two-thirds, staying in one gear throughout.

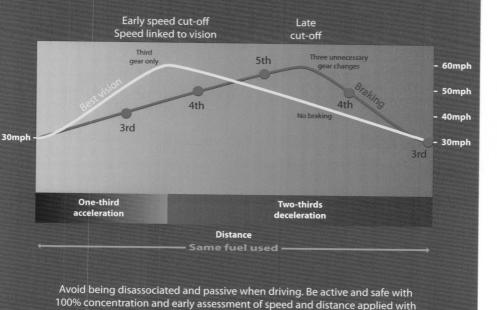

Avoid being disassociated and passive when driving. Be active and safe with 100% concentration and early assessment of speed and distance applied with deceleration and gearbox sense. Take one gear for one hazard.

Health and fitness is required for long hours at the wheel. The unfit tire easily and must take frequent stops to avoid fatigue. A considerable rest before a long drive is necessary to prevent potentially fatal drowsiness. Stop at the next service area for a coffee break if you sense tiredness. Do not press on regardless.

Perfect eyesight is the greatest physical asset for any driver, giving the ability to transmit information to the brain at a distance, as soon as it appears. If eyesight needs to be corrected by spectacles, these present an extra layer of glass in front of the eyes and they must be kept immaculately clean and polished. Normal hearing, undamaged by constant noise, is necessary to be able to sense approaching traffic at junctions with a limited view, to be aware of mechanical noise from the car in order to

*Above: The correct steering position –*
*hands relaxed at quarter to three to avoid*
*the airbag and be better able to react in the*
*event of an emergency.*

sense problems instantly, and for mechanical sympathy.

However, there is no point seeing and hearing early, if the driver is incapable of assessing the value of what is seen or heard. The best drivers are the most intelligent, able to anticipate to an uncanny degree. They are proactive, not reactive.

A master of roadcraft very rarely needs to make a quick physical reaction. Instead, he or she makes all driving, at whatever speed, look so easy. There is a blend and flow to all control movements because they are made so early and in total sympathy to the mechanical elements of the car and to its anticipated movement along the road as a whole mass on its springs. The influence of the weight of the car in relation to its speed becomes an instinctive sense.

## Acceleration sense

Acceleration sense is the ability to vary the speed of the car according to existing road and traffic conditions without braking. This sense is a skill found only in really good drivers, but it is latent in many. It can only be developed with improved judgement of speed and distance and considerable practice. One of the many differences between the average driver and the advanced driver is that for a given average speed and pace, the advanced driver will brake far less, if at all.

Acceleration sense is an essential skill for

*Steering technique 1. Left hand high in preparation for steering left.*

the advanced driver. The throttle works both ways. Lifting off the power early is preferable to unnecessary application of the brakes. An exception is when you deliberately wish to warn a following driver of impending danger ahead. Acceleration sense improves your forward planning and long-range anticipation coupled with gearbox sense, particularly when driving actively along twisting country B-roads – a great joy for any motoring enthusiast. Forward planning is essential with decisive, systematic method in the application of the driving plan; each feature, applied without hesitation and with perfect timing for the safety of others, as well as yourself. Have a defensive attitude of mind and then you will

avoid moments of sudden reaction.

Recognising the speed of all vehicles in the road scene, the expert takes account of any variation of their speed and position that may occur because of changing conditions that develop well ahead. Keeping a good safe following distance by deceleration, acceleration or maintaining a constant speed, the advanced driver will adjust road speed by skilful acceleration sense and will therefore avoid all unnecessary braking.

Steering is only part of the control of direction as there is always slight slip taking place between a tyre and the road surface when cornering and changing direction. Both acceleration and braking will also vary yaw (swerving) and pitch (tip) or roll (tilt) of the car to influence the behaviour of the suspension, tyre performance and grip.

## Steering technique

Most drivers are not taught the reason why you should avoid crossing your arms whenever possible, with the exception of reversing or manoeuvring in a confined space, or unexpected skidding.

For driving along the straight a light touch is sufficient with hands settled in the most effective position, at a quarter to three, particularly with a small-diameter steering wheel and the power steering systems fitted today. It is a position from which to react if an emergency occurs. Hands at ten to two is a little high and more appropriate with heavy unassisted steering in older cars.

In road cars with a relatively low-geared steering ratio it is best, for safety, to pass the wheel alternately, making large sweeps

*Steering technique 2. Change grip at the lower part of the wheel.*

before changing grip. Many drivers disagree, so let me try to explain the reasons why.

The objective is to have the hands on the wheel at a quarter to three, in the middle of the danger zone or hazardous area, to have something in reserve to deal with an emergency.

Obviously the wheel is a 360-degree circle. The two hands use 180 degrees before changing grip to use the full circle efficiently. To prepare to steer to the right, lift the right hand, to let you pull downwards, sweeping smoothly to change grip at 180 degrees, ending up with hands at a quarter to three. Pause, then recover the wheel with the same

*Steering technique 3. Hands back at quarter to three while going through a corner.*

preparation and sequence of movement.

On approach to a hazard, you may decide to go slightly past 12 o'clock and take a large sweep in advance. And do the same, on recovery, with the opposite hand at the exit of the turn, to take the steering back under control. Hand high in advance, corresponding to the turn, pause at quarter to three, then you can change the signal over on roundabouts, make minor course adjustments, without displacing the hands and react more efficiently, if you need to, safely.

With a steering ratio of two turns from lock to lock, the hands are only displaced twice in preparation and twice on recovery,

making the technique the most efficient, measured and controlled. This works even for handling on the limit, when powersliding and drifting powerful rear-wheel drive high-performance cars for demonstration, off the road.

For me the advantage was emphasised when I became a member of the Silver Arrows display team at Mercedes-Benz World at Brooklands and I could avoid crossing my arms except in advance, with a 225-degree sweep, before a 180-degree change of grip. Powersliding is not skidding. You mean it to happen and it is performed in perfect control. You are thinking in advance, in anticipation, and you know the steering requirements. You prepare your hand high first, corresponding to the anticipated turn

# STEERING TECHNIQUE
## *Avoidance of crossing hands*

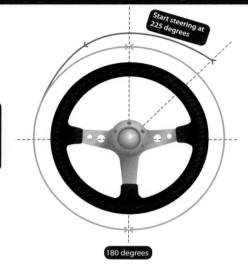

Start steering at 225 degrees

To be able to react or change line, the hand is best at 'a quarter to' in the middle of the hazard. This is a safe hand-grip if the airbag goes off.

To adjust the steering path or react, the hand is best at 'a quarter past' in the middle of the hazard.

180 degrees

And recovery

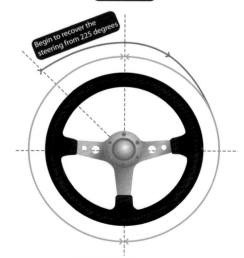

Begin to recover the steering from 225 degrees

Only two displacements of the hands for a sharp turn and two on recovery.

Measured, accurate, controlled and safe.

Change grip at 180 degrees

The sequence will be reversed for a sharp turn to the right.

of the wheel to correct the slide in advance. Proactive steering, not reactive: the mindset of an advanced driver.

With quick-steering competition racing and rally cars that have only one turn from one full lock to the other, using a fixed handhold up to 12 o'clock is quite correct, quick and efficient. To avoid crossing over in a hairpin, use the same technique of hand high first to prepare. Again the advantage is to be able to react efficiently, steer more accurately and have the flexibility to alter your steering path without having to displace your hands in the middle of the bend.

This flowing pull-push technique is not natural and it has to be taught. If your mentor does not explain to you why you should do it and, more importantly, does not give you sufficient practice, you will not continue with the technique. It takes only half an hour for a good instructor on an open area of tarmac to teach deportment at the wheel and this steering technique.

Many drivers are unable to use the full circumference of the wheel because they have not been taught to sit properly and so they sit too close to the wheel to use the bottom half. It is ineffective to cross hands using only small sectors of the wheel, awkwardly twisting to grip only one side. Poor deportment at the wheel leads to a nagging discomfort, with the driver fidgeting, keeping hands close together at the top of the steering wheel, or resting an arm on the window ledge (a traffic offence too infrequently corrected in my view).

## Changing gear

Many years ago it was appreciated that only a keen and knowledgeable minority of enthusiasts understood how a clutch and gearbox worked and could be bothered to change gear sympathetically. Enormous warranty claims had to be made, so much so that friction devices such as the clutch became considered 'consumables' and were not covered by warranties. The synchromesh

gearbox became universally accepted and new materials for clutch linings partly overcame the problem of lazy, thoughtless and ignorant bad driving. On old cars, synchromesh on second gear soon wore out.

Being mostly involved with town driving, the Metropolitan Police Force improved their maintenance costs by choosing mainly automatic transmissions for their police cars.

Disassociated drivers always preferred automatics. They could put the transmission into 'drive' and forget it. Without gearbox and acceleration sense around bends, down hills, or in give and take traffic, they just applied the brakes.

Today's automatic transmissions have been transformed with double-clutch semi-automatic systems and seven or eight speeds. Top gear may be so high as to be of no practical use, but it enables manufacturers to pass emission and noise regulations.

The double-clutch gearbox pre-selects the next ratio, changes up very fast and matches the engine speed precisely on the change down. On earlier gearboxes with a torque converter, the electronics do not do this and it is necessary to give a very light touch to the accelerator, a little after selecting the ratio manually at high road speed, otherwise stress will occur to the brake bands that change the ratios. In some old transmissions the friction in the gearbox was so violent that it would cause the oil in the box to boil at high road speeds, leading to failure.

On an automatic, the intermediate gear ratios can be held for control in the following situations:

- ↪ On the approach and through a series of bends or roundabouts, with acceleration sense allowing the fine control of speed, pitch and weight transfer, in order to vary grip between front and rear tyres.
- ↪ When descending hills, to help to control speed and to save the brakes going down an Alpine pass.
- ↪ To overtake a series of slow vehicles and

flow past effortlessly. You must know the maximum speed in each ratio to know which gear to select.

You should brake only once for each hazard. Keep both hands on the wheel while braking, then having acquired the correct road speed, select the correct and appropriate gear ratio for any of the three situations mentioned above.

For a single vehicle pass, with uninterrupted acceleration, kickdown can be used, but only in a straight line, particularly if the road surface is wet or slippery.

With an automatic transmission, guard against late braking, particularly if you occasionally drive a manual car. Automatic driving can make you lazy and a little careless when returning to manual.

One of the most admirable qualities of the advanced driver is the quality of car

*Gear-changing technique 1. 'Palm' the gear lever for first and second.*

sympathy. It is essential to have a basic knowledge of how a clutch and gearbox works – many do not. For gentle driving, set off with silky co-ordination, engaging the clutch at idle speed on level ground, certainly no more than twice idle speed to be sympathetic to the clutch.

The sequence many drivers use when changing gear is wrong. The tendency is to depress the clutch first, then make a wild grab at the lever, slashing through the synchromesh with no thought to how the engine speed falls or rises.

Changing up – the correct sequence is:
- ⊙ Hand on the gear lever, palm facing the direction of effort.

○ Cover the clutch.
○ Clutch down.
○ Move the gear lever with two
  movements to give the synchromesh
  cones a moment to assist you. The timing
  of these movements is in 'sync' with the
  engine speed falling.
○ When the engine has fallen to precisely
  the correct speed, let the clutch up to
  re-engage the transmission, with no
  perceptible jerk.
○ Replace the hand on the steering wheel
  (perhaps with the exception of between
  first and second gears), return the foot
  to the rest position and don't ride the
  clutch.
  Changing down – the correct sequence is:
○ Hand on the gear lever, palm facing the
  direction of effort.
○ Cover the clutch.

*Gear-changing technique 2. Fifth or sixth,*
*'palming' the lever for direction of effort.*

○ Clutch down.
○ Move the gear lever with two
  movements.
○ Raise the engine speed to precisely the
  correct engine speed for the road speed
  and gear ratio to be selected. Very few
  drivers do so!
○ When the engine speed is precisely
  correct, re-engage the transmission,
  releasing the clutch, returning the foot
  back to the rest position.
  For most small cars with light internal
components, at low engine and road
speeds, a single clutch depression is
sufficiently sympathetic. However, most
unthinking, lazy drivers will be braking while
changing down. They cannot be bothered

**39**

*Double-declutching technique 1. Learn to double-declutch at 60mph; here, note the engine speed in third gear – change up.*

to raise the engine speed and fail to see the need. If the road speed is low, when re-engaging a dragging clutch the engine compression is of negligible consequence and they sequentially change down through the gearbox ratios, not thinking about road speed or car sympathy. In my experience most drivers change gear this way. Do you? I hope not!

The problems arise when engine and road speeds increase, particularly with a large, heavy gearbox. When the driver does not match engine speed when changing down, clutch drag against a high engine compression will be severe, causing the transmission to drag against the driven wheels and road surface, affecting brake balance and possibly causing skidding in adverse conditions, particularly in a light rear-wheel-drive car. Also, inertia in a gearbox is in proportion to mass multiplied

by velocity squared. So the synchromesh will be stressed in proportion to the square of the increase in speed.

Notwithstanding modern baulk-ring synchromesh it is still essential that a driver should be taught – and use as necessary – the double-declutching method of changing gear at high engine, gear and road speeds.

The correct sequence to double-declutch when changing up at high engine and road speeds is:

- ⊃ Hand on the gear lever, palm facing the direction of effort.
- ⊃ Cover the clutch.
- ⊃ Clutch down, gear lever into neutral. Keep hold of the gear lever throughout the change.

◎ Clutch up, to connect the engine to the gearbox.

◎ Off power, time the drop in engine speed.

◎ Clutch down, into gear, clutch up.

◎ Return hand to steering wheel and foot to the rest position.

The correct sequence to change down by double-declutching at high engine and road speeds is:

◎ Hand on the gear lever, palm facing the direction of effort.

◎ Cover the clutch.

◎ Clutch down, gear lever into neutral. Keep hold of the gear lever throughout the change.

◎ Clutch up, to connect the engine to the gearbox.

◎ Raise the engine speed to precisely the correct engine speed to match the gear ratio being selected and the road speed.

*Double-declutching technique 2. Now note engine speed in fourth gear. To change down, you need the engine speed you had in third, to be sympathetic to the clutch and synchromesh.*

◎ Sustain this engine speed while you put the clutch down again and select the lower ratio.

◎ Re-engage the clutch to connect the drive.

◎ Return the left foot to the rest position and the hand to the steering wheel.

By double-declutching there is no stress to the clutch or synchromesh friction devices. There is no jerk or perception of changing gear, apart from a change in the engine note. There is no possibility of loss of adhesion and the clutch and gearbox will last the life of the car.

To practise double-declutching, find a quiet dual carriageway with a fair distance between

**41**

two roundabouts. Turn around at each one and drive at a steady speed, let's say 60mph.

In third gear, notice the engine speed on the rev counter, 4,000rpm? Now change up and, perhaps you see 3,000rpm. Prepare to change back into third gear. Hand first, clutch down, select neutral, clutch up, raise the engine speed to 4,000rpm exactly and sustain it. Clutch down, into third, clutch up again. Practise for half an hour and speed up the movements so you can change down in less than two seconds.

Double-declutching is part of the repertoire of the advanced driver, used as necessary at high engine speeds with heavy gearboxes. I have never found it possible to teach a lazy driver to change down sympathetically and cleanly without it. In my view it should be taught to and used by both novice and experienced drivers.

When making normal progress and driving gently, keep braking separate from changing down. When approaching a hazard, keep both hands on the steering wheel, assess the speed for it correctly and brake only once. Then, when you have finished braking and your right foot is free, make a single change down for the hazard, matching engine speed and double-declutching if necessary.

## Gearbox sense

The style of driving dictated by ever-reducing speed limits and heavy traffic is to spend a large part of our time cruising along, with a very light throttle opening. It is taught for the L-test and termed 'eco-driving'. The highest gear is chosen as early as possible with a very gentle increase in road speed. It is a habit encouraged from the start and it stays with most drivers throughout their driving lives.

Be guarded, because this top-gear cruising style may encourage a lack of concentration, observation and inadequate car control for the ever-changing road scene. This is particularly so when driving actively and safely on country roads, uphill, downhill and through a series of bends, or when an occasional burst of acceleration is necessary to overtake a slow vehicle.

So, let the engine sing. Enjoy the skill needed to drive. Have we forgotten? I am quite convinced that Britain is slowly falling asleep at the wheel! If you go to the continent you will see how they seem to drive with elan, and we can learn from them how to use a car effectively.

The best engine efficiency is between maximum torque (twisting power) and maximum power (which is a few rpm below peak engine speed). It may be harmful to over-rev the engine above the limit marked as a red band on the rev counter. For most motoring, it is sufficient to choose a ratio that enables the engine to be at peak torque with an appropriate throttle opening. In other words, 'ride the torque' and avoid letting the engine speed drop too far so you are in too high a gear for efficiency. Change down at the right time. This judgement is known as gearbox sense and is closely allied to acceleration sense. A driver without one quality is usually a driver without the other.

In an attempt to save fuel cost, a disassociated passive style of driver will tend to use light acceleration, change up early through the gearbox for two-thirds of a short straight on country roads and apply the brakes unnecessarily firmly for the remaining third. It is better to be active, hang on to the appropriate gear ratio, accelerate firmly for one-third of a short straight, achieve the appropriate speed where the view is best, then assess the speed for the next hazard early with forward planning and decelerate for the remaining two-thirds of the straight.

On country roads this style of acceleration sense requires a high level of concentration and long-range assessment of speed and distance. Fuel consumption is the same for the two styles of the driving. Safe overtaking is also achieved by passing during the first third of the clear straight. Halfway down, vision is only half as good. Advanced driving is both active and safe.

## Using the brakes

There is more to be learnt about braking than any other control function. More energy can be applied through the tyres during braking than with steering or acceleration. No matter how good the brakes are, it is the tyre contact with the road that produces grip.

Braking should be commenced lightly, increased to a steady pressure, then reduced to nothing as the wheels come to a stop to avoid a sudden jerk. The reason for this jerk is that stationary friction has a greater effect than running friction during the final stop, though it is not felt by the insensitive, inconsiderate driver. In emergency or fast driving, the brakes can be snapped on then tapered away.

The selfish unskilled driver can produce acute discomfort for passengers when

*Approach speed to this left-hand bend with limited view will have been anticipated well in advance by using acceleration sense and gearbox sense.*

braking. A bus driver can throw a person off their feet when trying to walk down the aisle. On the other hand, a good chauffeur will spread out braking lightly in a straight line so that there is no perception of a final stop. Consideration to passengers is his priority – and paperwork can be accomplished by the boss in the back.

The force applied when braking must not be greater than tyre grip. All of that grip can be applied in a straight line on a good dry surface. However, as you build up cornering force on the tyre, so must you release pressure from the brakes. This is known as tyre grip trade-off, or trail braking.

# VOICE OF EXPERIENCE

## Left-foot braking

Some people advocate left-foot braking in automatics. I don't. It could be dangerous in a car without ABS. How good would your cadence braking be in an emergency with your left foot? It's a lazy idea even with ABS. Reaction times are just the same with a conditioned right foot as with the left. In rallying, if a new hot shoe was becoming a threat, we would mention left-foot braking and they would be off the pace for the next two years! Only go-kart racers, when children on the way to Formula 1, would be able to condition their left foot to master it. For road driving, it's best to keep to what you know. In an emergency, which foot will you use? Don't be wrong-footed, it's not worth the risk.

*Left-foot braking has no place in road driving – go-kart racers and rally drivers only.*

This technique should only be applied with a good-handling car and by a highly skilled driver on a known good surface. In this case, heel and toeing is essential with a manual car. Electronic matching of engine speed with manual selection of a dual-clutch automatic gearbox also makes trail braking possible. I would recommend it only for exceptional driving, racing, rallying or emergency use. Guard against late and faulty assessment of approach speed.

The most amazing technology has produced cars that are as safe as possible.

Anti-lock braking (ABS) senses the tyre locking up under extreme braking and, before it occurs, releases sufficient pressure to avoid it. The best braking occurs just before the tyre slides. The biggest advantage of ABS is that you can change direction while braking hard, which gives you a chance to avoid an impact. Stability control (ESC) steps in to keep the car stable, and Pre-Safe will tension the seatbelt and shut the sunroof and windows when it senses a sudden brake application or swerve.

ABS and ESC will keep the car stable to

help you to prevent skidding, so if you skid, hit the brakes! With these systems today, it is old-fashioned prejudice to avoid braking in a skid or to brake in a straight line only. Always remember that nature will win in the end, and kinetic energy will always overcome a lack of grip if speed is too high. ABS and ESC will not save an impossible situation. Forward planning, long-range anticipation and total concentration will always be the hallmark of the advanced driver. Keeping a safe following distance (extended when you have poor weather) coupled with a sense of speed will save the day.

## Heel and toeing

Heel and toeing enables a driver to brake at the same time as changing down smoothly. When heel and toeing, one should brake firmly. It is essential for the right foot to be secure, with the ball of the foot squarely on the pedal, with no possibility of it slipping off. The side or the edge of the foot is used to sustain the engine speed, to

*Heel and toeing technique. Brake with the ball of the foot squarely on the brake pedal and 'roll' onto the accelerator, to match engine, gear and road speed together. Not difficult, or strictly heel and toeing. Don't forget, double-declutch.*

match the gear and road speed together.

Car manufacturers must be sure to keep to construction and use regulations. They must be certain that drivers of all shapes and sizes are able to handle their cars safely. Large feet, small feet, all should manage the pedal layout. The large-footed must not hit two pedals at once in an emergency! In consequence, it may not be appropriate for all drivers to heel and toe safely, and it may possibly be dangerous to try.

A competition car must be modified to do so, because in my view it is not possible to be competitive without using this technique. For road driving it may be used if safe, as necessary – as a technique kept in reserve for use under the pressure of circumstance and after assessing speed.

# 4 The driving plan

*The driving plan in action when turning left in traffic – the driving plan is a sequence of thought and action that forms the basis of advanced driving.*

All advanced drivers should have a consistent sequence of thought and action, what one might call a driving plan. It is the foundation of safe and measured driving, on which the finer elements of driving can be built. If there is any weakness or lack of judgement and timing when preparing the car for a hazardous situation, it will be evident in the driver's performance. It is my experience that very few drivers apply their driving plan sufficiently well, unless they have consistently repeated training over a lengthy period. It must be taught to be applied successfully. It is a method of safe driving, not a system of car control, which should have little to do with it.

When following a driving plan, the car should be positioned on approach, well in advance, to be in the best part of the road, to obtain the best safety, view and stability.

It must be travelling at a safe speed, to give you and other road users essential time to react.

The best gear ratio is then engaged, before the hazard, for flexible car control and acceleration through and away from a hazardous situation.

One may define an accident as a build-up of a set of circumstances, only one of which needs to be out of your control. It is not the first situation that may be a problem, or even the second, it is the third or more that overcomes you. In the light of training, coupled with long experience, you can develop an early driving plan on approach to any hazardous situation, applied with long-range intelligent anticipation and, most importantly, a sense of speed, so that situations do not build up against you. That is the value of the driving plan.

The result of this simple plan is that the car is always, at any time you drive, travelling in the correct lateral and longitudinal road position, safe speed and gear ratio for safety and efficiency. It only remains for the driver to communicate, with perfectly timed signals, for other road users to have

adequate and evident time to react.

A hazard is a physical feature of the road or potentially dangerous situation created by another road user that will, or may well, require you to change your course or speed. The practical application of the driving plan results in six separate sequences of thought and action, applied as necessary in turn, on approach to a hazard. If a further hazard develops, the plan is again applied, at any stage, flexibly fitting in to the new situation, all in good time. It is applied decisively and deliberately, with long-range application.

The elements of the driving plan are as follows: mirrors, signal, position, speed, gear and warning.

## Mirrors

All of them are scanned and checked frequently. However, if they are set perfectly, any movement will be detected in your peripheral vision.

In addition to using the mirrors, a life-saver shoulder check, using the same part of your vision, may be essential. Awareness of the ever-changing scene, both ahead and behind you, should be complete, in every detail, all the time you drive. Using the mirrors properly entails correctly assessing the value of what is seen and, most importantly, then taking the correct action.

## Signal

Signal your intention, if necessary, at the appropriate time on the approach to the hazard. It is essential for everyone's safety that sufficient time is given for other road users to react. It is unreasonable to expect another road user to react unless a signal is given for at least four seconds. Furthermore, there should be evidence of a reaction before the course is selected. Most drivers, even if advanced, do not do this and it is responsible for many incidents. Do not signal automatically; always have a reason to do so. This will further develop your all-round observation, awareness and, most

# DRIVING PLAN: TURNING RIGHT
## From major to minor road

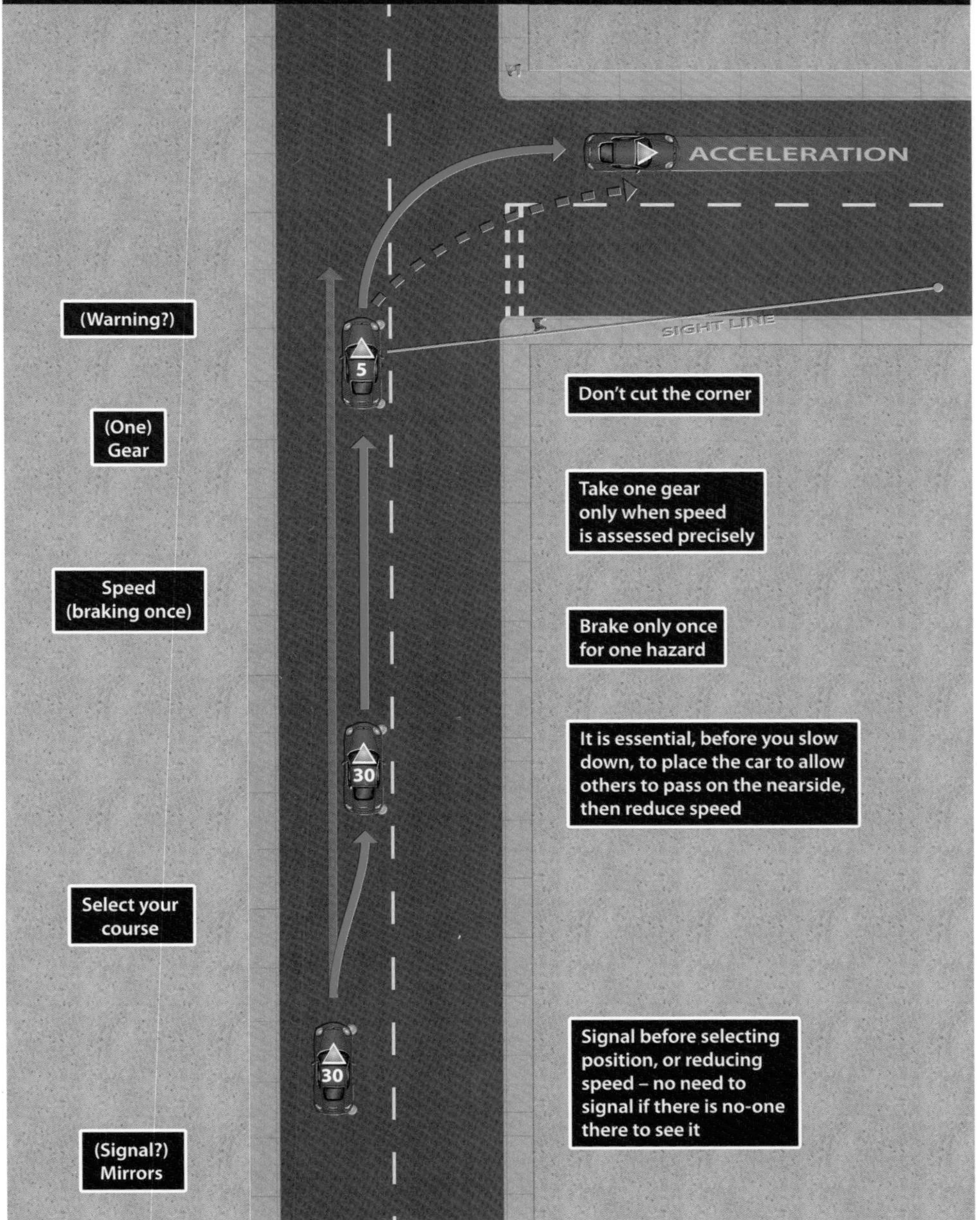

ACCELERATION

SIGHT LINE

(Warning?)

5

Don't cut the corner

(One)
Gear

Take one gear
only when speed
is assessed precisely

Speed
(braking once)

Brake only once
for one hazard

30

It is essential, before you slow
down, to place the car to allow
others to pass on the nearside,
then reduce speed

Select your
course

30

Signal before selecting
position, or reducing
speed – no need to
signal if there is no-one
there to see it

(Signal?)
Mirrors

**49**

importantly, your concentration. An essential signal should always be given in time. It is your responsibility.

## Position
Only now, select your course to put you in the best road position for the safety and convenience of other traffic. There is no better signal of your intention than an accurate road position. The lane is selected before you reduce speed or apply the brakes, so that you cause the least disturbance to following traffic.

## Speed
Speed must be assessed precisely. Braking is spread out and, if you have a limited distance in which to slow down, that is recognised and braking applied decisively, once for a single hazard. It is a mistake in speed assessment to be forced to apply the brakes a second time, after changing down. A physical feature like a bend in the road can be assessed accurately with forward planning and long-range assessment of speed and distance.

Remember, your priority with a limited distance in which to slow down is to brake in order to reach the safe speed for the hazard, and then make a single downwards gear change into the gear you need. It is the road speed of the car that dictates which gear

you require, so only select the gear you need when you know the speed. Look first, gear next, then go.

On some occasions, when driving gently, no braking will be required. If that is the case, having assessed the required speed correctly, a lower gear is selected that will provide sufficient retardation through engine braking alone. At a high road speed, double-declutching will be more sympathetic to the synchromesh in the gearbox.

## Gear
Once speed has been assessed precisely, the appropriate ratio is selected. If you have a semi-automatic transmission in manual mode, the correct gear is selected sequentially by you, in sequence from five to four to three, as appropriate, once your car's speed has been determined. If road speed is below 10mph second gear is selected automatically, and first if you become stationary.

## Warning
A horn warning is given only if it is essential to attract attention, and only then when every other reasonable precaution has been taken. One should not use the horn as a substitute for reducing speed, or in retribution, or to call out to a neighbour or an acquaintance! Many people are guilty of this. When driving, the warning is often given too late and this misuse gives the horn a bad reputation among the general population.

Use of the horn is not encouraged by driving instructors, and it may not be a requirement to demonstrate use of it during the L-test. The exception is if a vehicle is reversing into your car when you are stationary, even though it could be an offence to sound it while stationary in a non-emergency. However, there are situations when the advanced thinking driver will consider it to be essential to give an audible warning.

After making a safe approach to a hazard,

# DRIVING PLAN: TURNING LEFT
## From major to minor road

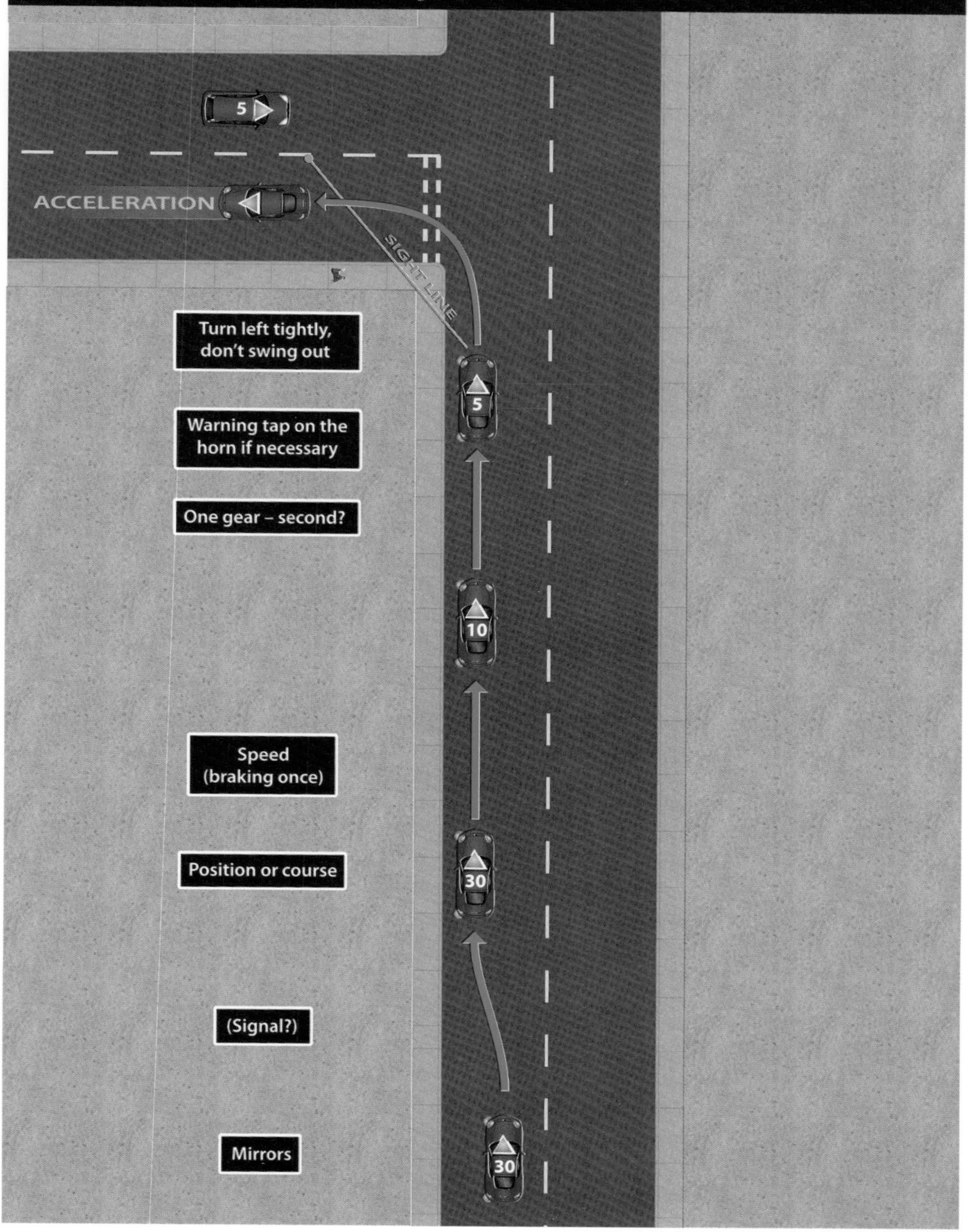

5 ▷

ACCELERATION ◁

SIGHT LINE

Turn left tightly,
don't swing out

5

Warning tap on the
horn if necessary

One gear – second?

10

Speed
(braking once)

Position or course

30

(Signal?)

Mirrors

30

**51**

acceleration through to the exit can be applied. In the dry, with good roadholding, firm acceleration may be applied at the exact time the hazard is considered safe, to exit out of the zone of danger briskly. In adverse conditions with a slippery road surface, the acceleration should be applied in a perfectly straight line. The acceleration is applied gradually, progressively and smoothly to blend the degree of acceleration with the grip available.

The safe and slow approach of the driving plan into junctions and low-speed hazards will not influence your overall journey time. Brisk, effortless acceleration to acquire the appropriate speed more quickly will assist concentration – and help to shorten your journey time.

This pattern of driving is not natural behaviour, and often has to be taught. Most think it is fastest to rush into a hazardous

*A tight turn, brake to 5mph, double-declutch into first gear for control, then give a warning note.*

situation. The difference in approach to driving is quite marked. The bad driver will brake harshly, and late, before giving any signal to turn, make a violent unsympathetic clutch-drag downshift while braking, then select another gear the same way. When emerging left into a major road, they will optimistically anticipate that the only danger can come from their right and swing into the turn with time only to glance one way! Where do you begin with a driver like this? The only way to try to change this thoughtless behaviour is to demonstrate advanced driving with a commentary.

The timing of each element of the driving plan is difficult to perfect and takes lots of hard work and practice. When it is displayed, it is easy, natural, logical and blends and

*Don't be rushed into making the turn, and turn tightly.*

fits into the traffic flow. It should not be disturbing to others, if signals are applied sufficiently early.

Timing should be measured back from the hazard, starting from where you may consider giving a warning. If the warning is given too late, it is because the gear change was late, the braking and assessment of road speed late, positioning on the road, the early start of signalling and even the look in the mirrors mistimed.

Instead, carry out this safe, consistent driving plan: consult the mirrors and observe all round, with shoulder checks; give a signal, if necessary, before positioning correctly; cut off speed early, with one period of braking; change down cleanly and give an early warning of approach, if absolutely necessary.

With early communication, the right position, speed and gear, what more can we do to prevent an accident situation?

Planning should be carried out not only on the approach to specific hazards, but all the time you drive, with total concentration. To be an advanced driver you must always be in the correct position on the road, follow safely, travel at the most appropriate safe speed for you to react and for others to react to you and to obtain the best view, stability and margin of safety from potential or actual danger.

Speed must be based not only on what you can see, but also on what you cannot see but you reasonably expect could be in the blind area out of sight. A healthy imagination is the first requirement for anticipation. Speed of approach may be difficult to judge, so lateral road positioning will help you to see before overtaking and cornering.

It will sound obvious, but try to be aware, at all times, of what is going on in the ever-changing scene, well in front and behind. Place the car to gain the best possible view, provided it is safe, to occupy the road in relation to actual or potential danger, for every moment of driving.

In town, danger sometimes lurks behind parked vehicles on the nearside, or in concealed junctions. It is best to have a safety margin away from pedestrians. There is nothing faster from zero to five miles per hour than a small child! An extended safety line position left of the warning line is best, for a better view, so you are able to react if required. A blind junction is passed more safely on a line that allows you to see into the mouth of the side road more deeply. One is better able to avoid the driver stopping too late or emerging over the give way or stop lines. Bad driving I know, but often witnessed.

Let's put the driving plan into practice with a few case studies of typical driving hazards you may encounter.

## Crossroads

Imagine a fast approach to a minor crossroads with restricted views into both side roads. At speed, you may see the warning sign and recognise the hazard at a very early stage; you check that the mirror is clear, and no deviation signal is required, as you wish to go straight on. You lift off the power to use early deceleration and avoid unnecessary braking. Speed falls away to a safe velocity at which traffic emerging will expect you to be travelling, so that they can reasonably assess your approach speed. You check early

*Arrive later, as this hazard becomes an 'opening' gap. Is the driver of the parked van about to swing his door open? He has retracted his door mirror, so he must be parked safely! The driver of the car parked outside the café should have a guilty conscience – the breakfast must be good there!*

*Read the road as well as the signs. The surface is wet, with standing water, providing less grip. The 'pinching' obstruction will put you out to the other side of the road on approach to the junction. If a driver emerges, he may not look your way. Watch out!*

right, left and right again. Speed is safe, you change down sympathetically by double-declutching cleanly. A medium warning note is given – a car's nose appears, the driver sees you and stops – a little lift of your left hand towards the top of the wheel to thank him and you accelerate firmly through and away from the crossroads swiftly and safely.

## Junction

You are driving through a long, gradual blind left-hand curve subject to a 40mph speed limit. Your road position, left of the warning line, gives you an early view. A road junction left warning sign comes into sight. You check your mirror, it's clear. You keep your position to give a margin for safety. The view into the junction is restricted. You apply the brakes gently, as there is a restricted distance in which to slow down. You finish braking at what you consider is a reasonable and safe speed, say 25mph. You change

down with the synchromesh, raising engine speed to match with third gear and road speed. A driver appears, he is not looking and rolls forward. You sound a warning; he looks at you and stops. You thank him and drive past with light acceleration up to 40mph again.

## Right turn

Driving in a 30mph speed limit, you see a direction sign showing where you wish to turn right at a minor crossroads. You check the mirror and there is traffic following too closely. You keep a steady speed and give an early signal. You look in the mirror again and the driver drops back. You select your course just left of the warning line. Traffic passes on your left. Judging the likely situation at the junction when you arrive, you assess that it is stable and will not change against you. Estimating the severity of the turn, you brake once to a safe speed. You then change

Advanced driving

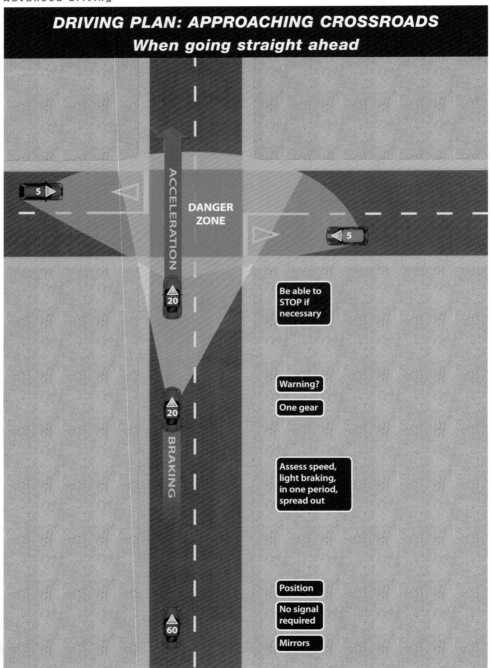

# DRIVING PLAN: APPROACHING CROSSROADS
## When going straight ahead

**ACCELERATION**

**DANGER ZONE**

Be able to STOP if necessary

Warning?

One gear

Assess speed, light braking, in one period, spread out

**BRAKING**

Position

No signal required

Mirrors

56

*Right turn. Look down the junction to be sure it is clear before you turn. Don't cut the corner. Prepare to steer.*

down into second gear, matching the engine speed. No warning is necessary. With a life-saver shoulder check, you confirm there is nothing in your blind spot. You look down the turn you are entering and when you can see all the way down it, you turn safely, without cutting the corner.

Next day, you are repeating the journey and you approach the same right turn. Your mirror is clear, this time no signal is necessary, yet. You select your course left of the warning line, still nothing behind, but there is traffic approaching from the opposite direction. You give them a signal. Braking gently, you have to stop to wait for a safe long gap in the oncoming traffic. You stop, apply the handbrake for security, take first gear and keep your steering straight (if your front wheels were already turned right, then in the event of a rear impact you would be shunted in front of oncoming traffic). Look to see that there are no pedestrians crossing, quick shoulder check, and you turn, without cutting the corner.

## Roundabout

The application of the driving plan is occasionally compromised. For example, when approaching a roundabout on a dual carriageway, I intend to turn right but I have difficulty seeing the advanced direction sign in the distance, as it is obscured. Fortunately the sat-nav confirms it.

I am in the nearside lane at 70mph. There is give and take, but light traffic, with drivers overtaking occasionally. I examine my mirrors, as I need to move into the offside lane. I must communicate any intention early, as there is traffic closing well back. Still in the nearside lane, I start signalling. There must be time for the following traffic to react to the signal. After signalling for four seconds, I check to see evidence of reaction. There is a car, but it is still well behind.

# DRIVING PLAN: APPROACHING A ROUNDABOUT
## When taking an exit at 3 o'clock

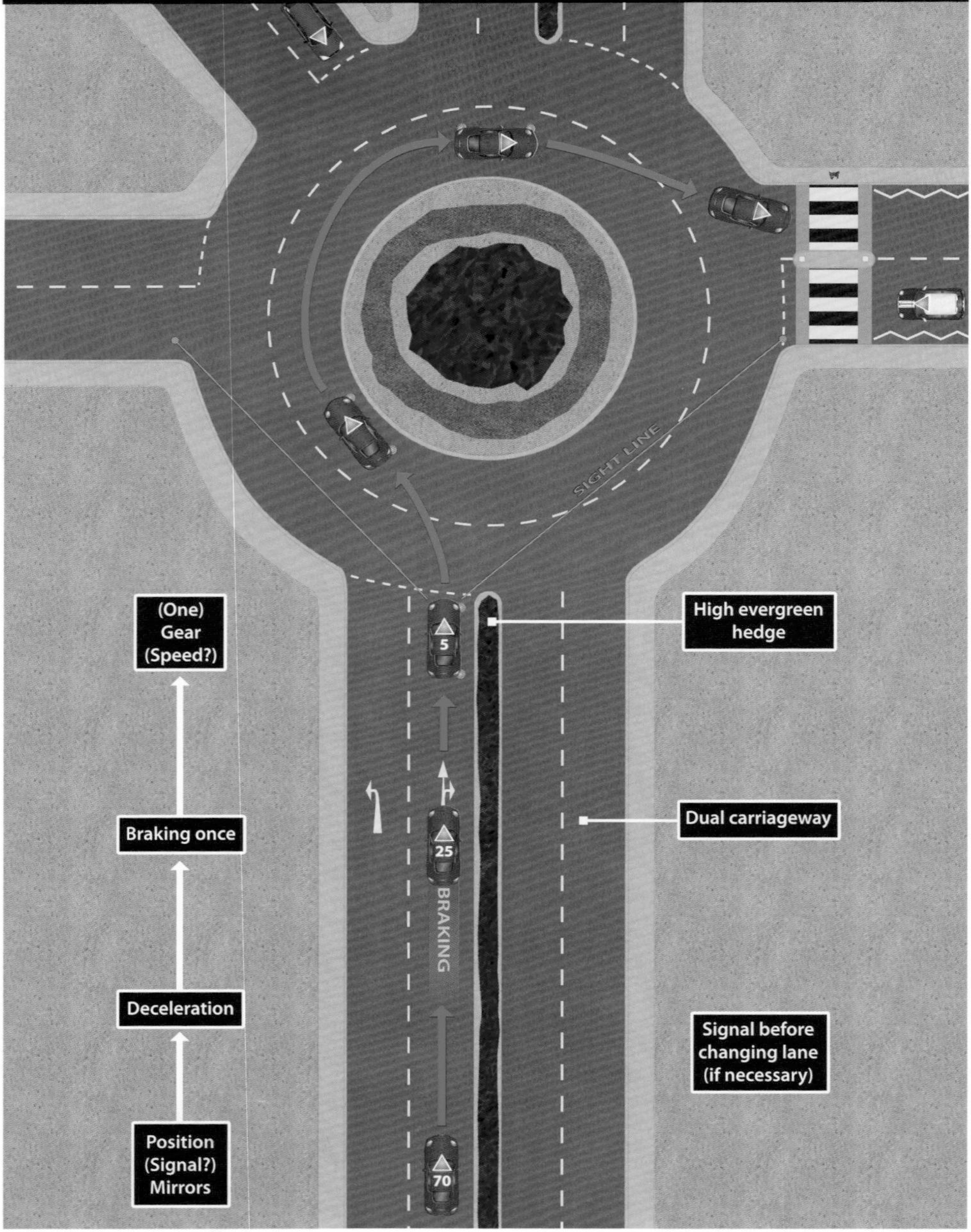

(One)
Gear
(Speed?)

Braking once

Deceleration

Position
(Signal?)
Mirrors

High evergreen
hedge

Dual carriageway

Signal before
changing lane
(if necessary)

SIGHT LINE

BRAKING

5

25

70

*Early morning and traffic is light; note how a thick hedge blocks the view for drivers approaching the roundabout at lower right.*

Before I move, I give a quick peripheral side vision shoulder check to see that the blind spot is clear. Only then do I point the car to gently change lane. I keep this signal going, as traffic cannot legally pass on my nearside unless the signal is communicating my intention to turn right at the roundabout ahead. Traffic is now passing safely in the left-hand lane, on my nearside. I look in the mirror before slowing down. Normally, if the roundabout were clear of traffic, there would be no need to brake. As I approach I cannot see into the roundabout because, to slow me down, the highway engineers have planted an evergreen hedge to block and restrict my view.

Checking the mirror, I brake lightly, to the safe speed that gives me time to look and assess the situation. It is the speed of the car that demands which gear I need, so I do not change into the correct gear until I have judged the safe speed to enter the roundabout. I have to be very slow, to give myself time to judge speed and distance.

I can now fit into a safe gap in the circling traffic. I change down cleanly, comfortably before the give way line. To blend in I use light acceleration. The sat-nav confirms I am taking the fourth exit. The highway engineers have restricted my view around the roundabout again, and to blend in with road users who are familiar with the route, I have very little time to select the exit lane. With use of the nearside door mirror and a quick left shoulder check, I signal left opposite the exit before the one I wish to take. Keeping a pace to blend with traffic, and taking a shoulder check to see evidence of reaction to my exit signal, I start to exit.

I now notice a pedestrian who has placed their foot on the crossing. There is no time for any warning signal other than my brake lights and I stop as gently as I can. When the crossing is clear, I can proceed with quick shoulder checks both sides. Flexibility, quick thinking and a slow pace will give essential time to react, which is not easy, despite my best intentions and forward planning.

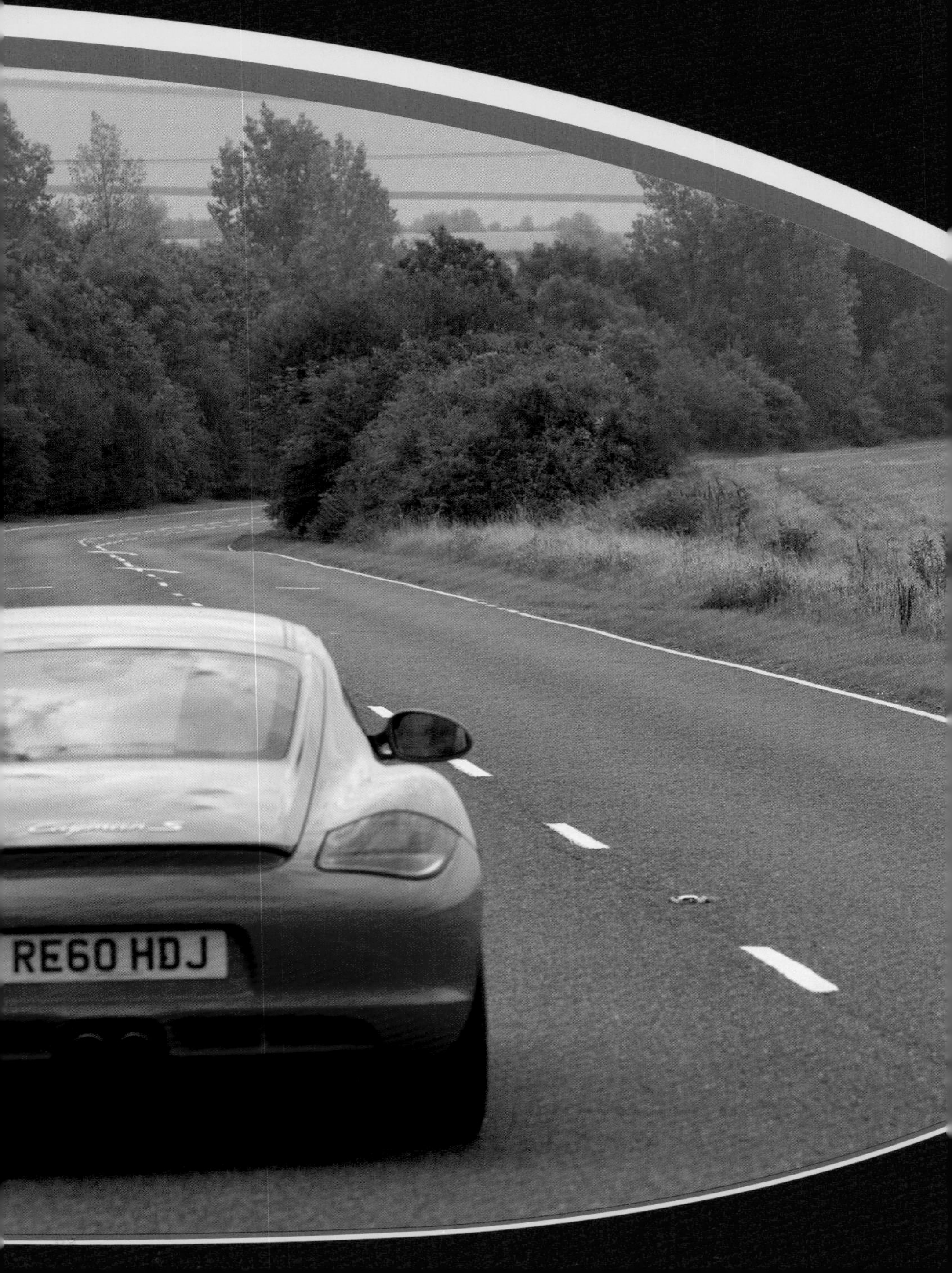
RE60 HDJ

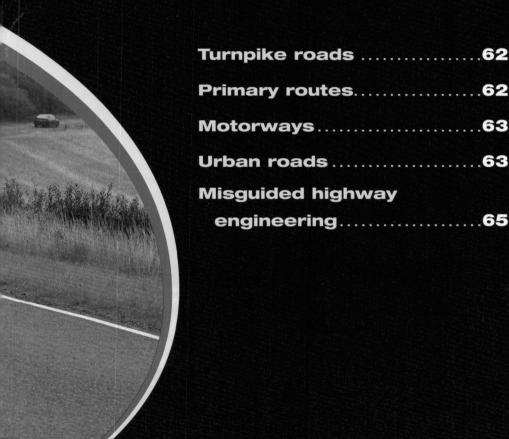

# 5 Road sense

*Road sense is required on this non-primary road: trees
block a crucial part of the view of the road ahead.*

# ROAD SENSE AT A MINI-ROUNDABOUT 2
## An LGV driving over a mini-roundabout to turn right

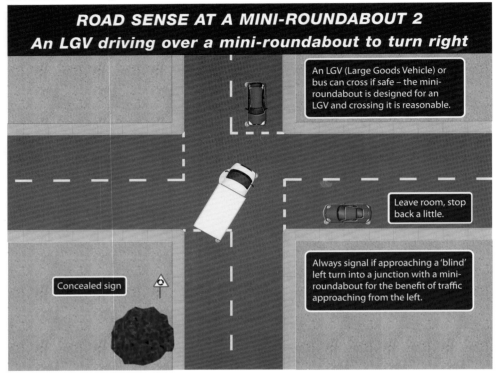

An LGV (Large Goods Vehicle) or bus can cross if safe – the mini-roundabout is designed for an LGV and crossing it is reasonable.

Leave room, stop back a little.

Always signal if approaching a 'blind' left turn into a junction with a mini-roundabout for the benefit of traffic approaching from the left.

Concealed sign

developed extraordinary skills to keep traffic moving at busy crossroads and junctions.

In 1927, land speed record holder Sir Henry Segrave was driving a journalist along busy London streets at a slow, steady and flowing pace. They approached a policeman on point duty, at a speed rather more slow and safe than the policeman thought reasonable. He shouted at him as he passed by, 'Hurry up, slow coach!' Sir Henry saw the potential danger of driving at an inappropriate and unsafe speed along crowded streets, yet he had just broken the speed record at 203mph a few weeks before!

When automatic traffic signals arrived to relieve the police of their uncomfortable job, the lights released the traffic in collective bunches. The length of waiting time at a red light is usually between 45 and 65 seconds. This allows a gap in the bunch of

traffic for drivers to have time to emerge safely at other minor junctions, further down the road. The current average speed across London in the rush hour is often below 9mph and this pace hasn't changed since the horse-drawn days. If you have nine miles to complete, give yourself at least an hour! Provide yourself with comfortable time to complete the journey and pace it with a flowing style. There is no point in rushing from one set of red lights to the next.

In traffic, match the general pace to blend and fit in with the give-and-take all around. Be decisive, use power if safe to extend the distance from the inevitable tailgater behind and hang well back yourself, at about one metre per 1mph. Then you will be able to scan the road scene for detail, rather than the back of that large bus! Leave sufficient space in front whenever you stop to be able to steer around any obstruction.

Many people, inspired by being constantly late and the intense activity around them, drive too fast in town, yet in the country they relax and fail to make progress. They mostly drive on roads they know. The hazards they meet are familiar to them and mistakes they have made in the past, such as taking the wrong lane, they have learnt not to make again. It is difficult when you are unfamiliar with the route to fit in with its pace and drive safely; so use power when it is clear, quiet and safe to do so, yet spread out your braking as early as you can.

Generally people who know the road do not see, or notice, traffic signs. As their eyes are cast down, they see the road markings immediately in front of them rather more readily. Many follow the preceding vehicle too closely and tailgate. This dangerous habit makes them look intently at the immediate vehicle ahead, in case they hit it! That prevents effective scanning for hazards ahead. Driving is often reactive, uncomfortable for passengers, with harsh braking and sudden reactions.

The streets are littered with roadworks, with little co-ordination between services. Their frequency causes congestion and pollution. It is estimated that approximately 7,000 people die from air pollution in London each year, compared with 200 in traffic accidents. It is best to keep traffic in towns gently flowing with mini-roundabouts at most junctions, not to stop and start the traffic unless it is essential for the safety and convenience of road users. More skill is required to deal with mini-roundabouts, but so much the better! It would be preferable to separate pedestrians and cyclists from buses, lorries and cars and keep the traffic moving. This policy would make the roads safer, particularly for cyclists and pedestrians, more efficient and less polluting to the atmosphere.

Speed humps are dangerous to injured passengers in an ambulance, damaging to the suspension, polluting and noisy to residents. The councils that lay them (quite legally) sometimes do not keep to the original design, recommended by the Transport Research Laboratory (TRL), which specified a gradual rise over six feet up to a height of four inches followed by a gentle fall over the next six feet.

## Misguided highway engineering

I am convinced that there is a misguided campaign by highway engineers to use disinformation and camouflage to slow and confuse the motorist, almost as though they are waging a war against speed. Direction signs are hidden behind undergrowth and other visual obstructions to keep to the shortest sight lines permitted. Is the idea to give you limited time to read the information on the sign in an attempt to slow you down? Then there are the direction signs that give a picture of the roundabout that is not quite what you experience when you negotiate it. It causes confusion, hesitation and lack of confidence, in an attempt to make you take more care and to slow you down.

Hedgerows hide and conceal. An evergreen hedge may be planted in the centre reservation of a dual carriageway, right up to a roundabout, to block your view and slow you down. It leads to bad driving, if the driver is optimistic and approaches too fast to give way safely, which is potentially dangerous to drivers on the roundabout.

Negative camber in a corner engenders the feeling that approach speed is too fast, 'leaning' the car away from the turn. One degree of negative camber gives five per cent less roadholding. When negative camber is accompanied by tightening radius through a bend – something that occurs in literally thousands of places throughout the UK – the result is uncomfortable at the very least, but also adds danger.

The 'reason' given is railway engineering, to introduce the train to the bend

*Bad road engineering 1. Here the inside kerb points you out towards the offside of the road into any vehicle approaching – watch out! You must be into the nearside at the exit.*

progressively. However, a driver in my experience is likely to misjudge the bend by approaching too fast for the tightening radius that is out of his sight, until it is too late. Many incidents may be caused, in particular to motorcyclists.

Perhaps highway engineers have chosen to forget the work carried out in 1990 at Aberdeen University* into the statistics of accidents that occurred in 'clusters'. They opened the view across the inside of these tightening bends, and designed in a constant radius to the inside curve. Accidents were dramatically reduced. This research is conveniently ignored!

More recently, in 2010, Yetkin v London Borough of Newham concerned the case of a pedestrian run over while crossing a dual carriageway at a point in the central reservation where the authorities had not cut back vegetation that obscured the pedestrian's view of the road. The judge stated: 'This highway authority owed a duty of care to all road users (whether careful or negligent) to use reasonable care in the manner in which it exercised its powers... The planting of vegetation in the raised beds of the central reservation is obviously a reasonable exercise of the authority's powers but to plant shrubs which will grow so large as to obscure the view and then not to ensure that they are trimmed back is a negligent exercise of those powers.'

In my view I should not have to point out to you such man-made hazards. If they are

* D. Stewart and C.J. Chudworth, 'A Remedy for Accidents at Bends', Traffic Engineering and Control, Vol. 31 No. 2 (Feb. 1990), pp88–93.

'natural' they are relatively easy to anticipate, but not if they are professionally designed to deceive and sometimes catch people out. If you drive at a moderate or slow pace, they may occasionally make you feel slightly uncomfortable. But if you are required to drive at high speed, like an emergency service driver, watch out!

The answer is always to leave sufficient in reserve in your approach speed. It is necessary for the safety of your passengers and other road users, to link vision to speed and grip, over the brow and round the blind bend. A roundabout may be just over the crest of the hill, and so may be the tail of the traffic queue!

Don't expect the road to be straight over the crest of the hill. There might be a built-in hazard like 'pinching', where your half of the road has a restriction and is taken away from you, or it goes from two-way to single track just over the brow.

*Bad road engineering 2. Proof of stupidity after the same corner – the tyre marks of someone who lost control of his car. This driver was reckless, but deceived by highway engineers.*

A lay-by is often hidden, just over the slight rise on a two-way road where you may be confronted with a vehicle slowly setting off or, worse still, an approaching vehicle attempting to pull into it from the opposite direction.

Frequent roadworks are a major influence on our average speed; they often seem to go on for an inordinate time, with little evidence of work in progress. Low speed limits to protect the work force have to be enforced by average speed cameras. But what about tailgating, which has a far more serious consequence, if a sudden stop is required? It would be better to combine speed limits with safe distance cameras in roadworks.

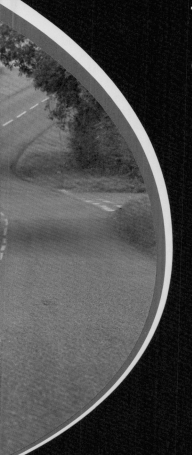

# 6 Observe to anticipate

*Observing to anticipate: the sign warns of a crossroads but the hedge blocks the view of the road joining from the left.*

Concentration, observation and anticipation are vital elements of advanced driving.

Concentration is defined as the complete application of the mind to a particular endeavour, to the exclusion of anything irrelevant. The result of not doing so when driving could well be serious and result in prosecution after an accident.

Observation means scanning the road scene 360 degrees all around, into the far distance as far as you can see, then to the middle and near distance, in order to assess the value of the smallest relevant detail and take prompt, appropriate action if necessary.

Anticipation is to be able to foresee what you reasonably expect is most likely to occur.

Progress in the development of safe driving skills is acquired in four progressive stages through training, practice and experience.

Unconscious incompetence as a novice, where you require driving instruction from an Approved Driving Instructor (ADI), is the first stage. Instruction should be given to you the moment it is required, so that you begin to understand the difference between right and wrong, as it occurs when driving.

Conscious incompetence is the next stage in your development, where you still require practical driving instruction from an ADI to learn the difference between what is considered to be good or bad driving technique.

Conscious competence is the stage where driving instruction should no longer be required but occasional advice and coaching still is. The novice stage should now be over. You should now know what to do and how to do it. You should be able to pass the driving test.

Unconscious competence only becomes so after many years of experience of the right kind, deep thought and sheer hard work. At this stage coaching will be of great assistance, as two brains are better than one. The coach, however, must be a master of the driving art, lead from the front and be able to demonstrate to you the style that you wish to emulate. You must be able to work together as a team. After long experience, you will acquire your own style of correct and safe driving. Your own character will shine through, and that is to be encouraged. You should now be able to pass the advanced driving test, as conducted by the Institute of Advanced Motorists (IAM).

## The hallmarks of advanced drivers

Being a passenger with a really good driver is a rare and fascinating experience, not only for their smooth, sympathetic skill in handling a car at speed, but for the driver's mental ability to anticipate far ahead to the horizon. Intelligent anticipation can be developed to a most uncanny degree, so that it appears to be almost psychic. It is only found in motorists with considerable experience of driving.

A supremely good driver is often able to visualise possible difficulties before they arise, and to sense potential danger when it seems no outward sign of it exists. Anticipation, developed to its highest pitch, is frequently based upon the smallest detail seen. But occasionally, it is an instinctive reaction and the clue cannot be seen. This instinct is natural to some, but is often developed only in the light of many years of experience of human behaviour and observation of the smallest detail.

Just as a hunter possesses a keen sense of observation, noticing by a broken blade of grass or their sense of smell which way the quarry has gone, so does a very good driver notice every clue and detail in the road scene. Take for example a pedestrian wishing to cross the entrance to a side turning; if they glance down the turning, but then step back to the kerb, they are obviously waiting for an approaching vehicle. A smoking cigarette at a deserted bus stop indicates the possibility of a bus around the next blind bend. You will deduce a similar sort of

# INFLUENCE OF WORKLOAD ON PERFORMANCE
## *Ability of driver to concentrate*

This diagram represents the additional stress of mistimed and inappropriate questions from a passenger upon the ability of the driver to concentrate, to the complete exclusion of anything irrelevant to the task. Stress also occurs if you are unwell, late for an appointment or lost.

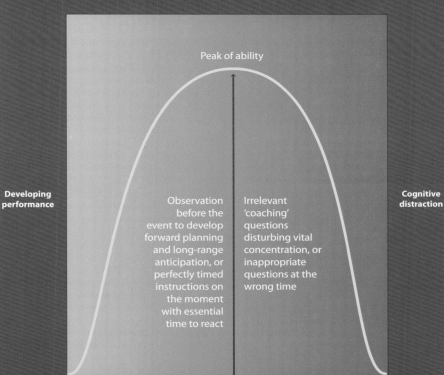

Peak of ability

**Developing performance**

Observation before the event to develop forward planning and long-range anticipation, or perfectly timed instructions on the moment with essential time to react

Irrelevant 'coaching' questions disturbing vital concentration, or inappropriate questions at the wrong time

**Cognitive distraction**

**Excessive workload leading to a potential crash** ⟶

EXAMPLE A passenger states random numbers out of any rational order. The driver tries to answer by repeating the correct digit two numbers ago. The effect upon concentration and driving performance is dramatic. The same detrimental deterioration in performance can be created by information overload delivered by a driving instructor, or a driving 'coach' asking questions at a time when the driver is under the pressure of circumstance. Questions requiring profound and thoughtful answers are best asked when the driver is in a café having a cup of tea! Similar distraction can be created by noisy, out-of-control children, an intense argument or road rage.

# TURNING LEFT INTO A MAJOR ROAD
## *Observe to anticipate*

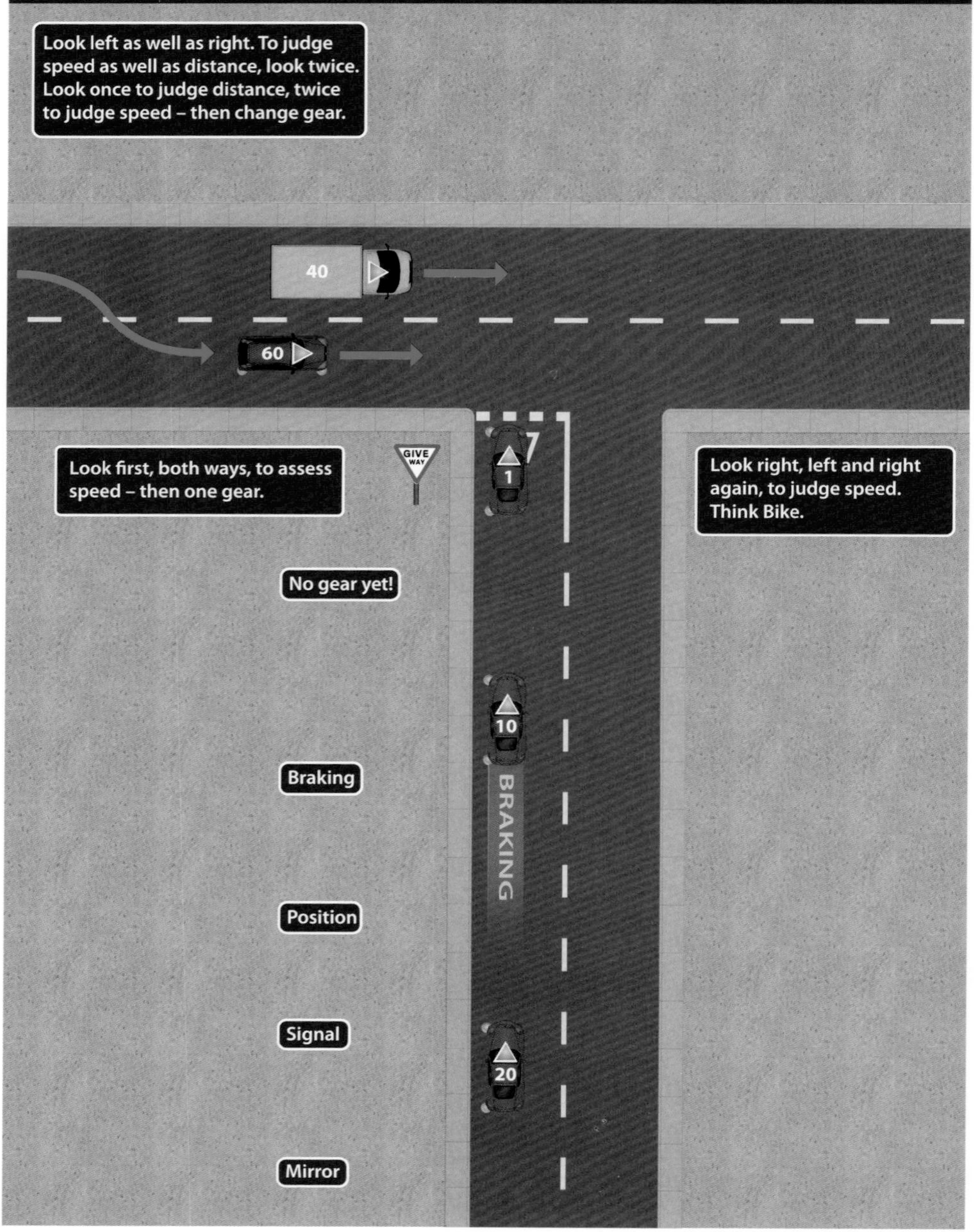

Look left as well as right. To judge speed as well as distance, look twice. Look once to judge distance, twice to judge speed – then change gear.

Look first, both ways, to assess speed – then one gear.

Look right, left and right again, to judge speed. Think Bike.

No gear yet!

Braking

BRAKING

Position

Signal

Mirror

# VOICE OF EXPERIENCE

## The inadequacy of the L-test

Are candidates truly competent when they pass their L-test? Let me give you a true story to explain my point of view.

In the 1960s I was asked by the British School of Motoring (BSM) to accompany a lady driver in a Triumph Herald, just after passing her driving test at Basingstoke, with a man from the press in the back seat. I was instructed not to say anything at all, but to use the dual control if a situation was dangerous. We drove towards London down the M4 in the evening rush hour. This lady had never driven on the motorway before and knew only one road speed – 40mph, everywhere. In the first instance she was in the central lane, then in the outside lane, being passed at high speed on the nearside. She was too frightened to move back to the nearside! Of course, I helped her out.

We came into London in the dark, still at 40mph. I had to ask her to switch the headlights on. We turned left at Hyde Park Corner up to Marble Arch, then left again in the dark along the A4 still at 40mph, past a bingo hall just as they were spilling out into the street. I had to use the dual brake many times during the drive, at one time when trying to negotiate a roundabout in top gear at 40mph. I could feel the knees of the poor journalist sitting behind me, as he pressed hard into the seat, every time the many potentially dangerous incidents occurred.

It proved to myself and the journalist how inadequate the basic L-test was in those days. BSM, rightly in my view, put an embargo on the press reporter and I apologised to the poor novice for saying very little to help her. I offered further instruction, but she refused! Since then I have always taught people to drive, not just to pass a test. So has BSM. People however, will want any driving school to get them through the driving test as quickly and as cheaply as possible, and it is a real problem to ask them to pay extra for further instruction.

situation when you see fresh animal manure on the road.

With concentration, you will be able to see a small detail, assess its value and judge the possibility of any reasonable situation. The law does not expect you to anticipate what is unreasonable. Bricks thrown off a motorway bridge may be considered to be unreasonable, for example. However, I must say, if I see children larking about on a bridge, I am likely to change lanes if I can – and report the incident later.

The very experienced driver will not only be able to judge what is right or wrong, but good and bad, safe and unsafe. It is only a question of knowledge to tell the difference between right or wrong. It is all there to read in any official publication about the rules of the road, such as the *Highway Code*. Swot up on the latest edition, as it is getting to be quite a volume and evolving all the time.

The difference between what is good or bad driving is a matter of opinion, and the view of the majority of road users matters. But the majority where? Certainly, a French motorist will have a different opinion than an Italian, and what he believes to be good, safe driving is, in my experience, totally different from the British point of view.

It is important to appreciate and understand the opinion of all types of road user, to get to know how they think on the road. A high degree of sympathetic understanding, respect and patience is required. Imagine what it is like to be in their shoes. We all have a responsibility towards each other to be calm and calculating, to blend and fit our driving into the pattern and pace of the majority of road users, and behave in the manner that other reasonable folk expect us to behave.

Sadly, only the very best drivers know the difference between safe and unsafe driving, at whatever speed. Some are dangerous at the speed limit down a busy high street. There is no substitute for experience and training of the right kind.

# TURNING RIGHT INTO MAJOR ROAD
## Observe to anticipate

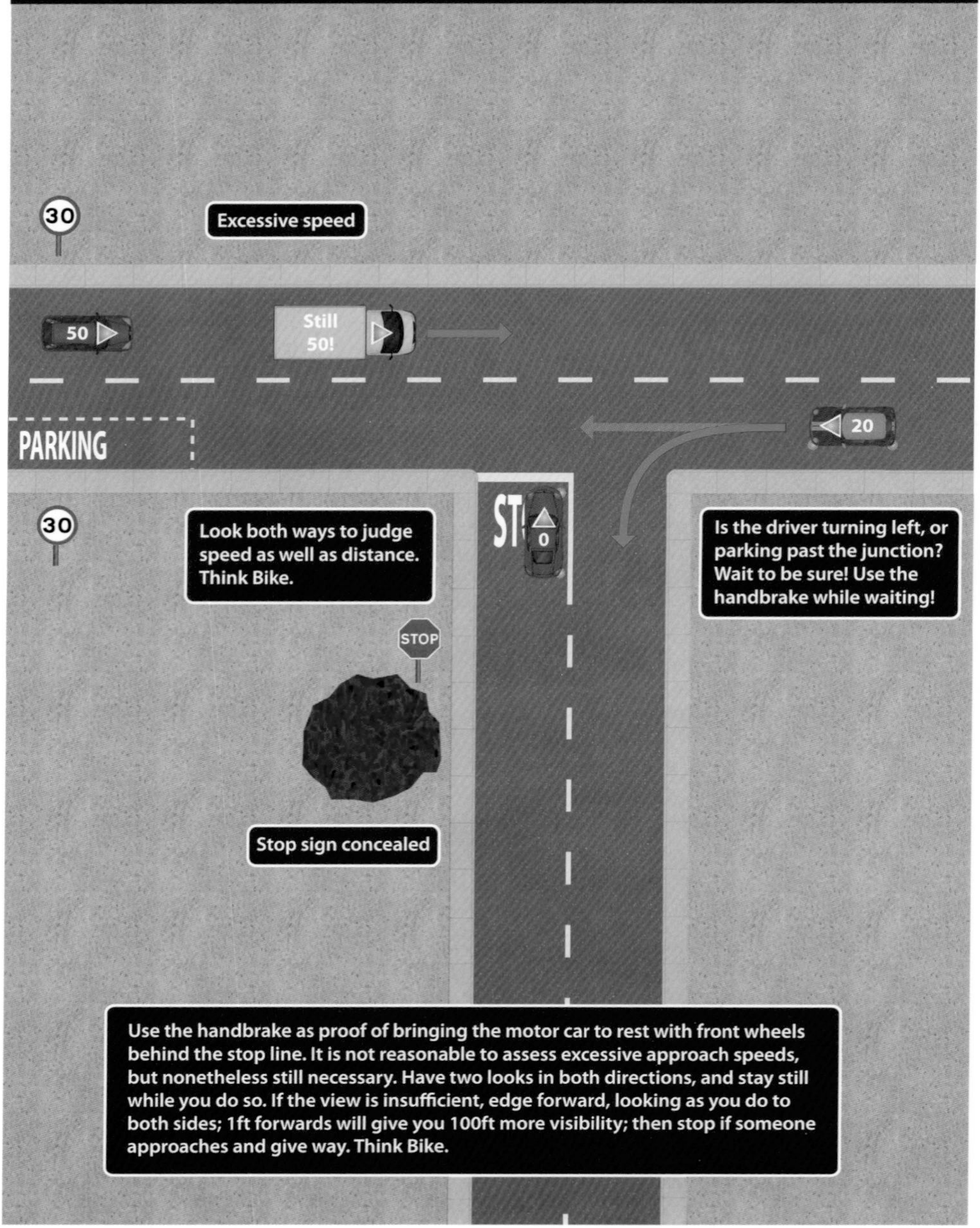

(30)

**Excessive speed**

50 ▷

**Still 50!** ▷

◁ 20

**PARKING**

(30)

**Look both ways to judge speed as well as distance. Think Bike.**

ST 0

**Is the driver turning left, or parking past the junction? Wait to be sure! Use the handbrake while waiting!**

STOP

**Stop sign concealed**

Use the handbrake as proof of bringing the motor car to rest with front wheels behind the stop line. It is not reasonable to assess excessive approach speeds, but nonetheless still necessary. Have two looks in both directions, and stay still while you do so. If the view is insufficient, edge forward, looking as you do to both sides; 1ft forwards will give you 100ft more visibility; then stop if someone approaches and give way. Think Bike.

Discipline and skill are essential to be safe, deliberate and decisive.

It has been my fortunate experience to be driven by some of the finest drivers, not only as a civilian instructor at Hendon, but also as a co-driver with the High Performance Course. They are not only naturally gifted and born with a flair for driving, but they display patient understanding towards others, coupled with a technique that is honed by fine timing, sound judgement and perfected by years of self-criticism. They are high achievers, people who are never satisfied with their own performance, always searching for perfection.

What the very best drivers seem to possess is extreme intelligence and an enquiring mind, which leads them to investigate and analyse the smallest detail. The ability to drive under pressure is essential in poor conditions, and with long experience, this eventually produces an almost bottomless pit of skill, held in reserve. They possess a sense of speed that enables them to travel safely, more relaxed but at a higher average pace than the majority, with the minimum of engine speed and braking. They always seem to have a vast margin of safety, something in reserve, something left, which is what advanced driving is all about. Yet they are able to estimate the time they will arrive, within five minutes either way, without the aid of a sat-nav, even after a long journey. They have a sense of pace, as well as speed, which takes years of experience to develop.

An advanced driver is unobtrusive, having the ability to move quickly and discreetly across the countryside, hardly noticed on the way. Their smooth, effortless and flowing style looks deceptively easy and is in complete sympathy with the car. They use acceleration and gearbox sense to ride the torque of their engine, not noisily screaming the engine to disturb others and draw attention to themselves.

Great skill and self-discipline will eventually hone driving into a fine art that makes it

## VOICE OF EXPERIENCE

### Reckless racers
Most racing drivers worry me when on the road. They are either reckless or disassociated passive, having got into so much trouble by driving like maniacs that they have given up and dismiss all elements of roadcraft as boring. The Government should not try to demoralise the spirit of the young. They should give realistic driver training, then impose discipline if that training is ignored.

almost impossible for the less able to copy. A very respectable reproduction can, however, be made by any fit, intelligent person with the right mental and physical qualities, after many years of hard work, enthusiasm and practice.

Having the flair to handle a car well is not often linked to a humble approach. The gifted are invariably overconfident and rely on their reactions to keep them out of trouble. They drive only for their own pleasure and enjoyment. They show off, frighten passengers and make violent use of the controls. They are downright selfish and make good racing drivers and little else. Track day and competition driving technique has no place on the highway and encourages a belief that that is all there is to driving skill. I have found it relatively easy to be successful in racing and rallying, in relation to roadcraft. The world champion racing driver is not the best road driver in the world. That person is unknown, and it may well be you!

When driving, we must all recognise and appreciate our own limitations, our own built-in speed limit and have self-discipline to drive within these limits. Advanced drivers are deliberate, decisive, calm and calculating, carrying out their driving plans with early, slow and smooth control movements, after quick correct thinking, based upon the safety of others as well as themselves.

The highly experienced possess good judgement. This is not only the physical assessment of space, speed and distance, but a balance of mind, between progression and restraint, and when and where to apply it. Decisive deliberation also engenders an ability to be not easily perturbed when under pressure.

A driver will only inspire confidence in their passengers if they are completely confident in themselves. Any weakness, like moments of indecision prior to overtaking, or secondary, harsh brake application, can turn a passenger's hair white.

Confidence and maturity of character engenders a degree of firmness, not to be intimidated or easily perturbed by the bad driving of others. There is nothing so effective in this situation than to show a good example to the less able. Self-discipline involves self-criticism too, and enthusiasm is essential to provide the inspiration to improve.

*Give a cyclist a wide berth. Six feet?*

Advanced driving is an art that can be acquired. The secret is concentration, not only for every moment that you drive, but for many years of study and self-criticism. Humility is an important part of the make-up of the advanced driver: whenever you learn something about driving, it falls into insignificance in comparison to what there is still to learn.

An advanced driver is someone who makes every mistake there is to be made but who decides never to make the same mistake again. The art of driving never stands still. To be advanced, you must always search for perfection. Discipline yourself hard, never give up, so that advanced driving evolves gradually, within yourself. Drive with the very best advanced drivers you can find. Have an enquiring mind, ask as many questions as you can think of and try to learn something new every day.

# VOICE OF EXPERIENCE

## A Bentley moment

I remember my father driving fast from London to Oxfordshire, in his pre-war 4¼-Litre Bentley. I was a little boy standing up, looking down the bonnet, watching his every move. Way ahead in the far distance was a countryman on his bike. My father selected an early, wide berth, but when we were right on top of him, the cyclist stuck his arm out and rode across the front of us. We missed him, just! My father hit the brakes and locked up the wheels, the Alsatian dog in the back seat hit the back of his head and the dog's saliva covered the windscreen. Dad angled the front wheels a bit and released the brakes, missed the cyclist, corrected a big slide, cursed the old man and parked to clean the windscreen. I told my father off for driving too fast! You can imagine what he said to his precocious son. I haven't changed!

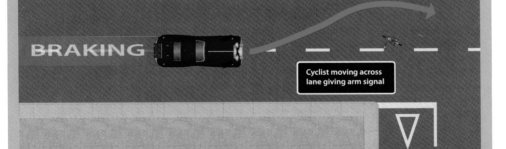

Hitting the brakes, locking the wheels (no ABS in those days)

Apply the steering angle while the front wheels are locked

Release the brakes and steer around

BRAKING

Cyclist moving across lane giving arm signal

## Observation and anticipation

Develop and condition your observation, exercise your eyesight and scan all around, far, middle and near distance, and far again, because if you do not observe well, you will not be able to anticipate in time. Don't just look at the vehicles, look at the people inside them. Don't just look at their faces, look at their eyes and see if they are looking at you!

Watch the tilt of the head and their facial expression. Notice their hands, the position they are holding the wheel; are they about to turn it? Watch a pedestrian's feet when walking. The toes turn out when about to turn onto a crossing, the head turns to look a little after and they will lean forward a fraction before they run!

A cyclist may wobble uphill and in crosswinds, so keep well clear, at least six feet away. Remember, they stop pedalling

*Respect horses: stay behind and wait well back until it's safe to pass unobtrusively.*

just before they turn, to look over their shoulder to see what is approaching and before deciding to signal to cross your path.

A cyclist will see and swerve to avoid potholes and gullies that you may not notice, and they may be influenced by your draught as you drive by. After all, they are balanced on two skinny little tyres and no suspension. Remember that in the wet it is an offence to splash pedestrians or cyclists, so watch out for puddles and standing water.

Notice the ears of horses. If they are laid right back the horse is upset. Set forwards, they have found something of interest. You may be just that, and the horse could shy when you come fully into focus. Horses are short-sighted, and sometimes difficult to deal with. They take a dislike to anything peculiar or noisy – such as rattling diesel-engined taxis or noisy Super Sevens like

mine! Keep well away and drive slowly and quietly by. The rider will invariably thank you. In my opinion, it is not pretentious to thank someone and equestrians are the most polite of all road users. If we were all to behave as well as them, there would be fewer problems on the road. The value of training at a riding school perhaps?

Mountain driving is most enjoyable, with open, clear views – but once across the cattle grid, there are sheep to contend with. If their heads are down, no problem. Then one out of many lifts its head, something takes its interest and off it goes. They are predictable, easy to anticipate and no problem for the local drivers; however, they seem to recognise and pick on tourists! If you hit one, you must report it. Ponies are wilful and will not move, so be careful with them. If they are spooked, they set off at high speed.

It is relatively easy to assess what an animal is going to do, it will let you know decisively, in no uncertain terms. People however, can

# VOICE OF EXPERIENCE

## Respect for horses

When I was a lad I was keen on horse riding, and I had my own pony called Betsy, who I used to ride bareback around the farm where we lived. My father thought I was getting a few bad habits and sent me off to a riding school. He chose well – the proprietor was an ex-cavalry soldier who was a strict disciplinarian. He would not let anyone ride one of his ponies, a gorgeous but almost uncontrollable Arab stallion, except me. It knew only two speeds, flat out and dead stop. Then backwards or sideways.

We rode around the sands of Hyde Park.

'No matter what happens to you, do not let go of the reins,' commanded the proprietor.

'Yes sir!'

It turned out that one thing the Arab did not like was perambulators, of the Silver Cross variety, pushed by uniformed Nannies. Being short-sighted, he saw the pram quite late, lit the blue touch paper and leapt high in the air. When he hit the ground, he was in full gallop. Some moments later, I also hit the sand, hard.

Hanging onto the reins with a vice-like grip, I was dragged along at high speed. Eventually we both came to a stop long enough for me to gather the reins, find one stirrup and remount. This was his chance to show what he could really do! Somehow I managed to stay on for the next mile or so. I think the boss was impressed, as he asked me to represent his school in various competition events afterwards.

The message is: have respect for horses, drive slowly and quietly by them and watch each one like a hawk, to anticipate any trouble.

*The building on the left severely restricts the view ahead. Is it clear? 'Tap' the horn in case.*

be far more difficult; 'nowt as queer as folk', as they say up north. On occasions, you will come across someone who is crafty. They will intimidate you into reversing priority, for their own benefit, by edging out of a junction, setting off from a parking place, or starting a u-turn in front of you. The answer is to be decisive and deliberate. In slow-moving traffic, give and take is sensible and works well. However, to reverse priority in all circumstances is to breed anarchy. Keep to the rules, then everyone will know what to expect. Decisive driving, without being self-righteous, will make a driver realise that you are not going to be intimidated. Give them a pleasant smile and thank them afterwards. Don't try to teach them a lesson, and try not to be easily perturbed.

It is relatively easy, with experience, to anticipate the intended action of a road

user you can see, but rather more difficult to anticipate a road user that you can't see, but who you might reasonably expect to be there. Some road users find this obvious element of roadcraft impossible to imagine. They make the sort of thoughtless pedestrian who will rush around the blind corner of a building and collide into you. They charge around when driving, around blind bends and brows, unable to stop if someone turns out to be in the way.

Take the example of a blind entrance to premises in an old town. In the horse-drawn days, the carter would lead the horse's head, to emerge after a good look, not leave it to the horse. Now, six feet of bonnet has to emerge before the driver can see up and down the road. Most folk are 'nosey parkers': they like to drive nose first into a driveway, and reverse out into the road (despite this being a traffic offence). This means that at least ten feet of car length has to emerge before the driver can see you.

So when you approach a blind entrance, expect someone to be there and about to emerge. Select a course that gives a sufficient margin of safety, slow to an appropriate speed, change down and give a medium horn warning of approach, which is essential in this situation. It is better to make a noise than have an accident.

At all times you must be able to pull up and stop within the distance you can see to be clear. The length of your sight line has to be matched with your ability to stop, which depends on the grip of your tyres on an ever-changing road surface. You must base your driving plans upon what you can see and what you cannot see but might reasonably expect is likely to occur.

Develop your powers of observation, constantly changing your focal point. If your attention is required in the foreground, or at the sides of the road, scan the road scene for potential danger or concealed areas. Down the busy high street, hang back to see the whole scene and try to drive with the minimum of braking. Arrive at each hazard as it opens out, not as it snaps shut – when the pedestrians have finished crossing at the zebra, or when the lights are changing to green. Pace your driving, avoiding unnecessary stops or application of the brakes, and flow along.

Be wary all the time of busy folk who rush about and take a quick glance that allows them to judge only the distance and not the speed of approaching traffic. You must give time for people to make mistakes. It is for this reason that you must drive slowly in a busy town environment. Although it is important to blend with the pace of traffic, to fit in, don't be intimidated to drive too quickly if you sense potential danger.

Look to see if stationary vehicles are occupied. If they are, keep at least a metre

*Hazard perception in action. A moment earlier this pedestrian had appeared and, yes, he did run out.*

*An example of observation and roadcraft – to be warned in advance. The reflection of an approaching car is visible (above) in the cottage windows, and then (below) the car appears.*

away, or a door's width. Notice exhaust smoke, and check the road wheels for any movement. Building lines and street lighting above the traffic often show the road's future direction and the position of junctions, so look way ahead occasionally, even though your speed is low.

Be a pessimist and anticipate the potential danger that lurks around every blind entrance, humpback bridge, dip, crest or bend. Anticipate that other road users may do something rash, illogical or foolish. Optimism is achieved when you clearly know what others are doing, by seeing evidence of their reaction to you.

Concentration and road observation are linked together. If you apply yourself totally to driving, to the complete exclusion of anything else, then your advanced driving will improve. Guard against fatigue. If you are tired, recognition and assessment of situations may become late and inaccurate. It takes practice and the experience of driving for long periods; pin-sharp eyesight and physical fitness will help enormously. The more experience you have, the better you will be able to sense if you are becoming tired and inefficient. My advice to the less experienced is to stop and rest quite frequently. If you are unused to driving far, two hours is long enough to drive without a break.

Speed must be varied for safety, as your focal points are lengthened and shortened over blind brows and bends. A short sightline indicates a situation that demands your attention and needs a slower speed to give you time to deal with it. So vary speed with acceleration and gearbox sense only, to give you time to react, without unnecessary braking. Flow along and try to avoid having to make any sharp evasive action in traffic.

Dips in the road are potentially dangerous and are blind until you can see all of the road surface throughout the dip. Dead ground is an army expression, perhaps to be taken literally if you ignore the simple advice not to commit yourself to overtaking until you can see all of the road surface before you pass.

It is an offence to splash someone, so alter your course if you see puddles or standing water. Holes in the road can cause damage to your suspension. There is no reason to hit a pothole – they do not move. So hang well back and plan well ahead to see them early. Do not run over and hit any object with your tyres; they need to be kept in top condition, internally too, to travel at speed. A plastic bag may have a brick in it, a plank of wood could have nails embedded in it and will cause a puncture. It is obvious folly to tailgate, as the vehicle ahead may jink and swerve past an obstruction and leave you to hit it.

In the country, range your eyes across the landscape and take notice of its general shape and configuration to assist your forward planning. Use your height to gain far views and read hilly country to decide where it is likely that your sight lines will be lengthened and shortened by crests, dips, curves and bends.

An exceptionally sharp bend will be signed. In Wales in particular, you had better take notice and be warned. But there is rarely warning of a steep crest or summit where, if there is a sign, it is often placed too soon where it will be forgotten by the less experienced. A sharp crest will dramatically shorten your sight line, and anything could be over the brow. The A68 in Northumberland is renowned for its blind crests, and is very dangerous to the reckless driver. I once witnessed a Porsche 928 cut in half on this road, with its engine thrown 300 metres away. The driver was lucky to survive. I was towing my racing car, and he passed me at enormous speed before the crash.

*Telegraph poles can provide useful clues to the road ahead; here they clearly run alongside it.*

Wooded country may have deer running across, mostly at night, perhaps when they think it may be safer. Trees cast a shadow and keep the road wet, or icy, and drop leaves to make surfaces slippery. A shadow or window reflection will indicate the presence of a vehicle a fraction of a second before it appears at a blind junction or bend. In summer, a shaded area, or tunnel, can be so dark as to make it difficult to see, so take off your sunglasses before you reach it. In winter, anticipate the angle of the low winter sun as you change direction. Around the back of the hill, in the shade, the road surface in the winter may be frozen – as it may be on a bridge. In the Alps, the warning sign 'fallen rocks', caused by cascading water, may indicate ice.

Notice an unbroken line of trees, square across your path; the road will go round the side of the wood. Odd trees are usually planted along the edge, following the line of the road. Telegraph poles march across country taking the shortest route, whereas the road may take a different direction entirely.

A church spire in the distance marks the probable location of a village (although the Black Death may have caused a relocation of its people, who upped sticks and moved their timber framed cottages, but left the stone church behind). A village is easily seen in the distance and demands an early lift off the power, to arrive at the speed limit without braking. Often, however, the limit sign is concealed around a bend, to make you feel uncomfortably guilty if you have failed to see the buildings in the distance.

If you do not look, you will never see! Try to take full advantage of open spaces, breaks in the lines of buildings, hedges, walls or fences, to obtain that brief but valuable view into converging roads. To the less observant, they may appear to be totally obscured. Often, you can see more further back from

*But do the telegraph poles follow the road here? Sometimes they march across fields.*

the hazard when you look down from a hill, than you can see when you arrive.

Vision into a minor crossroads with a limited view will only open up quite late. Potential danger can approach you from all directions, and someone could possibly cross your path at high speed if they do not notice the signs or road markings. It requires full consideration of each feature of the driving plan and perfect timing to apply the last feature, a long horn warning note. Remember, you should be able to stop before the zone of danger if required. Go in slow, out fast and safely, as vision widens and acceleration is applied.

Look at the road surface for clues of potential danger. Black lines left by a skidding vehicle indicate trouble in the past, a tangible reason why the 'danger of skidding' warning sign has been erected, perhaps having little to do with surface

conditions. It is cheaper to erect a sign than it is to re-engineer the road, to open the view and make it safer. They say the better the view the higher the 'inevitable' impact, so it seems the road safety agenda became the speed agenda.

Animal droppings, or mud from a tractor are most relevant if fresh and damp. Seeing them at the turn into an entrance warns you to select an early course away.

Constantly position your car to extend your view and safety margin when it is safe, without overdoing it, but never over a warning line into a blind area. This advice is often not heeded by many, who needlessly over-position into acute blind bends. The increased length of sight line gained by doing so is negligible.

When you see another road user in the distance, try to imagine what the driver is thinking about. What motivates their road behaviour? Is it road safety, pressure of business or lack of money to run their car? What vehicle have they chosen to own; is

*Arrive at the hazard when it's clear.*

*Apart from the cars, notice the pedestrians.*

*Wobbling cyclist. Is that crossing clear?*

it new, sporting, mundane or just an old banger? Is the driver linking vision with speed and driving up to the speed limit when safe and clear, or is the driver holding up the traffic by cruising inappropriately slowly? They may be a pensioner conserving fuel and the life of the car. If so, they may need to be passed when it is safe to do so. This driver's presence on the road is causing a potential hazard; you will have to begin your driving plan the moment their car appears in view. Look out if the driver slows down even further, it is most likely they wish to turn. Extreme patience and caution is required.

To follow a skilful good driver, well back, is a rewarding experience. There will be no need to pass. They give early warning of hazards on a winding road; watch the pattern of brake light application, pace and positioning. It is sadly a rare occasion to follow another driver who is driving both swiftly and safely. Evidence of roadcraft is so apparent when the driver is police trained.

Try to use your skill and experience to help others when driving, even if that means just not becoming involved with the bad driving of others, by hanging back a little in traffic. A balanced point of view is not easy to acquire, if your only experience of driving on a regular basis is heavy traffic in the rush hour, in town and on the motorway. It is easy to become frustrated by the incessant heavy traffic. Like unfortunate animals in a cage, people become badly behaved if bunched together. Limited by roadworks and speed limits, they may have road rage and react aggressively towards each other. This environment can lead to having the wrong attitude towards other drivers. Be calm, it is so easy to be drawn in, there is so much mischief and intimidation in big city driving. Patience is a virtue!

## Running commentary

Anticipation, roadcraft and discipline can all be improved by giving a running commentary as you drive. A fluent, articulate

commentary that blends well with your driving needs lots of practice and demands total concentration on driving, to the complete exclusion of anything irrelevant. It will encourage observation and anticipation because you will need to give a brief explanation of the actions you have to take to deal with a hazard and the reasons why, all before they occur.

You will feel self-conscious at first. So start when you are alone in the car and simply practise by identifying all the traffic signs and painted road markings, giving them their correct titles. If you don't know how to describe them, buy the official publication, *Know Your Traffic Signs*, and swot up – discipline starts by gaining knowledge. Mention each sign as it appears in view, to improve your forward planning. Don't just give it its correct title, but say what it means to you. Eventually your self-consciousness will disappear and your knowledge of sign observation will improve your confidence, fluency and concentration.

Eventually, with practice, you can attempt a full commentary. Start by introducing it. Imagine your passenger is sitting alongside you, but cannot see, or understand what is going on, before you set off.

# VOICE OF EXPERIENCE

## Slow doesn't mean safe!

Years ago I met a lovely old couple on holiday in Devon. They had the most immaculate Austin A30. I admired the car and mentioned it to them at breakfast. 'Oh, I am so glad you like it. You know, I never extend her, 50mph at the most and I have had her almost 25 years now.'

The couple were missing at teatime and I was told that they were OK, but in hospital. I immediately went to see them. He said, 'I was driving ever so slowly down this lane, with high banks either side, when there was a hell

of a crash and it all went black. A great big cow jumped over the bank and flattened us!'

You can drive slowly and carefully all your life, conserving fuel and your car, but if your number's up, that's it, you cannot anticipate the unreasonable.

I dread to think (and I don't!) of someone losing control coming the other way, or objects falling from high, even more so when driving my Caterham Seven as its secondary safety doesn't bear thinking about. Still, I am not here for a long time, I am here for a good time!

State your location, road classification and road number. If in the country, the distance to the next town. Describe the weather conditions and visibility, the state of the road surface and whether it is good for braking, steering and acceleration.

State that the car has been thoroughly checked by you personally, and is legal, serviced and fit for purpose. Mention if it is front-, rear- or four-wheel drive. State the make, model, year and whether it is familiar to you.

Run through the cockpit drill from left to right, with the static brake test and precautions before moving off, all achieved with dispatch and reasonable brevity.

Once under way, if it is not safe to do a running brake test, state why. It can be carried out as soon as you reach a clear road, front and rear, but not on the approach to a pedestrian crossing! Describe the road layout, if it has a pavement, is single or dual carriageway, the prevailing speed limit, traffic density and any traffic signs visible, and mention whether the road is familiar to you. Then, be specific. Lead into talking about the most important situation that is happening, say what it is, how it is going to affect you and what you are going to do about it, well before you arrive. If there is something more pressing to talk about, bring that in immediately and change the subject.

The quality of a commentary is not the quantity, or content; it is the correct assessment of the value of what you see and your judgement to take the appropriate action, in good time. Base your judgement on not only what you can see, but also what you cannot yet see but reasonably expect may occur. Although you cannot be expected to foresee the unreasonable, what is unreasonable to the inexperienced driver may be reasonably expected by the advanced motorist and is no problem, dealt with without fuss with minor adjustment to the flow of driving.

Plain, simple language is best, avoiding

*A warning sign to be taken particularly seriously – have your accident here!*

jargon. Use words as you would in everyday conversation. But don't drop into repetitive phrases. Where words of one syllable are available, use them. Simplicity will help you to avoid becoming tongue-tied trying to find the correct pronunciation. Be current and towards the future tense, never historical. Constantly mention the ever-changing scene behind.

Brevity is essential. You will have no time for long sentences, no matter that they may be quite correct to an English teacher, as long as the essence of what you say covers the facts and what you intend to do. Keep your voice clear and lively. Avoid a monotone voice (like some famous sports people), confidential whispers or muttering – try enthusiasm for a change!

Listen to the commentary of a professional pilot, calm, calculating, deliberate and decisive (even when he is about to crash); all the salient facts are there, delivered with professional brevity. Not easily perturbed, no panic or shouting, or even an excessively raised voice. Just professional to the last.

Make sure you draw a conclusion from your advanced observation. For example you might say, 'there is a garage.' So what?

'It has a forecourt, which may not be clear. A car is moving towards the exit. I am moving away.'

'That's better,' I might say.

Commentary is an excellent aid to extended training but can be highly inhibiting at first. You may need help with the technique and will then develop your own style of delivery. Any nervousness, lack of confidence or wrong attitude will be exposed. It will broaden your observation allowing an early decision to be made as to course, speed and gear. If you are early in thought, and time the driving plan to perfection, you don't have to move the controls so quickly. With practice, commentary driving will not slow down the pace of your driving, although it may do when you first start. What it will expose is any lack of roadcraft skills.

Observation and forward planning will be extended on fast-flowing roads, looking to the horizon, working back to the foreground and locking on to all relevant hazards. This is glance observation, done at lightning speed to scan and search the whole scene. It is essential in the fast-changing situations that are occurring, to the front and rear, to be able to formulate your driving plans, instantly, with long-range anticipation and judgement of speed and distance. Speed is time, multiplied by distance. Your brain is assessing millions of moving pictures that are changing, with distance, content and size, to assess depth and speed. Only long experience will develop your judgement.

Be sure that your phraseology is sufficiently descriptive, with the brevity required, for example: 'Junction on the left, good open view across the fields – clear junction right, but there is a potential danger from behind the farm.' In rural areas like this, observation is often not extended sufficiently far forward, behind or laterally. Houses in the far distance may indicate a speed restriction. Tree lines often show the direction of the road over a brow. A farm building in a field will pose the question, where is the entrance? Farmers are often wise enough to ask the authorities for a cattle crossing warning sign, but this is not always so.

In town traffic, it is not often necessary to break your flow of commentary, but you frequently have to prioritise and mention something new and more pressing. Your view is sometimes restricted by large vehicles, so reflections in shop windows and shadows may provide clues. Feet under vehicles, a hand to the bell of the bus, a lean of the head, turn of the feet, all these are vital details to be observed. Moving hazards are the greatest source of danger. Think of the vulnerable, the elderly pedestrian, cyclist or children, as an essential priority. Comment on the position of these people, their probable movements and actions.

When you comment on traffic, identify what people are driving. Is it a truck, a car or a motorbike? If several vehicles are present, use colour to identify them, rather than the make or model of car. Continue the commentary, even when stationary at traffic lights or in a jam. Use this time to gather information before moving off, and remember to check your gauges and warning lights. Try to avoid long pauses and drying up. There is invariably something interesting to talk about, even the child picking his nose and pulling faces at you!

The commentary can be broken down into three basic elements – observation, assessment and the driving plan. For example, take the approach to a right-hand bend:

# VOICE OF EXPERIENCE

## No unnecessary braking!

On a long, straight decontrolled autobahn in Germany, when you can see that the road to the horizon is clear and will remain so, high speed (as when flying) can be completely safe.

A few years ago now I was given the privilege by *Autocar* magazine to drive a Lamborghini Diablo along the A31 autobahn in Germany, from Bottrop, close to the Dutch border, up to the north coast. The objective was to drive this supercar quickly and safely, extending its performance fully with no element of danger whatsoever. With vision absolutely clear to the horizon, we achieved 201.4mph on four separate occasions in perfect safety, despite the road surface being slightly damp. The car was designed for this

speed and its condition was frequently checked by the engineers. I did not apply the brakes at any time at speed, I made sure there was no need to do so. It was always our policy to avoid unnecessary braking on the motorway on the High Performance Course, before the 70mph speed limit was imposed in 1965. As Ettore Bugatti once said to a customer who had the audacity to complain about the brakes on his car, 'brakes are only for people who want to stop!'

*The Lamborghini Diablo that I drove at 201.4mph on a deserted German autobahn for* Autocar *magazine: the photos show me with the car before the exercise and the travel-stained beast afterwards.*

# LINKING VISION TO SPEED AND GRIP
## *Using the landscape to assist your forward planning*

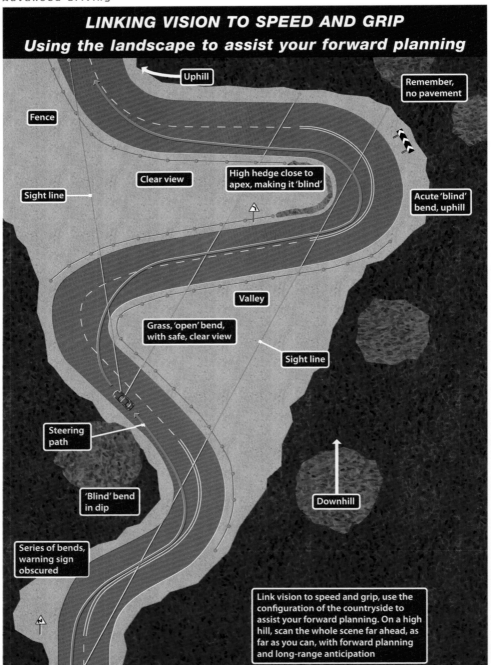

Uphill

Remember, no pavement

Fence

Clear view

High hedge close to apex, making it 'blind'

Sight line

Acute 'blind' bend, uphill

Valley

Grass, 'open' bend, with safe, clear view

Sight line

Steering path

'Blind' bend in dip

Downhill

Series of bends, warning sign obscured

Link vision to speed and grip, use the configuration of the countryside to assist your forward planning. On a high hill, scan the whole scene far ahead, as far as you can, with forward planning and long-range anticipation

- Early observation of both the warning sign and the bend means they are seen as soon as they appear on the horizon.
- The assessment is described as 'right-hand bend is acute and blind with no view, I lost it behind the hedge. The visibility is static.'
- The driving plan is described as: 'mirror clear, on course and holding in to the left, not too close – view is still closing – speed off on approach with light braking – speed now fits vision and grip – third gear – view and speed constant, engine pulling – there is the exit now, increasing speed with view, as I blend power with steering recovering – firm acceleration now, to gain the best from the car.'

Another example is overtaking a single vehicle on a straight clear road:

- Long-range observation begins as soon as the vehicle appears in view.
- Assessment describes a 'slow-moving van ahead with a nearside, now, offside

view far ahead – I intend to pass at the first safe opportunity, there is nothing behind.'

- The driving plan describes 'positioning out now, still well back – long headlight warning, slight reaction – situation stable and clear, no entrances, so overtake is on – speed maintained to pass, mirror, moving back – acknowledge to mirror.'

With simple phraseology you can convey your thoughts with brevity and improve your concentration with training of this kind. It will bolster your passengers' confidence to talk through complicated hazards in potentially dangerous situations. There is no doubt that an occasional commentary sharpens the quality of driving and will help you develop the easy driving flow of the advanced driver.

*A single-track, 'blind' bridge. It is reasonable to expect an oncoming vehicle or other road user, so slow down, change down and sound the horn.*

# 7 Language of the road

*Two pieces of vital information conveyed by road markings: the end of the centre line shows that the road ahead narrows; the solid white line at the roadside is broken wherever there's an opening*

Signs and signals are a language that it is advisable to learn. It may be surprising to realise that road users often fail to see or understand road signs and interpret their full meaning. Equally, it is important to give early and clear signals to communicate one's intentions, yet visual signals are often given too late and audible signals not at all.

Most journeys by car are short and on roads that are familiar. This may cause sign blindness and lack of sign observation. With experience of a route, most learn the usual hazards to be encountered and ignore the mandatory and warning signs.

To develop your sign observation, try a commentary, giving the correct titles of all the signs and road markings on a familiar route.

There seems to be so much information given to us, particularly by local authorities, that it clutters and blights our environment. When giving a commentary, your attention can be given to seeing and interpreting signs and road markings, almost to the exclusion of what is really important – other road users. The Government should encourage more common sense.

When you drive abroad, their system of controlling and advising the population is not only different, but considerably less complicated. When you return to the UK, it is likely that you will feel overwhelmed by the unnecessary clutter of signs and road markings, often concealed behind trees, hedges and buildings, and often so clustered together that is difficult to absorb their messages in the time available.

We will simply divide the language of the road into three parts:

- Signs and road markings, laid down by authorities.
- Visual and audible signals, given and received by drivers.
- Natural elements of the highway that have evolved, such as weather and surface conditions that need to be assessed and read.

## Signs and markings

There are three classes of sign, giving orders, warnings and information. Each have a different shape, which makes them easier to recognise in snow, fog or low winter sun.

- Circles give orders. Blue circles are a positive instruction, red circles a negative one.
- Triangular signs warn you of an approaching hazard or potential danger.
- Rectangular signs give information. Blue rectangles give general information, brown is for tourist interest and yellow for roadworks. Direction signs are also rectangular: blue on motorways, green on primary routes, and white for non-primary A- and B-roads.

The inverted triangle of the give way sign is easily recognised, and the double broken line across the road is the place where you should give way. A single broken line gives the approximate position where you should give way.

The octagonal stop sign is also easily spotted, unless it is obscured, and is supported by an extra thick continuous line across your path which you should stop your front wheels behind. Use the handbrake as proof you have brought the wheels to rest. Then, passengers can witness you did! Many drivers say they stopped, but most do not. Having stopped, search for a view by edging forward; one foot forward may give an extra 100 feet of vision each side. Think bike. Approach speed is time multiplied by distance so look right, left, right and left again, computing the distance covered between each glance, to assess the speed of approaching vehicles.

Note the difference between the blue circle signs meaning turn left, turn left ahead and keep left, where the white arrow gives a positive instruction. These mandatory instruction and prohibiting signs are 18 inches across. Sadly, like all the others they are often obscured, giving limited time to read them. If the speed of approach is too

# VOICE OF EXPERIENCE

## Emerging from a side turning

When emerging from a side turning, drivers should assess any reasonable approach speed, as well as distance, but often they don't. Driver training would address this weakness, but does it? I suggest not.

The authorities call 33 per cent of accidents 'speed-related', but in my opinion only 5 per cent of accidents are caused by excessive speed. Therefore, sadly, 95 per cent are caused by other factors. Appropriate speed may not be the speed limit, it may be less. And it is always the responsibility of the driver emerging to do so safely.

I think there is a case for altering speed limits according to time of day. After all, it is necessary to check the time of day when a bus lane or parking restriction applies. So, why should we not do the same for speed limits? For example, a lower limit should apply near schools at setting-down and picking-up time, but not at all other times.

high there will be insufficient time to read the sign.

Officially, you are not to accelerate towards a higher limit sign when it comes into view, but you should wait until you reach the sign before you can legally increase your speed. It may be surprising for you to discover that the local authority is not obliged to place any national speed limit sign for your information. If it is there, change down for acceleration and wait for the sign to disappear from the corner of your eye before you go.

Roadworks are often inconsistent and you never know what to expect. They can have a dramatic influence upon journey time, so take them into account. In Germany, and

*Why is this sign concealed round the corner? If there is no approaching traffic the level crossing may be shut – be prepared for stationary traffic.*

other large countries in Europe, perhaps because journeys are longer, most of the roadwork is done at night.

The 'slippery road' sign (or 'have your accident here' sign) you so often see when the road surface is obviously of good grip, simply because there have been more accidents than usual on that particular section of road. You may see long black lines signifying the incident.

A large yellow surround to a warning or mandatory sign also signifies there have been more accidents than usual at that location, and if the warning line is more than four inches wide, the approaching hazard is considered to be extra hazardous.

The sign for a railway level crossing may be concealed over a crest or around a blind bend; of course, it could mean there is the tail of a queue just out of sight. If there is no approaching traffic, the crossing is most likely to be closed.

It should be appreciated that a 'single bend' warning sign on a winding country road means that the next bend may be sharper than the rest. A 'sharp deviation of route' chevron should obviously lead to even more respect. The 'double bend' warning sign should display which bend comes first, left or right. Many drivers I have sat alongside have not been aware of this useful distinction.

The 'series of bends' warning sign is different, something which, again, is sometimes not appreciated. This should inspire the driver of an automatic transmission to manually select the appropriate gear ratio for the best and varying control of road speed for each bend. Underneath the warning sign, there will invariably be an information plate to tell you how far the bends will continue. But, is this information noted by the majority of drivers? I doubt it and, even fewer would think of linking the distance to the mileometer. It is handy to know if you are following a large vehicle, enabling you to hang back safely until the distance to the end of the bends is down to one- or two-tenths of a mile, when the opportunity to overtake will become more likely. Instead of course, the authorities now place a double bend warning sign, repeated every half mile. Perhaps the highway authorities don't want us to overtake and are trying to teach us patience?

When you see a number of warning signs on the same post, you read from the top down, as that should be the first hazard to deal with. But occasionally the signs are in the wrong order because the person who put them up got them the wrong way round. I joke not!

The 'dual carriageway ends' warning sign is frequently mistaken for 'road narrows both sides' and is not linked with a two-way traffic warning. This is potentially lethal, so why are they so similar?

The 'end of dual carriageway' sign should be a rectangular information sign, so that there is no possibility of confusion, and this should be linked to a double line system, at the edge of cross-hatching, to prevent overtaking. It's a daft place to overtake anyway, better to do so at the beginning, but it takes an age for drivers in comatose cruising mode to realise that the dual carriageway has started.

Many don't know the difference between the 'steep hill' warning signs, uphill and downhill. Read them from left to right: a steep hill downwards means braking to a safe descent speed and changing down into a lower gear to give adequate engine braking to hold you back. The lower gear

# MISLEADING ROUNDABOUT SIGNS
## A potential problem for drivers unfamiliar with the area

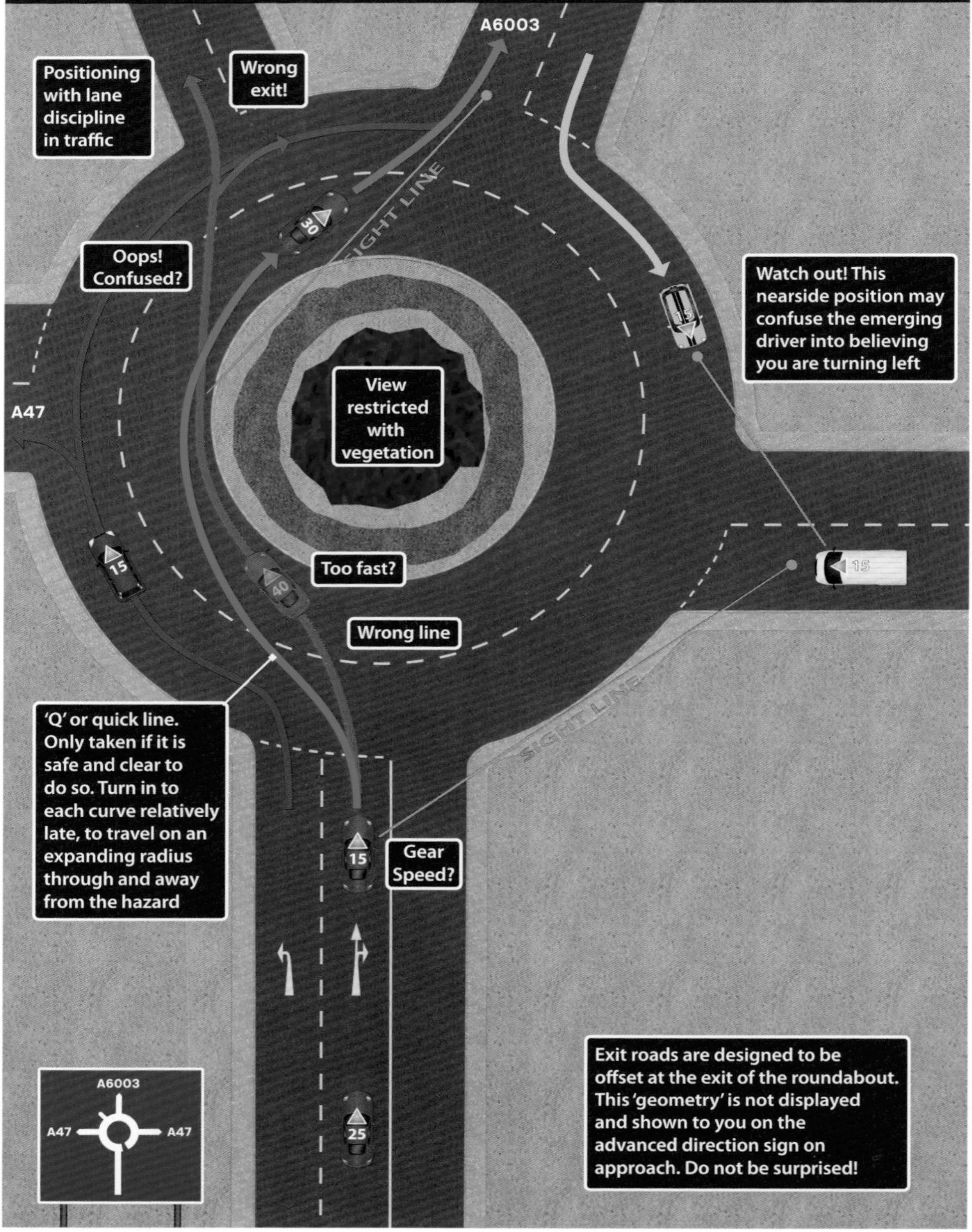

A6003

Positioning with lane discipline in traffic

Wrong exit!

SIGHT LINE

Oops! Confused?

Watch out! This nearside position may confuse the emerging driver into believing you are turning left

A47

View restricted with vegetation

Too fast?

Wrong line

'Q' or quick line. Only taken if it is safe and clear to do so. Turn in to each curve relatively late, to travel on an expanding radius through and away from the hazard

SIGHT LINE

Gear Speed?

Exit roads are designed to be offset at the exit of the roundabout. This 'geometry' is not displayed and shown to you on the advanced direction sign on approach. Do not be surprised!

A6003

A47 —⊙— A47

should be taken at the 'low gear now' sign at the top of the hill, not, as some do, halfway down or not at all. Anticipate that a heavy lorry (LGV) may speed up on gentle down grades, so don't pass unless you have plenty in hand. Climbing a steep hill, however, an LGV can be passed much more easily, perhaps when the driver changes down.

Red paint on the highway is an unnecessary blight on our countryside, in my view; I just don't see the point of it. On the other hand, the yellow box junction is sensible. The instruction 'do not drive onto the box junction unless your exit is clear' is confusing to some drivers when turning right. The positive instruction, 'go into the box to wait for oncoming traffic, if your exit is clear', is an instruction that I often have to give in this situation.

They may be only white paint, but the white markings along the road give a continuous message, not understood by many as they guide, warn and inform. A line often not noticed is the warning line on the approach to hazards, almost continuous with small gaps. Do not position over the warning line, unless you can see well ahead that the road is clear, particularly into blind bends and

crests. It is supplemented by a continuous edge line marking, if the road is considered to be extra-hazardous.

For a double-line system, when the line nearest to you is continuous, you must not even touch the line with your right tyres, except if it is safe to do so when you want to enter or leave a side entrance on the opposite side of the road, pass a stationary obstruction, or overtake a road maintenance vehicle, cyclist or horse rider moving at 10mph or less. Avoid clipping the end of the continuous line, wait until the broken line begins and signal early, before it arrives, to communicate your intention to pass. It should be obvious to the impatient driver behind and it may prevent them committing a traffic offence by stealing a march.

A restriction where the majority see good sense is where it is an offence to park on zigzag markings on either side of a pedestrian crossing. Very seldom is this parking restriction abused. Confusion reigns, however, among moving traffic on the approach to the crossing. The impatient will overtake a slow-reacting driver. Remember, it is overtaking if you pass the front bumper of the lead vehicle before it is clear of the crossing, and if the lead vehicle is the first

## VOICE OF EXPERIENCE

### Problems with road signs
Signs are often designed or concealed in an attempt to slow you down.

A common example of disinformation is the map-like layout in the direction sign provided on the approach to a roundabout. It may display the exit you wish to take at 12 o'clock, when in reality the exit is at 2 o'clock. It may also be somewhat concealed from you by vegetation that has been allowed to grow in front of it.

Perhaps it may confuse you, to give you a mild shock, to make you hesitate, to make you feel you have made a mild error, to try to convince you that you are driving too quickly? In a bad instance you could find yourself heading for the outside kerb if you haven't

selected the correct steering path and an accident could result.

It is vital that we are given correct early information on the advanced direction sign, to select the correct lane on approach: left lane for an early exit, before 12 o'clock; right lane for an exit past 12 o'clock; either lane to go straight on. Advanced driving should be assisted!

It is best to turn into each bend of a roundabout slightly late, so the exit is progressively straighter as you emerge. This will give more in reserve and a greater safety margin. Only in traffic is lane discipline essential, and we should all have the confidence and competence to drive alongside each other as we drive around.

to arrive, it must be the first to set off. You can slip by the second or subsequent vehicle in another lane, but not the first, moving or not, unless it has parked there illegally. Protection of concealed pedestrians is vital. You must give way if their toe is on the crossing. Many drivers push on not knowing or caring about these sensible rules and how to interpret them.

When planning a motorway journey, it is essential to check your exit junction number before you set off; this is shown clearly on the map. In order to keep the blue direction signs easy for you to read at the pace of motorway traffic, it is seen as sensible to limit the number of destinations shown on the first direction sign, usually positioned one mile in advance of the exit, but the exit number is clearly marked in a black panel at the bottom left-hand corner of the sign. The next sign at half a mile will add the main destinations in writing. Downward-pointing arrows on urban motorways display which lane to select and an inclined arrow points you to your destination. There are three 100-yard distance markers before the deceleration lane, where there is a third sign giving the principal destinations. A further route direction sign is located in the deceleration lane with a route confirmation sign to follow.

The exit from a motorway bend often tightens with a contracting radius, which may make you feel uneasy if you are travelling too quickly. There may be a visual obstruction as well and, if the tail of the traffic queue is around the blind tightening curve, it will give you a moment.

On urban motorways, signals are fixed overhead at approximately 1,000-yard intervals. Red flashing lights above a lane command you to stop before you reach them, not after. One driver I travelled with stopped too late. He passed the gantry and was unable to see when to set off again, until I pointed out the changing lights 1,000 yards away!

Orange telephone boxes are situated at one-mile intervals on the motorway. If you have to stop on the hard shoulder, angle the car with its wheels pointing a little to the left, and don't wander about. There are marker posts every 100 metres, numbered. Take a mental note. The blue arrow points the way to walk to the nearest phone. Get the family out of the car and put them behind the barrier. Most of the people killed on the motorway are on the hard shoulder. Noise is horrendous, particularly if the road surface is concrete, or if it is raining. These marker posts at 100-metre intervals have reflective stripes to be seen more easily in bad weather, and this can help you to judge distance.

The phones connect you to the police – not the AA or RAC. Tell them what service you require and your location on the motorway.

## VOICE OF EXPERIENCE

### Zebra crossings

I was a passenger in the back of a Metropolitan Police Driving School car, observing the driver receiving his coaching. We were in a traffic jam, starting and stopping. The student inadvertently stopped astride a zebra crossing. The sergeant instructor said, 'Open your door', to the young driver. The sergeant also opened his door. About to cross was a middle-aged lady with heavy shopping bags. He said, 'Come along madam, there is plenty of room through here', gesturing her to make her way through the car.

She laughed, the student learnt a good lesson and, I am sure, never did that again. It also taught me that if you can bring humour into coaching, as long as it can be taken without offence, it will always be remembered. One of the motorcycle instructors was a talented cartoonist. At the end of each day, if there was an incident, he would illustrate it and give it to the student. I hope they are all framed.

# PEDESTRIAN CROSSING
## *No overtaking on the approach*

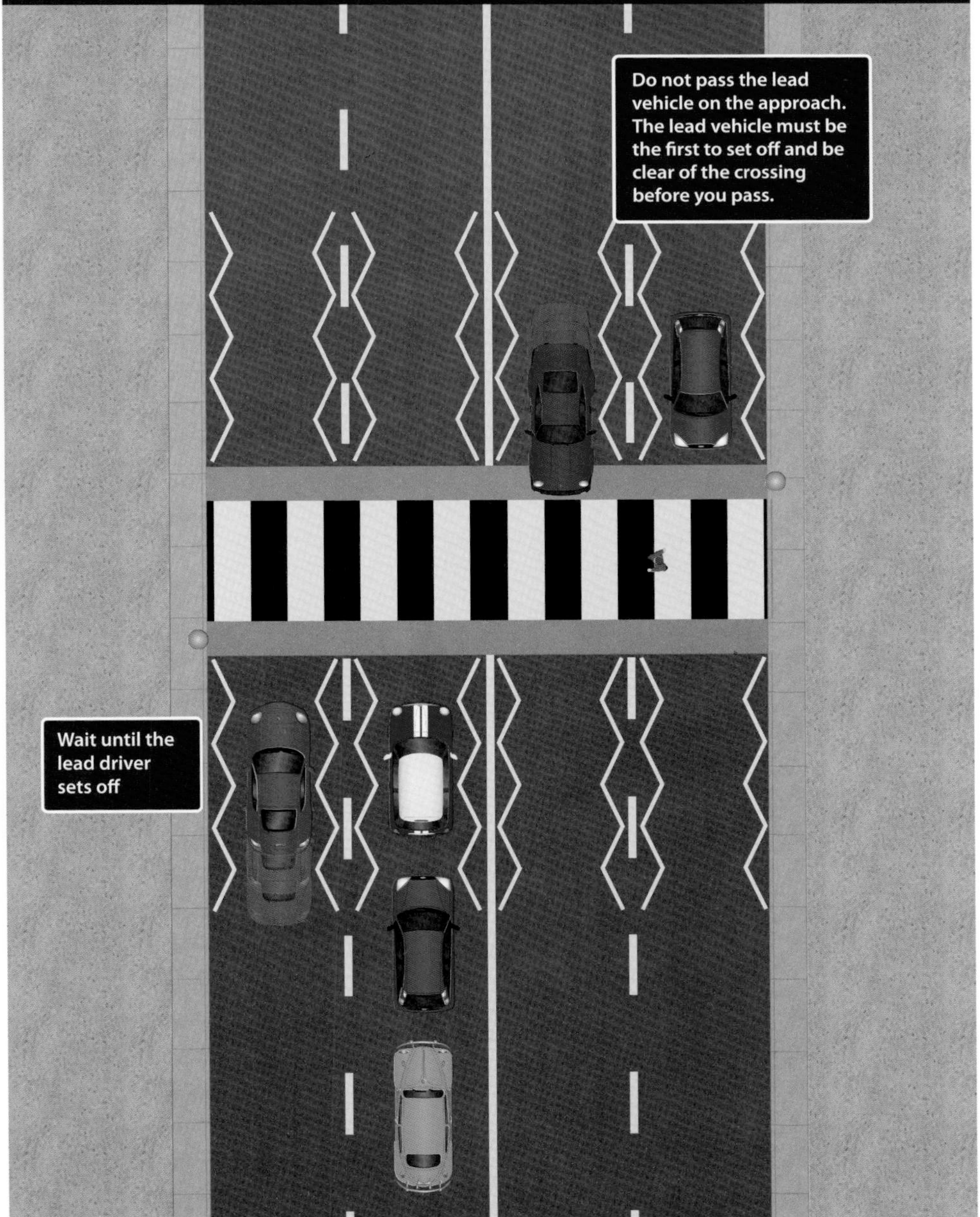

Do not pass the lead vehicle on the approach. The lead vehicle must be the first to set off and be clear of the crossing before you pass.

Wait until the lead driver sets off

# VOICE OF EXPERIENCE

## Flying Ferrari

In the 1960s we ran the High Performance Course for a short time in France, staying in a lovely farmhouse. One morning two of our clients were late arriving and Roy Wheeler and I were sitting in the garden having our breakfast. In the distance, we heard the exotic sound of a high-performance Ferrari engine howling across the country. Roy and I looked at each other and said together: 'He's mine!' We tossed for it and I won.

The driver arrived sideways, covering our table in dust. He was Italian and had a beautiful girlfriend (whom he left with Roy) and a very nice Ferrari 250GT California, which now would be worth a fortune. He spoke a little English and we got on fine at first, although I expected the worst. I gave a short but swift demonstration with simple commentary, which he seemed to understand.

After we changed sides, he drove flat-out. I didn't want to spoil his fun as the road was deserted and arrow-straight.

After a while, travelling at very high speed, I spotted a level crossing with a train approaching. I casually pointed this out.

'Si, si,' he acknowledged, foot to the floor.
'Train!' I said. Still no lift.
'There is a train coming!'

The barriers were still up and we shot through them at very high speed and left the ground, flew through the air and landed slightly askew. With lightning correction, he held each slide with great skill. I glanced in the mirror and the barriers closed behind us! With both hands in the air my client said, 'No problem!' I managed, eventually, to get him to stop. I drove gently back to the farmhouse and gave him a lecture. I ordered another breakfast and enjoyed the sunshine, glad to be alive.

Reflective white studs mark the lanes on the motorway; the left-hand edge has red studs, green for the exit and entrance with amber studs and a solid white line for the right-hand edge and central reservation. This is particularly useful to be aware of in fog, the most potentially lethal time on the motorway.

On primary routes, the green rectangular advanced direction signs display the next primary destination and route number, some distance before the junction. They should display the junction layout, but perhaps deliberately, on occasion they do not. They are also concealed on occasion too, behind a visual obstruction.

When the sign comes into view, there is much to read so, as the authorities wish you to do, you have to slow down if the road is strange to you. The more important road is shown as a thicker line. Road numbers in brackets can be reached along the road indicated and, for simple junctions, or where the sign size is limited, destinations can be stacked. Directions to motorways are in blue, and white indicates local or non-primary routes leading from the junction ahead. A route confirmation sign confirms the primary route number, as a check for you, and gives you the distance to a main town, which you should mentally note. Zero your mileometer.

On fast primary routes at multi-level junctions, advanced primary route signs are seen every half-mile, with green countdown markers and a final direction at the junction. On busy primary routes, signs in green are placed above the road, similar to those found on urban motorways, with either downward-pointing 'get in lane' arrows or offset panels informing you of no reduction in lanes on the primary route.

Non-primary A- or B-class roads – what I call 'white-signed roads' – are more natural and formed gradually over a very long period. Maintained by local authorities, they are not changed, engineered or redesigned to the same degree as primary routes. They are more demanding to drive safely and skilfully. They generally have less traffic, with greater opportunity to overtake the odd slow vehicle. They are fun if your roadcraft is advanced. If you enjoy your motoring, use them safely, as much as possible.

Plain white signs with black borders are used on non-primary roads. They may have green inset panels, if the road crosses a primary route, and like other advanced direction signs they can display a warning or prohibition. Blue insets are for motorways and green for primary routes. A pointed direction sign will identify the junction location.

The language of signs is difficult to acquire, so it is best to take time to learn it. Swot them up, if you are not aware of all this information already. Many drivers I have accompanied are not aware and sometimes admit to getting lost. Sat-nav is not assisting drivers' navigating skill. I do not use sat-nav when coaching and will always tell my client to follow a route, with a number and the next destination, and look to see any evidence of a lack of sign observation – which is surprisingly often the case.

In my briefing, I use an Ordnance Survey map to plan the route beforehand. Link your planning with mileage between towns. Estimate the potential value of overtaking on single carriageways to shorten your journey, with distances between dual carriageways noted, to zero your trip. There is no point in passing with a town or dual carriageway over the brow of the next hill. And what is the point of overtaking when you intend to make a turn a short distance down the road, around a blind bend? This is not the sort of motoring to make anyone popular.

The first principle of progressive motoring is to have your route planned, clear in your mind and noted on your strip route, before you set off on your journey. If you don't know where you are going, how can other people guess?

# CLOSING SPEED IN YOUR MIRRORS
## Time x distance – and check frequently

The following driver is seen as they appear in the rear mirror, and is closing up.

Closing speed is time x distance.

The driver behind is now tailgating. Be sure you plan and anticipate further ahead, spread out your speed reduction as soon as you can. Tap the brake lights, then decelerate and see evidence of safe reaction. If not, look for escape!

# Signalling

When following other drivers, try to estimate their degree of concentration, competence and consideration. It's a sort of one-way telepathic communication, sensing good or bad drivers by their position or speed. Even the type of car they are driving may give you a clue.

The driver ahead may be lost and unfamiliar with the area, have poor sign observation or be looking for an address, a most vulnerable time for any of us to make a mistake. It's a time to be deliberate and to keep out of the way. If you sense an inconsiderate bad driver, do not intimidate them. Keep well back and give yourself room to work. Plan to pass them when it is safe; maybe it will be essential to give a tap on the horn as a warning. Pass decisively, with a cheery wave afterwards.

The pattern of hesitant driving is easy to recognise. The driver's pace is slow and does not match or fit in with their environment. They may be a pensioner conserving fuel, which is to be sympathised with. We may all be in that position one day, although if I do drive slowly I will do my best to help others to pass, or I will use the first lay-by to retire into and let others overtake.

When turning, the inconsiderate bad driver will slow down first, brake, signal late if at all, then look in the mirror, I suppose to see what effect their bad driving is having upon others behind. Then they fail to position properly and cause an obstruction; it is painful to watch. Never sound the horn aggressively, in retribution, to teach them a lesson – it is the height of bad manners.

An element of bad driving which is highly dangerous on all fast roads is to pull out, change lane and signal at the same time. The majority of drivers do this. I have tried to analyse why. The habit starts with poor driving methods from the beginning. Mirror, signal, manoeuvre, degenerates into the reverse sequence. This dangerous, inconsiderate, bad habit will develop unless the instructor insists that the correct assessment and the proper use of mirrors and shoulder check is made. It is not only a question of glancing in the mirror; it is a question assessing the value of what is seen, using anticipation and the fine judgement of speed and distance.

We learn to judge distance in the light of experience, but speed is more difficult. It is time multiplied by distance. To estimate it, we need to look in the mirror at least twice on high-speed roads when wishing to change lane. The first look is to establish the distance involved, as soon as the closing vehicle appears in the mirror (if your driving position is correct, the movement in the mirror will attract your peripheral vision). The second look is to judge closing speed.

Signal only to inform, to ask, 'Please may I?', if it does not disturb an approaching driver. Do not ask to change lane if it will cause a problem, particularly if the closing speed is high. Wait until they are past. Do not instruct others with the indicator. The crafty, bad drivers will keep their intention

## VOICE OF EXPERIENCE

### Police presence

One of my HPC clients is a motorway traffic patrol police officer of 20 years' experience. He considers the habits of signalling late when changing lane and tailgating to be the cause of most motorway accidents. Why does it seem that the so-called experts take no notice of officers like him? There never seem to be sufficient numbers of police officers on our road system. I know it is expensive, but after all we do pay enormous sums in motoring taxation and surely deserve a high-profile police service. They are all highly trained, sensible and display a superb example on the road to inform, educate and if necessary, enforce motoring law.

secret, and chop across your bow, signalling without giving time to react. They may do this deliberately, with malice aforethought. Many are guilty.

A signal to turn or change lane should be given very early, without a change of course or speed. You must give time for others to understand what the signal means to them and to react to your signal, to be able to change their driving plans. A minimum time for your signal is four seconds; longer on high-speed roads, up to eight seconds.

Your forward and rearward planning has to be carried out far in advance. Then, you must see evidence of a reaction from the driver behind before you can change lane, to the convenience of the faster driver. You may just decide to wait before signalling, for the next opportunity to ask. If you judge that it is reasonable to signal to gently closing drivers that you want to change lane, don't be timid or indecisive, ask. Don't delay. It is unreasonable to expect strangers to read your mind, so communicate; if you do not ask in plenty of time, you will not receive. By all means wait for a safer time, if you can afford to, but waiting to signal can cause more potential problems, late into a hazard. It is no excuse to give people the chop!

To follow a good driver is rare and an education to others. Their signals are properly timed and they allow time for others to react, before changing lane or course. When you witness that a signal is effective and you receive co-operation, cancel it before your right-hand tyres cross the lane line; but you must see evidence of reaction, first of all. The signal to change lane is given as a signal of intention! If it is given early, there is no value in continuing to signal when the lane is being changed. And don't forget an acknowledging 'thank you' wave, hand beneath the mirror, afterwards.

Pulling out and signalling at the same time is self-righteous, perhaps bloody-minded, and if you miss seeing a driver in your door mirror, there is no time for them to react. Don't rely on the door mirror, give a quick life-saver glance over the shoulder and use your peripheral vision to check the blind spot. Don't look around. A quick, side-vision glance is enough. You must not take your eyes off the road any longer than necessary on fast roads. For someone to drive into a blind spot, they must have been visible in the mirrors beforehand, but check to be sure.

Signal when emerging from behind stationary, parked cars when setting off. It takes time to manoeuvre and you are vulnerable. So be prepared to wait and take a final look, just before you get going again.

In town or country, there is no better signal of what you intend to do than to position your car accurately in the road; but positioning is only one of the indications of turning, and not every road user is another experienced driver.

## VOICE OF EXPERIENCE

### A terrible trucker

I have an LGV licence and I remember giving instruction to a tanker driver on the motorway. He was a Cockney from the East End of London, demonstrating the same bad habits he had learned driving around town, ducking and diving, but this time on the motorway, with 44 tons of kinetic energy at 55mph, six feet from the vehicle in front!

I instructed him to drop back to 55 yards and advised him to signal before changing lane, not as he was doing so. 'Ere mate, where do you come from? Cloud cuckoo land?' he said. 'If I signal like you tell me, they box me in. I give 'em no chance, mate. I give 'em the chop, dun'I!'

Where do you begin with someone like this? In this instance, I turned him off the motorway and established reason, with discipline. Drive safely or you'll have no job! I gave a demonstration drive, with commentary, and finally won his respect and reason.

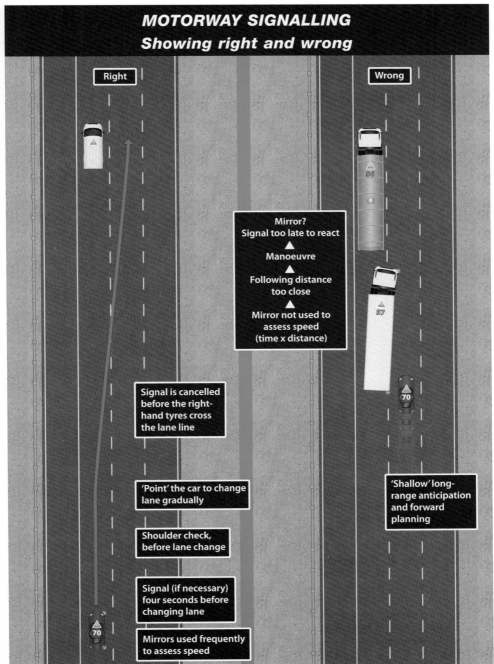

# MOTORWAY SIGNALLING
## Showing right and wrong

Right

Wrong

Mirror?
Signal too late to react
▲
Manoeuvre
▲
Following distance
too close
▲
Mirror not used to
assess speed
(time x distance)

Signal is cancelled
before the right-
hand tyres cross
the lane line

'Shallow' long-
range anticipation
and forward
planning

'Point' the car to change
lane gradually

Shoulder check,
before lane change

Signal (if necessary)
four seconds before
changing lane

Mirrors used frequently
to assess speed

**109**

# CAUSES OF MOTORWAY ACCIDENTS 1
## *Shallow planning, tailgating and late signalling*

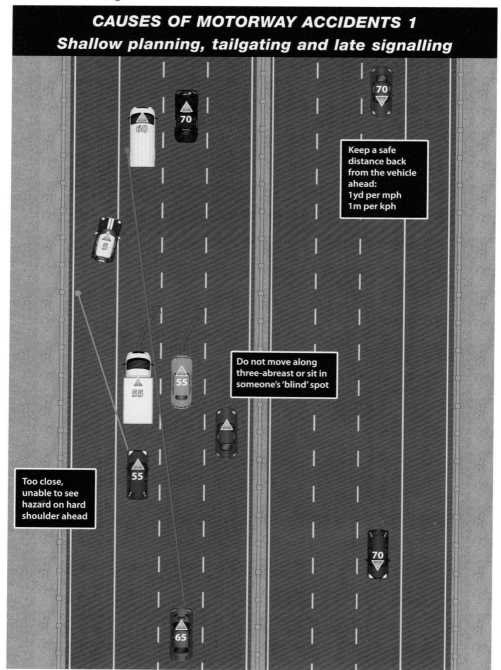

Keep a safe distance back from the vehicle ahead:
1yd per mph
1m per kph

Do not move along three-abreast or sit in someone's 'blind' spot

Too close, unable to see hazard on hard shoulder ahead

Modern cars are so easy to drive with excellent all-round visibility that I think they may lead to a degree of laziness, both mental and physical. Clear signals can be given with the mere flick of a switch. The lazy way is to signal automatically, irrespective of reason or timing, with nothing around the driver – a flick of the switch for any deviation, parked car, bump or pothole in the road or any excuse to operate the turn signal. It is done without looking or thinking, without rhyme or reason.

Establishing a reason to signal is vital. The type of driver who never fails to signal with the indicator, whether it is necessary or not, tends to signal too late, and fails to sound the horn when it is essential. It is simply to do with awareness. If all-around observation tells you there are no other vehicles around and no pedestrians or cyclists to see you, there is obviously no need to signal.

However, there is an exception to every rule. If your ability to see another road user is in doubt, it is better to be safe than sorry. A good example is when turning left at a blind approach to a mini-roundabout. Any driver approaching quickly from your left will want to know instantly that you are turning left, so they do not have to give way to you, so you need to be already signalling before they come into view.

This acute observation assists concentration, which is vital to safe driving. Most drivers, if honest with themselves, will agree that they signal automatically. Bad drivers will signal late, after braking, with little respect for the following situation. They will say after being involved in an accident, even if they are to blame, that it is always the other person's fault, because, 'well, I signalled didn't I?'.

Always be aware of the reason why you need to communicate to any other road user, who may or may not be in view. Operate the switch with perfect timing for each individual situation. It is always different: even at the same junction, the next day the signal will require different timing or even no signal at all. You may perhaps have heard of the old countryman who didn't signal and caused an accident. 'Well, don't you know, I always turn in here at half past twelve, every day!'

Do not flick the indicator switch automatically without thinking. Act upon what you see in the mirror and in front. For example, a signal to pass a parked car is unnecessary in most situations with cars following you. It can be confusing, even dangerous when approaching a right turn. Use the indicators with care and thought and give them the way you would like to receive them.

## VOICE OF EXPERIENCE

### Using the mirror

Driving examiners are trained to look across at the candidate's eyes as the command to turn is given, to watch and see that the candidate actually consults the mirror before the turn signal. I find this off-putting and disturbing. If the driver is competent, it will become apparent that any signal given is perfectly timed and given in the way you would like to receive it. To check if the signal is necessary, the mirrors have to be used and the correct action taken. To me it is the correct assessment of what is going on behind that is more important.

Many years ago I taught novice drivers in Central London. To encourage the proper use of the mirror, before deciding to signal, I found it vital to establish the reason to signal – to communicate to a cyclist, pedestrian or any road user in front, rear or alongside, in fact anyone anywhere in the environment who may have reason to know what you intend to do.

It became unnecessary for me to have to look at my clients' eyes as it was apparent through their driving decisions and actions that they were using the mirror and acting correctly upon what they saw.

# CAUSES OF MOTORWAY ACCIDENTS 2
## *Nearside passing, tailgating and late signalling*

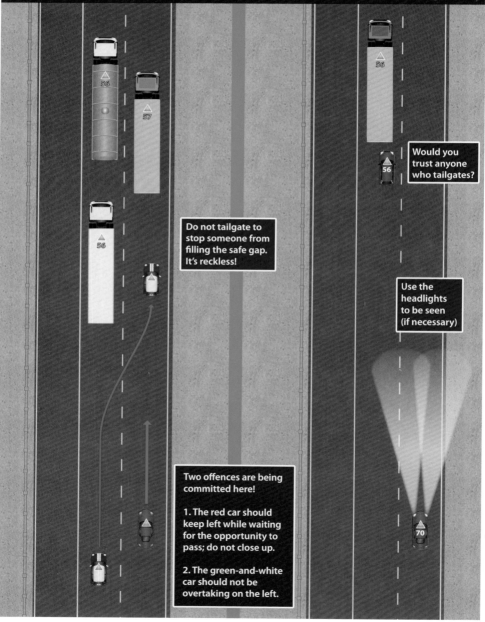

Would you trust anyone who tailgates?

Do not tailgate to stop someone from filling the safe gap. It's reckless!

Use the headlights to be seen (if necessary)

Two offences are being committed here!

1. The red car should keep left while waiting for the opportunity to pass; do not close up.

2. The green-and-white car should not be overtaking on the left.

Cancel any direction signal after use (I have to remember this in my Seven, as the indicator is not self-cancelling) particularly if the next junction you pass is a minor turn to the left. The driver emerging may think you intend to turn. It's the reason why, when emerging from a junction yourself, you should wait until the signalling vehicle begins to turn before pulling out. The driver may also be using the indicator to signal that they are stopping on the left, past the junction you are emerging from.

To emphasise an intention to turn right in a blind bend, a smartly given, clear arm signal can be invaluable; because you are giving the signal personally it is more decisive. Put your arm out straight, palm to the front, fingers together – don't point. An arm signal when slowing down should be given before applying the brakes. Two sweeps of the arm, shoulder height to the door panel,

*The hedge at this junction has been allowed to grow and blocks visibility. By edging forward 1ft you gain 100ft of further vision.*

wrist straight, and palm to the ground. It is unrealistic to expect it before braking in most cases. I favour the continental 'I am stopping!' particularly in my Super Seven, with arm straight up, palm to the front – to be clouted from behind is to be avoided! 'I am turning left' to someone in front is okay before turning into a minor road, but give it across yourself, not your passenger. We should also give up the 'I intend to turn left', arm rotating signal, which is plain silly. I would prefer us to adopt the continental signal, over the roof and be done with it.

Do not wave or beckon pedestrians to cross junctions or crossings. Just gently stop a little back from them, so you do not intimidate by your vehicle's presence. In a stationary queue

you should avoid t-boning a minor junction on the left, but don't beckon someone out of it. Just keep a blank expression and leave a gap for them to make up their own mind to emerge. If an accident occurs after calling them out, you will be partly to blame and possibly liable. You may, however, consider it essential to wind your window down and draw attention to a motorcyclist by waving him down with an arm signal, to do your best to avoid an accident.

The third form of visual signalling is to use the headlights, excellent when used on the approach to junctions at night and before overtaking. Wrongly, the headlight main beam is often used to reverse priority. Don't do that. Keep to the rules! Use headlights only as a visual means of warning of approach, not to call road users to cross your path.

Like any other signal, it should be given clearly and decisively and for as long as it is reasonable for it to be seen and understood – not as a quick flash. Four seconds is often needed before your signal will be seen. Only use this form of warning in daylight if the horn will not be heard. The horn is less effective in dead sound conditions when it is raining. Use main beam headlights to try to penetrate the peripheral vision of a lorry, or tractor driver, with a long light. Look for evidence of a reaction before committing to overtake, to see that slight movement of the offside wheels away from the centre line.

Never flash the headlights aggressively several times when someone is overtaking ahead of you on a motorway or dual carriageway and obviously cannot move in, it's just bad manners and antagonistic. Give them fair time to move over, even if they seem to be deliberately obstructive, which occurs frequently in this country. Then, if there is evidence that they haven't seen

you, use a four-second light on main beam to attract their attention, or until you see a reaction. Only expect someone to move over into a long, safe and reasonable gap. Don't tailgate or close up to intimidate them to move over – that's reckless and potentially dangerous, and a most serious traffic offence, if proven.

Headlights have only the same meaning as sounding the horn. They are just a visual means of warning of approach, or an indication of presence, and are not to be used to give instruction or information about your intention. However, if you have good reason to use headlights, do so; don't always expect others to be aware of your presence or to do the right thing. Communicate with a clear headlight warning, decisively, without feeling guilty. It is not an offence. It is better to give a warning than to have an accident.

Hazard lights can be used as a warning, if it is essential to alert following traffic to a sudden stop on the motorway (but don't use hazard lights when parking illegally or unloading). Tapping the brake light switch, on and off, may also be used to give a sense of urgency when slowing from higher speed, until you see evidence of a reaction from the fast-closing driver behind.

The last visual signal, but not the least, is to always acknowledge the courtesy and co-operation extended to you by others. This essential signal does more to further a spirit of road safety in others than any other and is so badly needed on our roads today. Lift your left hand, so it can be seen easily in the middle of the screen of a right-hand drive car. The hand need not leave the steering wheel, just lift it to 11 o'clock high, except after overtaking, when to ensure it will be seen, lift your left hand up to the centre mirror.

## Voice of the car

The horn is the voice of the car; it can be aggressive and demanding, or polite and informative. It can save lives or give

*Never beckon a pedestrian to cross; if an accident occurs you will be partly to blame and possibly liable.*

offence. It should be used in the same way you would speak to someone and consequently has a great bearing on the way it is accepted by them. You are not shouting 'get out of the way!', you are saying 'I am here', like clearing your throat, as you would on occasion, rather than using the formal 'excuse me'. Followed always by 'thank you', irrespective of the situation.

Is the natural British instinct for discretion, the desire to try to avoid drawing attention to oneself, to avoid a fuss, the reason why, in this country, drivers object to sounding the

horn? Many think that if you drive carefully, you should never need to sound the horn. But sadly, others are not quite so careful. No matter how slowly you drive, a road user may not see or hear your approach and take the necessary precautions. I am convinced, by the near misses I have witnessed, that some drivers would rather have an accident than make a noise.

The driver who doesn't give audible warning when approaching a situation will then sometimes sound the horn aggressively, to tell off the other driver for not co-operating. The noise will be late, of no value and may give offence or shock that can on occasion have serious consequences. Many retaliate when some offence has been committed through inattentive driving and the aggressive driver will sound the horn in retribution – often the only occasion when the horn is sounded. This aggressive bad driving is responsible for the bad reputation the horn has in this country.

The horn note, sounded aggressively late and for too long, hardly encourages a spirit of good fellowship on the road and its misuse encourages its omission from a considered driving plan and its potentially valuable contribution towards road safety. The following question is hardly ever omitted from a motor insurance claim form: 'Did you sound the horn?' I would add, 'if so, when, and was there any evidence of reaction to the warning?'

The horn is often blasted unnecessarily by the inexperienced and very good judgement is required to decide when and where it should be sounded. It should be voiced only when it is really necessary and only to make one's presence known to other road users. They must be given time to react to the warning and you must see that co-operation before committing to the hazard. You must always see evidence of reaction – don't forget that a road user may be deaf.

The warning of approach is the last feature of the driving plan, only to be sounded after every other precaution has been taken. Never use the horn as a substitute for slowing down. In town, the worst type is the one who drives too fast for others to react and uses the horn aggressively, demanding the right of way from anyone who dares not to judge their excessive and inappropriate approach speed. This behaviour is the height of bad driving manners.

In heavy town traffic occasions for sounding the horn are rare; speed is slow and other precautions can be taken. Drivers in foreign cities are not prepared to do that, so life becomes unbearable with the constant cacophony of horns blaring – resulting in a ban, as is the case in the UK in built-up areas between 11.30pm and 7.00am.

In lighter traffic, the need to give a warning will increase and a light tap is often enough to attract the attention of vulnerable, unaware pedestrians or cyclists, but only if all-round traffic drowns the sound of your approach, or if they show signs of carelessness.

As speeds rise in the country, the need to give a warning will be seen more as a necessity on the approach to blind bends, humpback bridges, junctions or entrances. If you cannot be seen, why not be heard? Good judgement and discretion is still required, not to sound it for every unseen area of potential danger. It depends upon its importance; for example, on a blind bend on a narrow single track road it is a necessity to give a warning. At other times, an alternative driving plan might be considered.

The inexperienced driver who has difficulty in noticing and assessing actual danger that is visible will never see the need to sound the horn for a concealed potential danger – one that can reasonably be expected to be there, but cannot be seen. It is a question of intelligent anticipation that is developed in the light of long experience, some of it nasty!

To help you decide if a warning is necessary to any road user, try to decide if there is any evidence in their behaviour that shows they are aware of your presence. If it matters for the safety of both of you, and there is no definite clue that they are aware, a warning has to be used, as a final feature in the driving plan, after every other reasonable precaution has been taken. After all, that road user is a stranger to you. You cannot speak to them, can you? So, talk to them, communicate; use the voice of the car.

Only sound the horn once, at the correct time. Not so early that it cannot be heard or identified as being for the person intended. Nor too late for them to have time to react. Do not sound the horn twice; if it is done at

precisely the correct time and for the correct duration, there is no need. The exception will be for children, when light tapping several times has greater effect. Once you receive co-operation, always acknowledge it, with the courtesy signal, when they look.

There are three types of warning note:

⊘ Short tap, used at very low speeds to attract the attention of a pedestrian or cyclist.

⊘ Medium note, the most frequently used with a length of approximately one second. Once you see evidence of reaction, it is followed immediately with the courtesy signal. If you haven't time to give that wave, or a nod of the head if pressed, then the warning was too late – which means the gear selection and the braking was too late.

⊘ Long continuous note, used only when approaching at speed, for the note to carry. Sometimes, when the situation is vital, the signal can be supplemented

*Give a warning and sound the horn! Narrow road, 'blind' bend, no pavement – be able to stop and apply the last feature of the driving plan.*

with a long headlight main beam at the same time. Give this warning, for example, at the speed limit on a dual carriageway, if a driver is creeping out of a junction without looking, where the potential impact would be extremely serious. My Super Seven is a tiny car and in inclement weather, I drive on dipped headlights to be seen, as motorcyclists do. Others are less inclined to emerge at road junctions as the Seven is then more easily seen.

Never creep up behind old people (especially in your quiet electric car or limousine) and then blast the horn. It is an offence. In the country, when it is very quiet with no approaching traffic, pedestrians, cyclists and horse riders will hear you coming. You must refrain from making an

unnecessary noise. Just steer a wide course if there is room; if not, wait until there is. The authorities are intending to designate quiet lanes, and quite right too. The sooner the better.

If the horn button is situated in the centre of the wheel, where I personally prefer it to be, you are more aware of where it is. When travelling at speed, use your left hand along the spoke to help to hold the wheel with a steady grip, while pressing the button with your thumb.

At low speed just bop the button with your left fist or knuckles. My Super Seven's warning devices are wired in series; a peep for town or gentle country road situations, and a strident Italian air horn for speed or blind areas.

When planning to overtake, take all the precautions you can, by positioning out on the path to overtake, then, from this position, by sounding the horn, if necessary, before you accelerate. Give time for the

*When sounding the horn – the 'voice of the car' – use the left hand and 'steady' the steering while giving the warning.*

other driver to react and see evidence of this reaction before overtaking, such as a slight movement of the offside wheels of the overtaken vehicle away from the centre line. Do not accelerate to pass with commitment, and then sound the horn. Give a warning first, and then use power to pass, if safe, with the full co-operation of the driver to be overtaken. Not forgetting afterwards to acknowledge the courtesy extended.

Any driver who is travelling unnaturally slowly may be turning off without warning. They may not be concentrating upon what they are doing. They may be on their mobile phone with a hands-off set or listening intently to the radio or talking to passengers. If there is any doubt, sound the horn. It is far better to make a noise than have an accident!

**119**

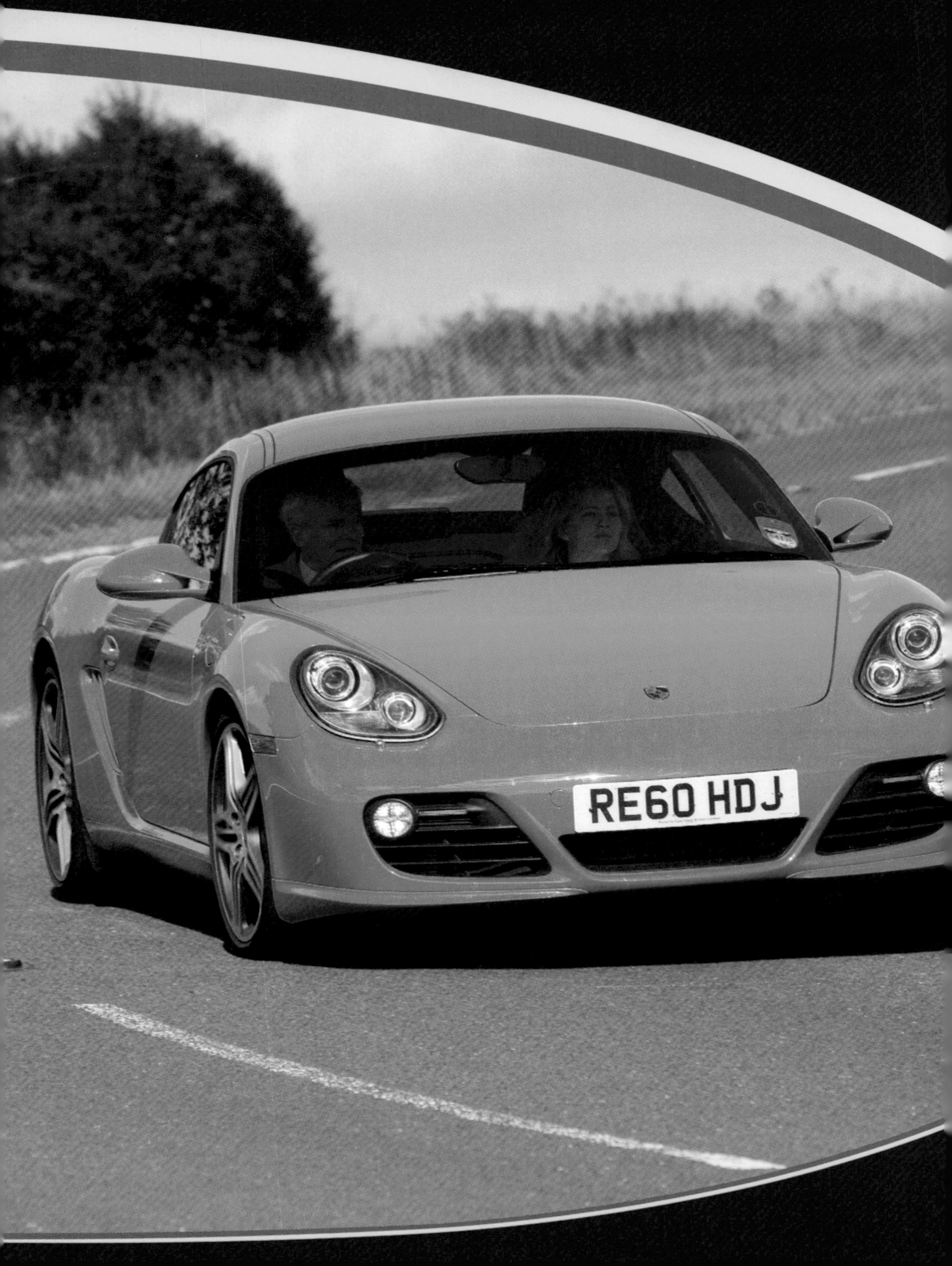
RE60 HDJ

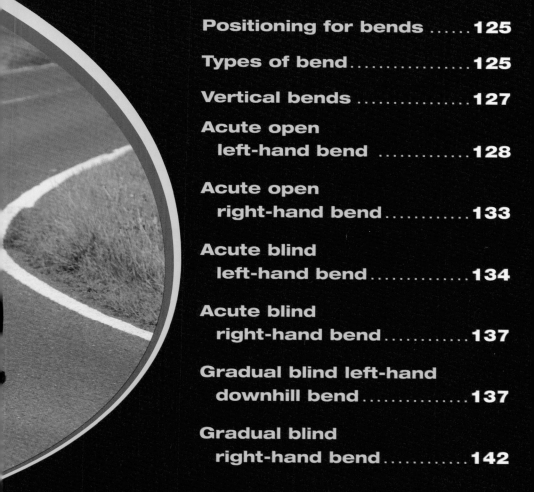

# 8 Cornering

*Cornering on a country road is a great
joy in a car like a Porsche Cayman S!*

For a keen driver, cornering is the most challenging and enjoyable aspect of driving. It should be approached with the knowledge, skill and responsibility that can best be established with training and confirmed with long experience.

Over the years car technology changes and improves, and an enthusiastic driver must keep up to date and preferably gain experience with every kind of car. You should also try to appreciate the problems of other modes of transport, from motorcycles to large goods vehicles; even race and rally cars, if you have the opportunity. It is important to have empathy with other road users. The more experience you have the better.

Most bends in the busy parts of the UK are blind and restricted in view. Elsewhere, the natural configuration of the countryside dramatically varies the view. It is vital that you vary your speed on country roads, to link vision with speed and grip, to drive safely, and to use acceleration and gearbox sense

to enable the car's engine to vary road speed without unnecessary braking. The type of driver who cruises along in fifth gear, to save fuel, is often the type of driver who is too fast in one instance of limited view and too slow in the next. The engine is the primary controlling influence to vary speed. Brakes are applied only when there is limited distance and space to slow down.

If the curve of the bend is blind or restricted in view, it is not the ability to hold the road which is the limiting factor, it is the ability of the car to stop within the distance seen to be clear that matters. This is undoubtedly where, in the last few years, advances in electronic technology have developed to the most extraordinary degree. ABS and ESC can now get the best possible grip from the tyres in an emergency and keep the car stable, without skidding. Most drivers have never experienced this ability, and some may say ignorance is bliss. The keen motorist will go off the highway to find out safely how they work.

## VOICE OF EXPERIENCE

### A near-death experience

If you need to know how essential it is to be able to stop within the distance you can see, consider this near-death experience I had as a young man, while I was serving in Hong Kong in the late 1950s. I had a tuned MG Magnette Tourer, which went very well, winning its class in various hillclimbs and sprints in the colony.

In those days, the road between Kowloon and our Army Air Corps base at the village of Shatin was a fabulous twisting mountain road that I enjoyed immensely. One morning at about 3am I was driving it in foul weather. It was the monsoon, and it had been raining hard for about three weeks. Positioning the car out a little to see around a blind left-hand bend, I came across a parked van up against the cliff without lights. I jinked around it, but then, I instinctively reacted and cadence braked to a standstill, because the headlights no longer reflected the surface. It was not

there! The engine had stalled in my panic to stop, and the car was shaking up and down on its springs. I fired the engine, slapped it into reverse and backed away, fast. My passengers leapt out and we all stood in amazement. The road surface fell away 100 feet into nothing.

It emerged that the water reservoir in the mountains had become dangerously high and, without issuing a warning, the Chinese officials had released a few million tons of water down the mountainside. It washed a valley away and nearly us with it! I turned to ask the Chinese van driver why he did not warn us, but he seemed to be in meditation, staring straight ahead. We took aerial photographs of the devastation next day, and I kept thinking, another five feet and it would have been our ghosts looking down there. Ever since I have always insisted my clients are able to stop in the distance they can see to be clear.

# SAFE STOPPING DISTANCE WHEN CORNERING
## A personal experience in Hong Kong

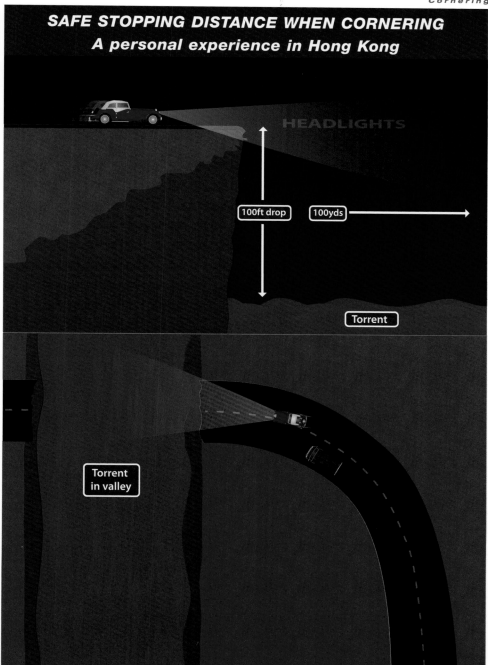

# CORRECT CORNERING LINE
## *How to maximise forward vision*

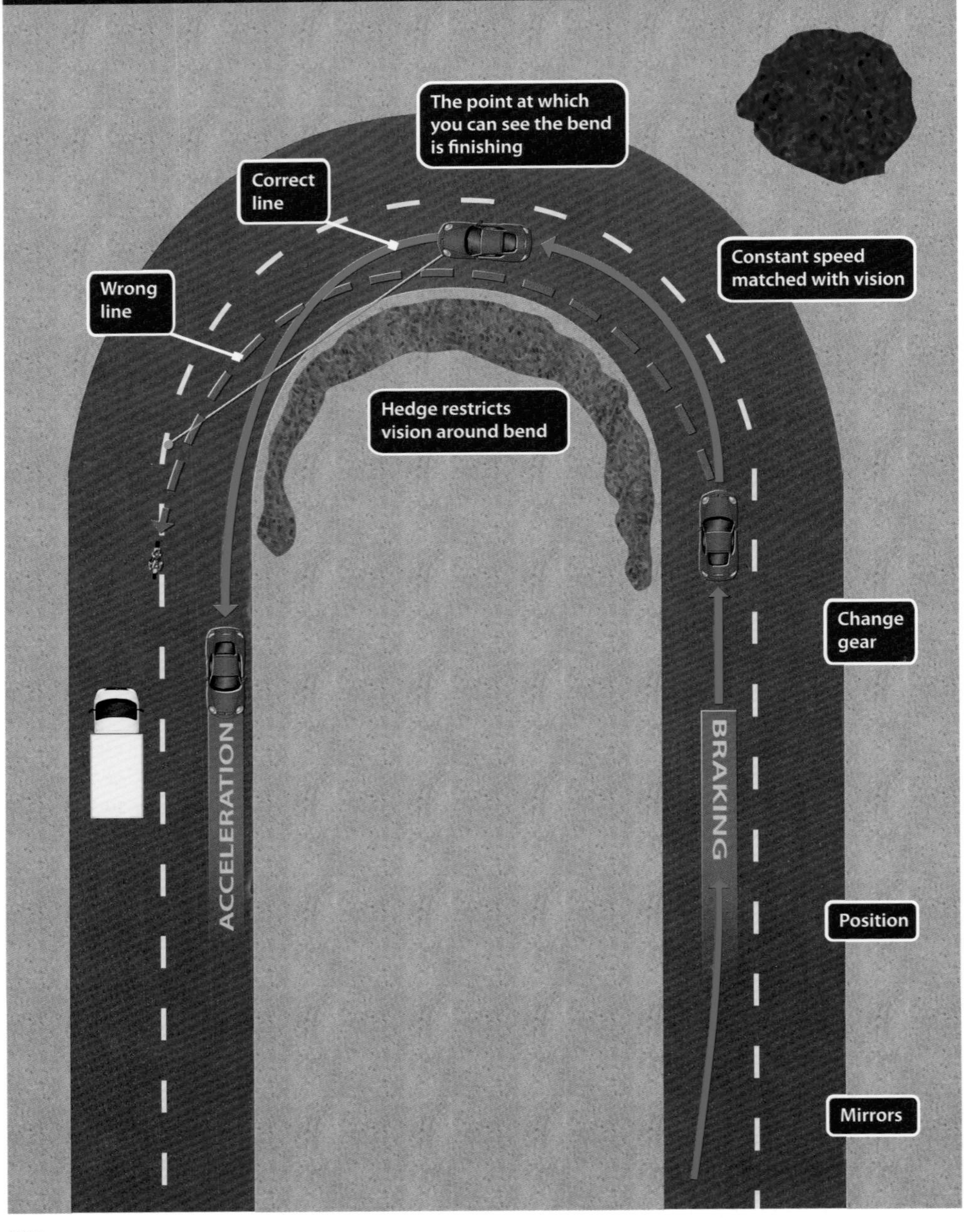

The point at which you can see the bend is finishing

Correct line

Wrong line

Constant speed matched with vision

Hedge restricts vision around bend

Change gear

ACCELERATION

BRAKING

Position

Mirrors

# Positioning for bends

Road positioning when approaching a bend is mostly of value on wide roads. On narrow blind bends, it could be dangerous and inconsiderate. This is why I do not recommend extreme road positioning to novices, as they may not discriminate where it is safe and unsafe to apply it.

Approaching any bend the driving plan must be applied precisely. The correct course and position is chosen as soon as the bend is sighted, speed is assessed with an early cut off and deceleration, and any necessary braking applied only once, decisively. One gear is chosen, cleanly selected. Problems of cornering are mostly solved by a precisely assessed speed of approach. If there are any flaws in judgement, it will be apparent when you arrive too quickly.

On approach and through the bend, there are three lateral road positions that you may consider within the bounds of safety along a single carriageway:

○ A safety line position would be a normal station in the road for driving, with an equal margin of safety between the edge of the highway and any white lines down the centre of the road.

○ A reduced safety line, in towards the left-hand side or nearside position, but not so close that you have to watch the edge of the road for too long, instead of taking a quick glance.

○ An extended safety line towards the offside, only if it is safe and not if there is any oncoming traffic.

It is important to range your eyes far ahead, to the limit point of your view, away from the road surface. The limit point is normally where the left-hand side (approaching a blind left-hand bend) intersects with the far edge of the road. If the two points hardly move in relation to each other, the bend is a sharp deviation and it is vital to link vision to speed and grip to be able to negotiate the bend with a sufficient reserve of grip left in the tyres, to be able to stop, if it is necessary.

# Types of bend

The first problem is, which type of bend am I faced with? The answer is found in good observation. The brain is triggered by past experience of the kinds of bend and curve you have encountered in the past. It is essential to train oneself to look across bends, through gaps in hedges or between buildings and use scanning techniques, to range your eyes across the countryside, to gain any clues and use the configuration of the landscape to assist your forward planning. Use a line of trees or a hedgerow, or a church steeple in the distance to give an idea of where the road may be going. What goes left, will go right. What goes up, will go down again.

Bends along a two-way country road may be categorised into six basic types:

○ Vertical bend. That is, any rise and fall in the road that pitches the car and makes it light or heavy.

○ Horizontal bend to the left or right.

○ Acute bend that is a sharp deviation, like a hairpin.

○ Gradual bend, usually engineered (but it may tighten).

○ Blind bend where only part of the road surface is visible at any distance through the bend.

○ Open bend where the road surface is visible throughout the bend. (Sometimes an open right-hand bend may suddenly be made blind by the presence of oncoming traffic.)

In addition, one has to consider all of the following considerations:

○ Safety and convenience for yourself and others.

○ View, to be able to stop if required.

○ Stability, to have sufficient handling, roadholding and cornering power in reserve to be able to stop safely.

If you have passengers, you must not be selfish or show off. Drive in the manner you would like to be driven yourself, safely and comfortably, with a smooth flow, polish and

Limit
point

*Positioning for a left-hand bend:*
*towards the centre line of the road*
*to maximise view through it.*

finesse with the engine maintaining road
speed to make a passenger feel secure while
you corner – like the Queen's chauffeur!
Praise a good taxi driver; he is probably an
ex-police driver. Report dangerous taxi drivers
to the local authority; they may hurt their
next passenger.

It is surprising what you can see if you
look, but if you do not look, you will never
see. Train yourself to look across bends. Plan
far ahead, because sometimes you can see
more long before a bend, particularly when
high up in hilly country, than you can when
you arrive. This forward planning is essential,
as soon as the bend appears in view. Some
people are lazy, saying to themselves, 'I will
deal with the bend when I get there', and
they brake and change gear too late.

It must be stressed that merely to look at
the limit point will help only to a limited

degree. If the bend tightens and shortens
your sight line, so you must slacken speed.
If you ease off the power, the change in
pitch will alter grip between the front and
rear tyres. It is wise to look across bends, if
you can, not only to make an assessment of
severity, but to learn of the presence of other
traffic over hedgerows, or through the odd
glimpses you may have of gaps and breaks
of vision.

To further help in your assessment of
approach, think of the definition of an open
bend: a bend around which the whole of
the road surface is visible. Not that one
should look at the surface too much when
cornering. Spend most of the time ranging
your eyes far ahead, with an occasional
downward glance, to gain a sense of
position.

Naturally, a car is most stable at speed
when travelling in a straight line. It is
inevitable that when the driver directs the car
onto a curved path, a degree of stability will
be lost, which is proportional to the curve

Limit
point

and, most importantly, in proportion to the square of any increase in speed. A driver can change the speed of approach but the bend is static. However, if the driver widens and straightens the path of the car, within the rules of the road, the greater the stability. If the radius of the curved path of the car through a bend is reduced to a minimum, then open bends are far safer. Apart from anything else, we can see other road users a long way off, especially approaching vehicles, and assess their behaviour.

## Vertical bends

Vertical bends or crests are open if you can see all of the road surface throughout; be absolutely sure you can. Safety is easily assessed if it is absolutely clear. Your car's stability will be affected if your course is not precisely straight. Use brakes and power to influence pitch.

Crests or humpback bridges are blind if you cannot see the road surface throughout. These are extremely dangerous, particularly if

*Positioning for a right-hand bend: towards the left-hand edge of the road to maximise view through it.*

they are single track over the crest. You must carry out all the features of the driving plan with an extremely healthy imagination.

Select the correct course for safety. Wind down the side window. Brake to an absolute crawl. You must be able to stop well within the distance seen to be clear. If the road is single track, be able to stop within half the distance you can see. Take the appropriate gear, sufficiently early, to sound the horn with a long continuous note (most do not, which is why this hazard is potentially dangerous).

With the side window already down, listen for an answering note (most unlikely). If the road curves the other side of the bridge you can often see anyone approaching the blind area.

Remember that your stability will be affected over an 'open' crest, and tyres do

*A 'vertical' bend – select the correct course for safety.*

not grip so well when lightly laden. Skilful use of the brakes and power can influence the pitch of the car over crests. Brake up the rise to slow and put the nose down, then just as the car goes light, swap to the power, ever so delicately, and the car should settle down on the other side, all square. Keep the steering absolutely straight otherwise you could lose control and skid. Different cars pitch differently, depending upon their weight distribution and aerodynamic balance. The worst I came across was a Lancia Stratos rally car, which did not fly very well at all. Everything else it did, it was brilliant, particularly traction out of corners. I found it a challenge, but most enjoyable to drive.

Downhill bends are hazardous in the mountains and the brakes can fade away in proportion to the length of time you are braking. Best to brake rather more firmly over a short distance, then release the brakes

for as long as possible, to let them cool. Stop in a lay-by if you can, occasionally. If you stop in a café at the bottom of a mountain, leave the handbrake off and do a static brake test before you set off again, as heat sink can overheat the brake fluid giving no brakes at all. Change down into a low gear at the top of the mountain and use engine braking all the way down the descent, then you should have less trouble.

## Acute open left-hand bend

An acute open left-hand bend must not be taken like some reckless racing driver, using the total width of the road on the approach and exit. The public highway is not a racetrack. Ask yourself the same question a judge in court would ask you: 'Is it necessary to drive a car so fast, that in order to maintain its stability you have to position it totally on the offside of the road on the approach and, worse still, to the total width at the exit?'

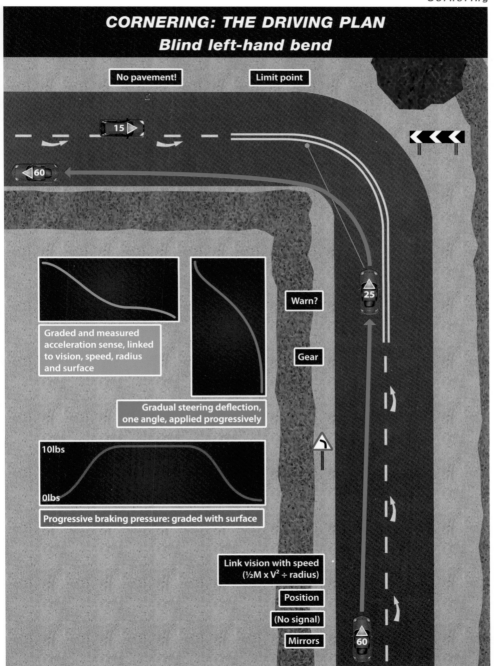

# CORNERING: THE DRIVING PLAN
## Blind left-hand bend

No pavement!

Limit point

15

60

Warn?

25

Gear

Graded and measured acceleration sense, linked to vision, speed, radius and surface

Gradual steering deflection, one angle, applied progressively

10lbs

0lbs

Progressive braking pressure: graded with surface

Link vision with speed ($\frac{1}{2}$M x V$^2$ ÷ radius)

Position

(No signal)

Mirrors

60

# VOICE OF EXPERIENCE

## Care with road positioning

I do not advise positioning very close to the edge of the road on the approach to a corner. A gust of wind, change of camber, or brakes pulling, can take you off the edge. It's a mistake so easily made into a downhill right-hand curve. I made this mistake driving a works Alfa Romeo 2000 GTV in a British Touring Car race at Brands Hatch. I had a brake-balance problem and locked up the rear wheels on the approach to Druids Hill bend and the back nearside wheel hooked over the edge. Although I released the brake to recover, I was then too fast, so I spun the car to a halt.

It was a pity, as I was running second overall at the time, leading some famous names. Gerry Marshall had told me I was fast, but too precise. I thought it may have been a bit of gamesmanship on his part, to slow me down – but he was right, as he usually was! A

*Racing the Alfetta GTV at Brands Hatch.*

good driver is one who makes every mistake there is to be made, but makes it only once. I vowed not to make that mistake again. So far so good!

---

Sliding wide at speed, rally-style through the curved path of the bend may frighten an oncoming driver into some evasive action. It is reckless driving, particularly sliding over the crown of the road towards oncoming traffic. Certainly at least, it shows little consideration towards other road users. Given the circumstances, base your judgement upon what you consider a reasonable person would do.

A safe, measured and reasonable driving plan for an acute open left-hand bend is:

- Select a course of approach to widen the effective radius in relation to the bend, for the best stability possible, within the bounds of road safety. Do not position on an extended safety line over a warning line and the crown of the road, unless the road is seen to be clear of anyone approaching in the far distance, as far as the eye can see, and will remain clear. The extended safety line can be considered to be using no more than two-thirds of the offside of the road on approach. There must be no offside entrances.

- Brake to a speed in relation to the radius of the curve selected, the condition of the road surface and change of camber or gradient, with a little roadholding in reserve.

- Take the one gear that the speed requires, cleanly, heel and toeing, if necessary, and trail braking to keep understeer to a minimum.

- Deflect the steering a little late with one smooth steering angle, to arrive at the apex late, around the back of the curve to be tight into the nearside at the exit, where the inside edge of the road is becoming straight. Use the throttle to maintain the road speed you have chosen, once the car is answering to the steering deflection. Do not accelerate too early, and most importantly, be able to remain tight into the nearside at the exit without drifting wide. This vital element of safety is often neglected. Then use power, blending it with a straightening steering path at the exit. There must be no drifting out towards the road centre at the exit of the corner.

# ACUTE OPEN LEFT-HAND BEND
## The driving plan

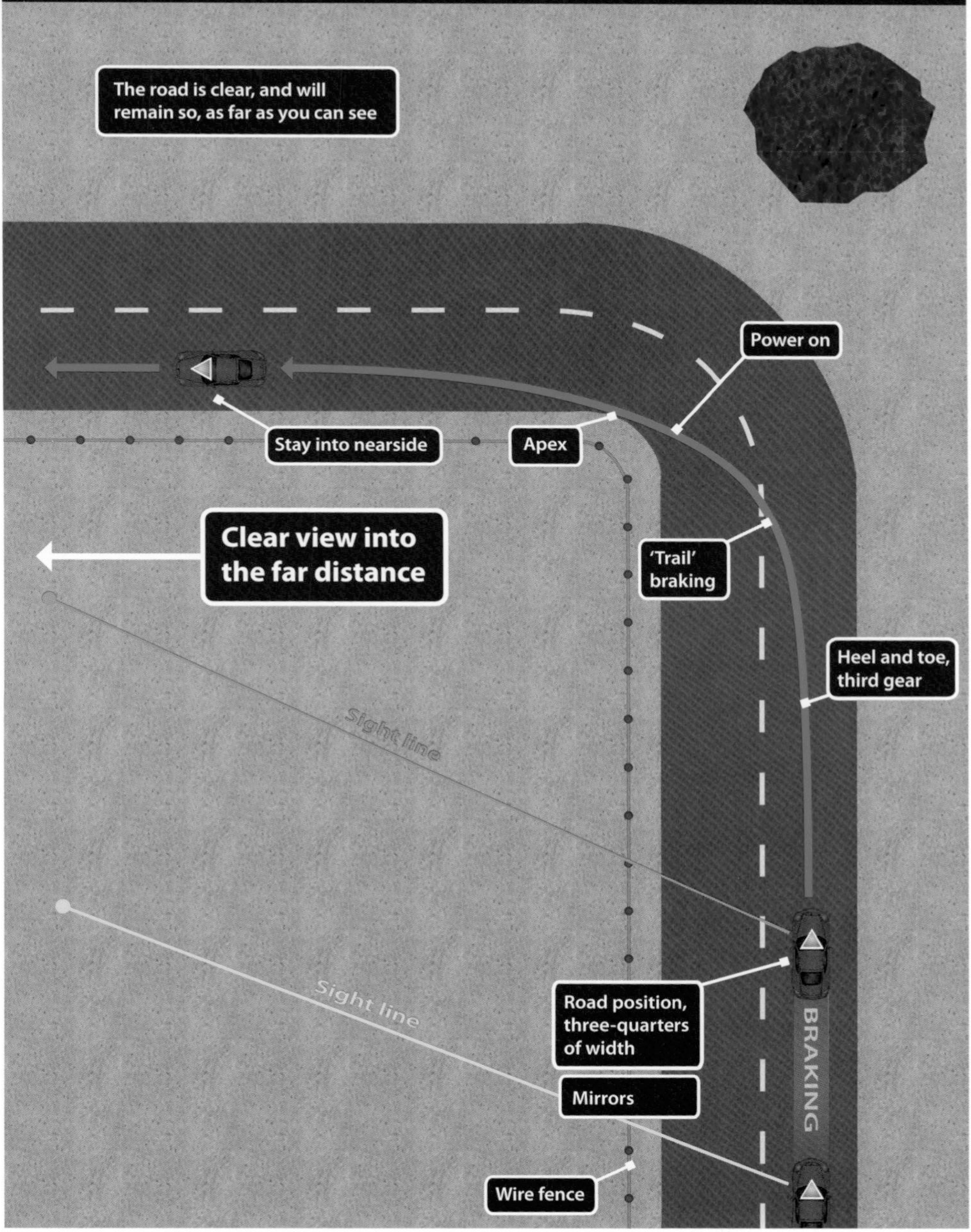

The road is clear, and will remain so, as far as you can see

Power on

Stay into nearside

Apex

**Clear view into the far distance**

'Trail' braking

Heel and toe, third gear

Sight line

Sight line

Road position, three-quarters of width

Mirrors

BRAKING

Wire fence

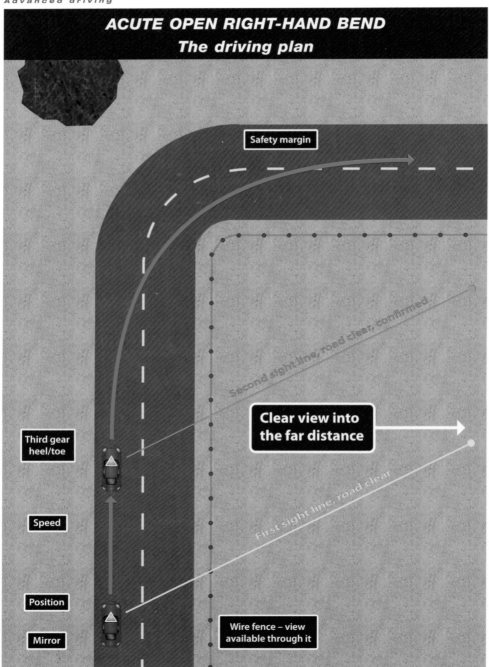

# ACUTE OPEN RIGHT-HAND BEND
## The driving plan

Safety margin

Second sight line, road clear, confirmed

**Clear view into the far distance**

First sight line, road clear

Third gear heel/toe

Speed

Position

Mirror

Wire fence – view available through it

This driving plan has ensured safety. There is sufficient reserve in roadholding. The car is in to the left-hand edge of the road at the exit and, most importantly, is able to remain there. There is a complete view of all of the road surface through the bend and far into the distance, which allows you to be sure it will remain clear. The mirror is clear. The effective radius of the curved path of the car is a wider radius than the bend itself, so the best stability possible is obtained relative to the road speed. The exit position from one bend is the approaching position to the next. Left-hand bends are usually followed by one to the right and vice-versa. One can flow into another.

*An acute 'blind' left-hand bend with no pavement – link vision to speed and grip.*

## Acute open right-hand bend

Approaching an acute open right-hand bend, you need to see that the road ahead is clear and will remain so, by ranging your eyes across the road scene, scanning far away over the landscape. You start the driving plan, knowing the road is safe and clear.

The driving plan for an acute open right-hand bend is:

⊙ Course is selected, mirror is clear. Almost the total width of the road will be used, as it is absolutely clear and will remain so, with no offside entrances or other road users in sight.

⊙ Speed is cut to the correct speed, with braking spread out precisely.

⊙ Heel and toe cleanly, into the correct gear. Trail brake, blending braking into

Apex

steering deflection. Position 18ins (45cm) from the nearside left-hand edge, clear of any gravel. The turn-in is late to take a steering path, initially tightening, but then expanding to a late apex, around the back of the curve 18ins (45cm) from the extreme right-hand edge. Progressively blend the power with straightening the steering path to a normal safety line position, with plenty of safety margin.

Again, safety has been complete, as the road is clear and will remain so, far into the distance and behind. There is an unobstructed view, across the bend and far into the distance. There are no offside entrances. The mirror is clear, so nobody is going to pass as you negotiate the bend. Stability is secure as speed is precisely assessed. Advantage is taken of the positive camber on the extreme right-hand side on the inside of the bend.

## Acute blind left-hand bend

On an acute blind left-hand bend, with no pavement either side, the view is expected to be restricted. In our example this is a sharp, blind, slightly downhill bend on a non-primary B-road, an old turnpike. There are wide grass verges, bordered by hedges, set well back. The bend is acute with a 'sharp left deviation to route' sign. The left hedge has grown closer to the edge of the road now, obscuring the left-hand bend warning sign. Both signs have a yellow surround, signifying that there have been more accidents here than usual. An earlier slippery road sign has already given the same message, along with an extra-thick warning line and continuous line edge markings, all demanding extra care. The hedge is right up to the edge of the road at the apex, closing down the view. Without a pavement there could be pedestrians walking on the road. The road is reasonably wide with a good surface.

Immediately the bend is sighted, a very early and decisive driving plan is started with forward planning:

⊘ Mirror is clear, so a course is selected out towards but comfortably left of the double line system, to gain an early view across the bend, with the longest possible sight line. Sacrifice this position if there is any approaching traffic. Remember, if there is only a warning line, your sight line will not be lengthened by excessive road positioning if the bend is acute and blind.

⊘ Following an early lift off the power, braking is spread out. The hedge is now right up to the road edge. The limit point is static, that is, the nearside and offside edges of the hedgerows are not moving in relation to each other. The bend is a 90-degree blind left and you must be able to stop if necessary. As the road is two-way, the limit point is up to the white warning line, as you must be able to remain on your side of the road if you have to stop. The sight line is going to be very short and confined to the warning line, as you must be able to remain on your own side, particularly at the exit. No fancy heel and toeing this time – if your foot slips, you will be in trouble. You finish braking sufficiently early to change gear separately, for a greater margin of safety.

⊘ Cleanly double-declutch into second gear (a block change from fourth if necessary).

⊘ Give a medium horn warning with the left hand, only if necessary.

⊘ Use a light throttle to maintain speed, over-coming any loss of speed through drag.

⊘ The far edge of the offside hedge is just beginning to go straight. At the same moment the double line system is becoming broken on your side, evidence that the bend is finishing. As the steering angle does not change once deflected, a slight adjustment of power is enough to vary the pitch slightly, to grow or reduce the front tyre contact patches and deflect the car towards

# ACUTE BLIND LEFT-HAND BEND
## *The driving plan*

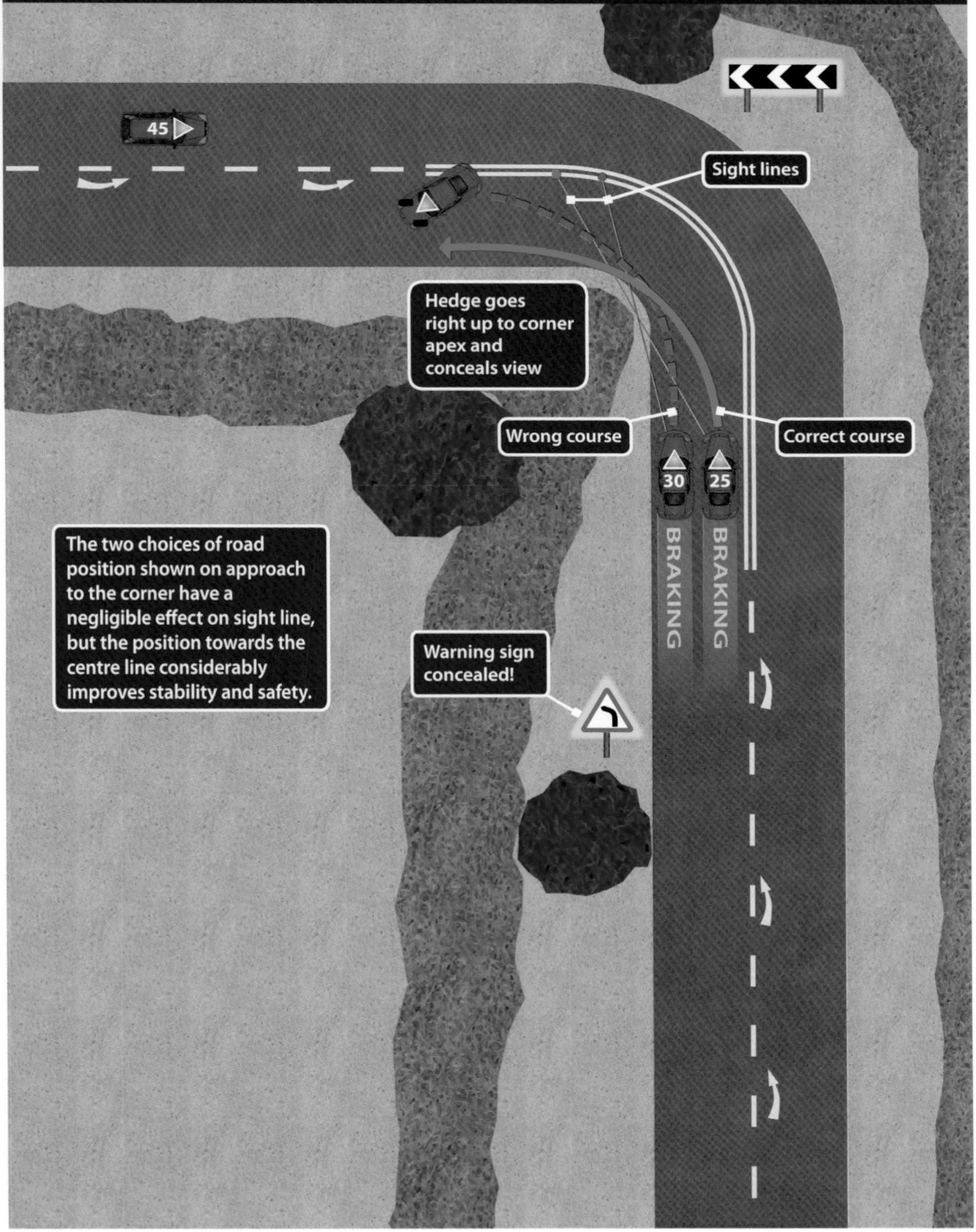

45

Sight lines

Hedge goes right up to corner apex and conceals view

Wrong course

Correct course

30

25

BRAKING

BRAKING

The two choices of road position shown on approach to the corner have a negligible effect on sight line, but the position towards the centre line considerably improves stability and safety.

Warning sign concealed!

# ACUTE BLIND LEFT-HAND BEND, SINGLE-TRACK LANE
## The driving plan

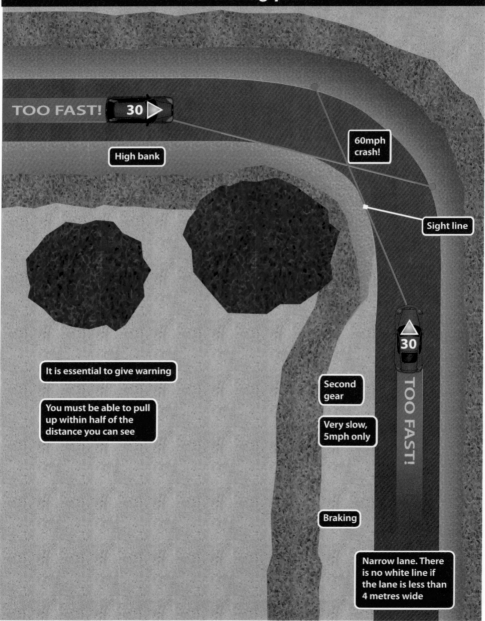

TOO FAST! 30

High bank

60mph crash!

Sight line

It is essential to give warning

You must be able to pull up within half of the distance you can see

Second gear

Very slow, 5mph only

30

TOO FAST!

Braking

Narrow lane. There is no white line if the lane is less than 4 metres wide

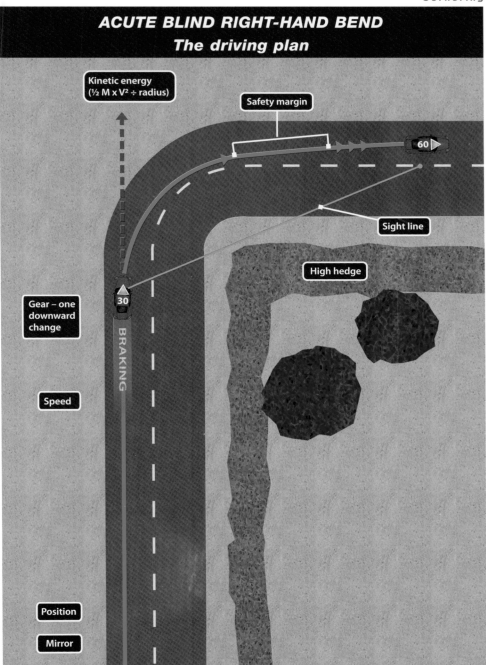

ACUTE BLIND RIGHT-HAND BEND
The driving plan

Kinetic energy
(½ M x V² ÷ radius)

Safety margin

60

Sight line

High hedge

Gear – one downward change

30

BRAKING

Speed

Position

Mirror

# GRADUAL BLIND LEFT-HAND BEND
## The driving plan

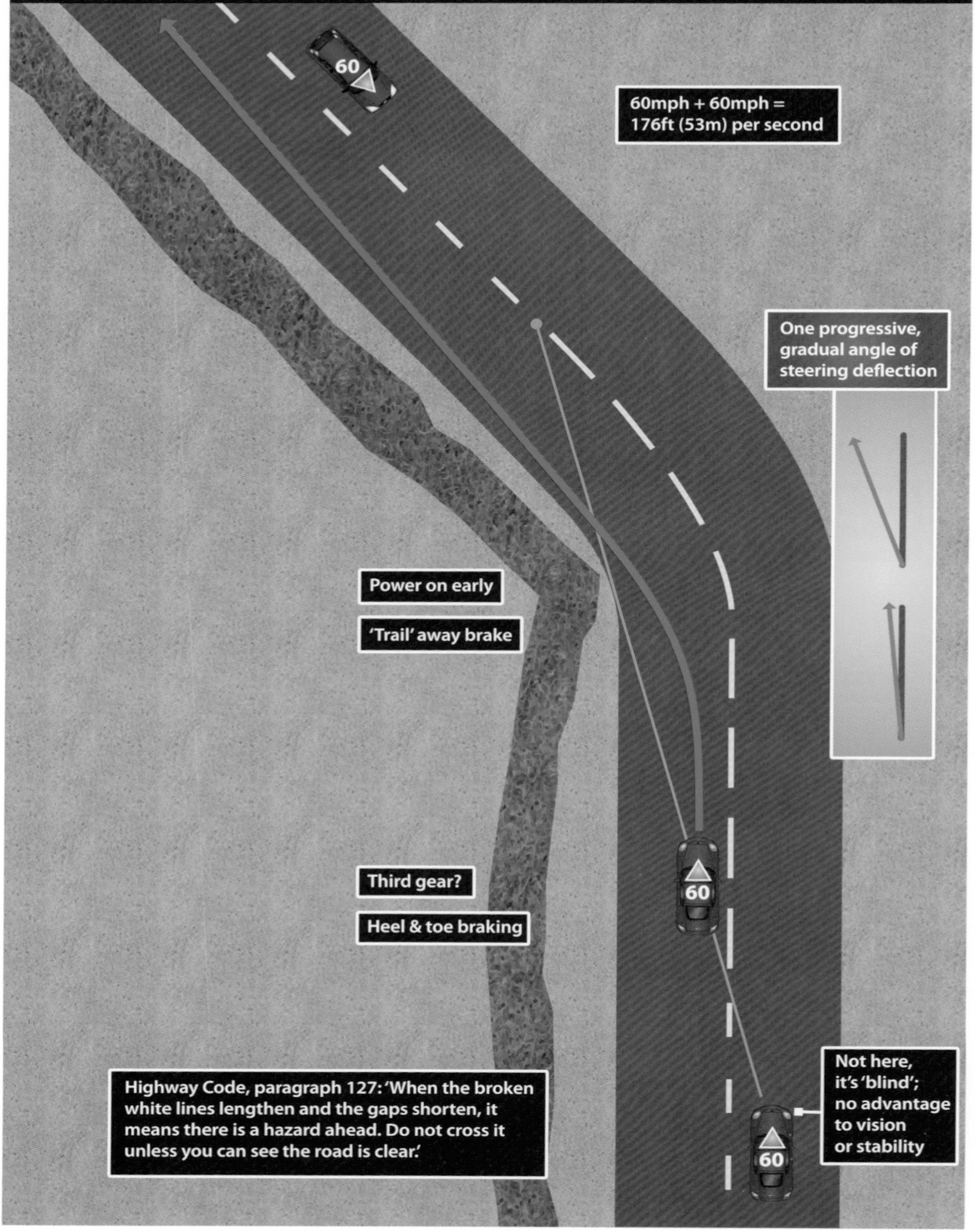

60mph + 60mph = 176ft (53m) per second

One progressive, gradual angle of steering deflection

Power on early

'Trail' away brake

Third gear?

Heel & toe braking

Highway Code, paragraph 127: 'When the broken white lines lengthen and the gaps shorten, it means there is a hazard ahead. Do not cross it unless you can see the road is clear.'

Not here, it's 'blind'; no advantage to vision or stability

the nearside edge of the road, for the best margin of safety. The sight line is lengthening rapidly now, so accelerate firmly and gain speed quickly, still able to stay into the nearside.

Again, safety is complete, as at any time the car could stop well within the distance seen to be clear, with a sufficient safety margin. Even so, a warning horn note may be essential. Although the view was shut off dramatically by the tall hedge up to the road edge, you were not deceived by the same hedgerow being set back along the straight on approach giving the initial impression that there would be a good view across the bend. The reason? Limit point technique, linking vision to speed and grip. There was always sufficient in reserve for stability. The steering path could be slightly changed, altering pitch with power.

If a lane is very narrow it is essential that no position towards the centre of the road is taken if the bend is blind. All you will gain is an early view of the vehicle about to hit you! Local drivers tend to drive too quickly along lanes they know well, and 99% of the time they get away with it. That 1% may be the time you are approaching. Look for skid marks and if the bend is blind on a single track road, slow to a crawl so you are able to stop within half the distance you can see. It is essential to sound the horn for a blind single-track bend.

## Acute blind right-hand bend

This is how you would give a commentary for an acute blind right-hand bend, with no pavement:

- ⊘ 'Mirror, bike behind, he slips by, no problem – we both see the sharp right-hand bend – mirror clear, select a course into the nearside – no nearside entrance so reduced safety line is OK – mirror clear.
- ⊘ 'I brake early, drop back from the bike, leave time for separate gear selection – warning is now considered.

- ⊘ 'I pick up the drive now – there is no nearside danger – condition of the road edge is good – no gravel.
- ⊘ 'My road position gives the longest sight line view – this gives the greatest possible safety margin from oncoming traffic – best to remain in this road position, all the way round.' (commentary continues)

Safety has been achieved, by being able to stop if required. The view is the best that can be obtained (allowing the driver to see any pedestrians on the roadway). Stability is maintained, in slow, out fast, under progressive acceleration. In the wet, acceleration to increase speed is not applied firmly, until the car is quite straight and true. The exit position gives room if a skid occurs.

## Gradual blind left-hand downhill bend

This gradual blind left-hand downhill bend is on another old turnpike, now a non-primary A-road, maintained by the local authority. The road is gently curving, rising and falling with wide verges. There is a 'slippery road' sign, but the surface is perfectly sound, until you discover there are skid marks, giving a clue as to what is meant by this sign. Just after this sign we notice a gradual left-hand curve. The hedge is set well back either side, giving the impression of space and good vision across the curve to the left. No problem then, or so it seems. We start the driving plan:

- ⊘ Mirror is clear behind. We select a course left of the warning line, but not over the line, because the bend is blind and we cannot see sufficiently far ahead to be sure it is going to remain clear.
- ⊘ Lift off the power sufficiently early, but the approach is slightly downhill, so we apply the brakes delicately, establishing precisely the correct safe speed in relation to the available vision. The limit point is moving, indicating a gradual blind curve. The surface is assessed, to give grip in reserve.

↻ Third gear is chosen, double-declutching to match engine, gear and road speed precisely. There is no need for a warning, as the view is quite good.

↻ Use the throttle to maintain a speed matched to available vision, as the sight line is the same length through this part of the bend. The gradient is not too steep, only slightly downhill – so far so good. As the bend curves around to the left, the hedgerow has been running straight and is now right up to the edge of the road, cutting off the view and dramatically shortening the sight line through the bend. We have to ease off the speed and power – this drops the nose and unsettles the tail on our old Porsche 911! Then, surprise, surprise, in the blind area the curve tightens, the road surface deteriorates and the camber falls away even further downhill into a negative slope. By now we feel distinctly uneasy. Thank goodness, we had something in reserve regarding road position, to give an early view, and

moderate speed, to give a reserve of grip – and we have a good-handling sports car. At last we see evidence that this nastily engineered bend is finishing. The far edge of the road is becoming straight; we now point the car tight into the left, able to remain there.

In terms of safety, this bend was potentially dangerous. The view was deceptive and shortened dramatically by the hedge leading up to the edge of the road, in the middle of the bend, out of sight of the approaching driver who may not have the skill or experience to cope. The message is to slow down. Stability was seriously affected leading to potential danger to the untrained, inexperienced driver. Think of the fast motorcycle rider leaning into the bend taking an early apex race line, but not thinking about vision.

*A gradual 'blind' bend, with a pavement – position the car to see earlier. Are the yellow bars warning of a 'limit' in front or behind?*

# TIGHTENING, CONTRACTING-RADIUS LEFT-HAND BEND
## *The driving plan*

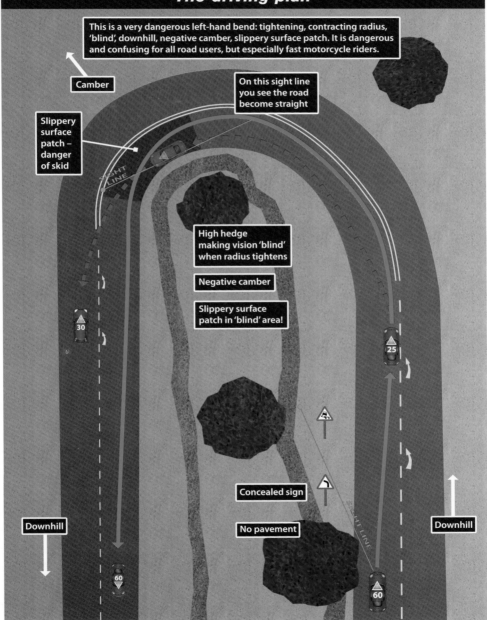

This is a very dangerous left-hand bend: tightening, contracting radius, 'blind', downhill, negative camber, slippery surface patch. It is dangerous and confusing for all road users, but especially fast motorcycle riders.

Camber

On this sight line you see the road become straight

Slippery surface patch – danger of skid

SIGHT LINE

High hedge making vision 'blind' when radius tightens

Negative camber

Slippery surface patch in 'blind' area!

30

25

Concealed sign

No pavement

SIGHT LINE

Downhill

Downhill

60

60

## Gradual blind right-hand bend

On a gradual blind right-hand bend, the driving plan will start as soon as the bend is sighted. That is why it is so important to see any warning sign in advance. So why are warning signs so often obscured behind foliage? It doesn't make any sense for the authorities to erect a large sign and then allow vegetation to grow and conceal it. The driving plan is:

- Mirror, course is a reduced safety line if there is no nearside problem like an entrance or gravel.

- An early lift off the power will bring the speed down sufficiently. Accurate speed assessment is essential.

- Double-declutch, cleanly and smoothly into third gear, and continue to decelerate, as you assess that no braking is required.

- Slight delay in finding the throttle to keep the nose down for more grip from the front tyres, then keep the engine just pulling to maintain a speed that is matched to vision and grip.

- Road position towards the nearside to gain an early view, with an occasional glance down to maintain position. The nearside position is maintained until evidence is seen that the bend is finishing, then, as all of the remaining road surface is in view, a blend of steering and power will flatten out the exit, towards the double line system as the lines go straight, for the best margin of safety at the exit.

Safety is established by being able to pull up if necessary, the best view is obtained, and stability is achieved, with a progressive change of pitch between front and rear grip (what some racing drivers call balance).

Cross-country driving provides the greatest challenge to drive well and, for the enthusiastic driver, is one of motoring's great joys, when driven swiftly and safely. Not all people drive safely and are motivated by many other distractions. All you can do is to drive as well as you can and apply technique with skill and discipline.

## VOICE OF EXPERIENCE

### You cannot anticipate the unreasonable

Correct cornering technique will possibly save you from an accident. It did for me once.

I had just finished racing at Castle Combe with my Super Seven, when I received a telephone call to go to Chester to see my father, who had been taken ill. The Seven was road-going, so I tore off my racing numbers, left the tow car and trailer for the mechanic to take home and set off in the Seven. There was an accident on the M6, so I turned off across country. It was quite twisting and hilly, but good going.

Approaching a downhill blind left-hand bend, I spread out my braking, changed down to third and kept the little car towards the warning line for the best view, searching for evidence of the exit, such as the far hedge becoming straight. I then swept the car into the left-hand side, tucking it in, able to remain there, without drifting wide. It is a steering path that undoubtedly saved my life.

Approaching flat-out were two vans, both from the same depot, racing each other, taking the whole width of the road. I had to react instinctively to swing that little Seven instantly up a steep bank on the left, like a wall of death to miss the oncoming vans. I eventually managed to stop.

With good grace, surprisingly, so did both the van drivers, who ran back to me still sitting in the Seven, trying to recover my composure. 'Sorry mate, having a burn-up,' one of them said. The reason for the story is this: there is no way I could have had the reserve ability to take the Seven off the road to the nearside and miss the vans if I had taken an early apex in the corner, with the car pointing towards the centre of the road at the exit. It turned out to be okay too for my father, who recovered quickly, and told me to take more care next time!

# VANS RACING ON THE ROAD
## A personal experience driving my Super Seven

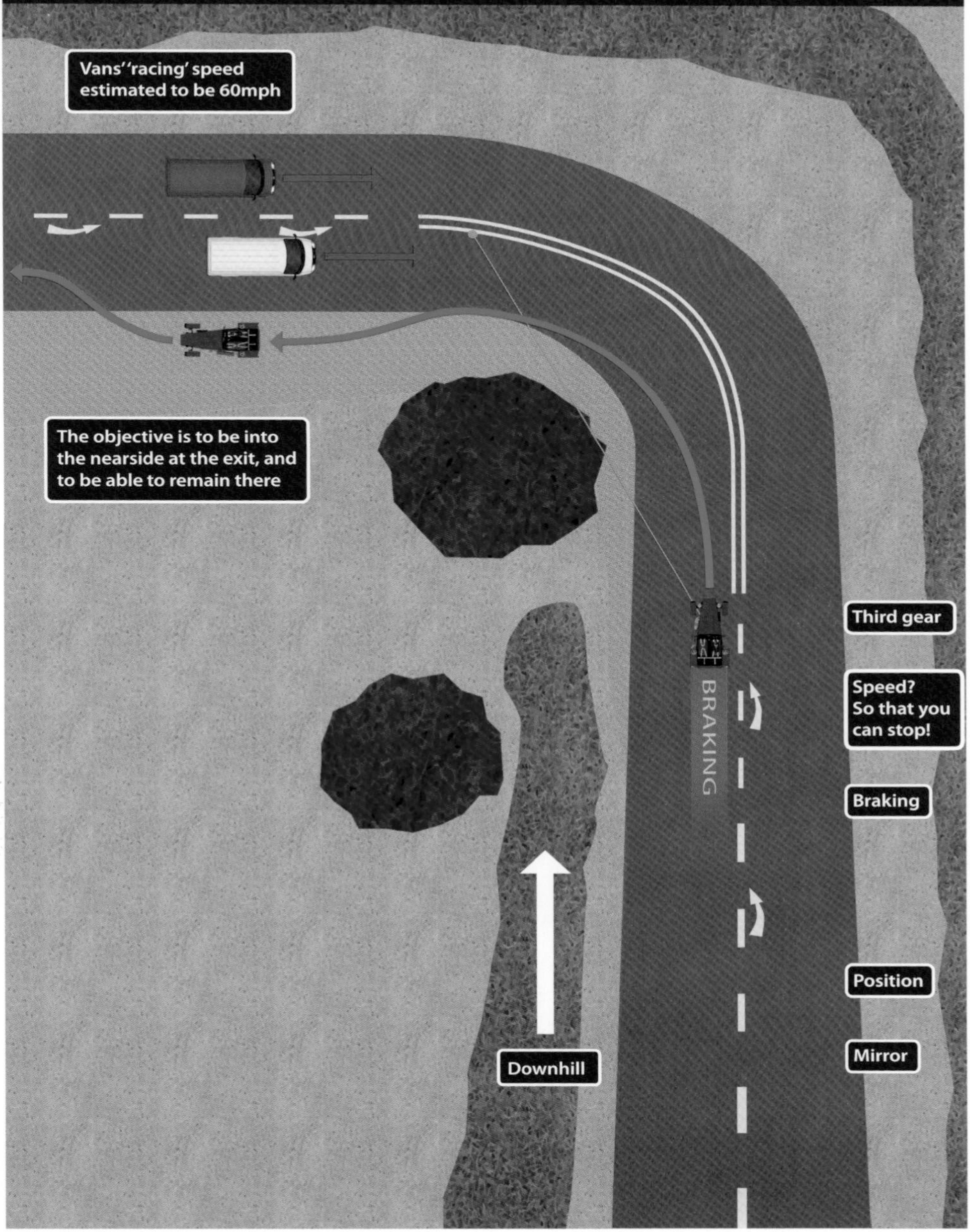

Vans' 'racing' speed estimated to be 60mph

The objective is to be into the nearside at the exit, and to be able to remain there

BRAKING

Third gear

Speed? So that you can stop!

Braking

Position

Mirror

Downhill

# 9 Past the limit

*Power oversteer is fun on the proving
ground, but demands skill to be safe.*

Every driver has a responsibility to drive within their own ability, in such a manner that the car should be completely under the driver's control on the public highway. A little slipping and sliding is perhaps unavoidable, when the road is covered with ice and snow, even though one should try to avoid it if possible. It is safe to affirm that many accidents, which are alleged to have been due to skidding in wet weather, would never have occurred if tyro drivers had a better understanding of the causes of skidding and better control over their vehicles when in a skid. The only way they will get this is with practice, off the highway, safely.

## Why practise skidding?

Causing, controlling and preventing skidding is a practical skill that can only develop with many hours of practice, with one particular vehicle, on every kind of road surface – and then, when you change your car, you must start all over again. It is not the desire of every driver to do this, but it is necessary if you are to become a master of every situation. With long experience you learn to avoid skidding like the plague!

A little experience can be a bad thing and lead to overconfidence and more accidents. I think this is why the official view is that knowledge of what to do in the event of loss of control should be kept a mystery, except to give some very basic advice. That it is best not to provide any official places to practise apart from an occasional police driving school allowing their officers to volunteer their services outside their normal hours of duty for a short period on a skidpan. This is insufficient. Slipping about on a pan is not the same as emergency car control in your own car. Racing circuits are potentially

*Demonstrating the art of the power slide in my Super Seven HPC at Spa-Francorchamps.*

# THE TRACTION OVAL
## *Tracing the outer rim*

Trace the outer rim of the traction oval (because of the square of the tyre contact pattern) by progressively easing away the brakes as you deflect the steering, or blend power with steering straightening as you exit the corner.

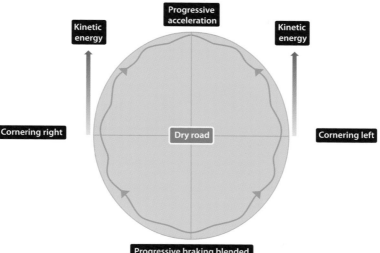

**Progressive acceleration**

**Kinetic energy**

**Kinetic energy**

**Cornering right**

**Dry road**

**Cornering left**

**Progressive braking blended with steering deflection**

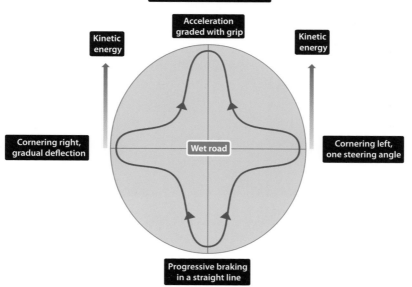

**Acceleration graded with grip**

**Kinetic energy**

**Kinetic energy**

**Cornering right, gradual deflection**

**Wet road**

**Cornering left, one steering angle**

**Progressive braking in a straight line**

# USING BRANDS HATCH FOR DRIVER TRAINING
## Druids bend, anti-clockwise, two-way traffic

Sight line

25

35

Best vision

Skid?

1. Constant radius: one steering angle constantly applied

35

Apex

25

3. Expanding radius: more progressive acceleration

2. Transition: changing the pitch with delicate deceleration sense

25

When you see the warning line becoming straight, you have evidence that the bend is finishing

dangerous and unsuitable for teaching drivers. The answer is the facility we use on the High Performance Course. We use the same proving grounds that car manufacturers use for testing, at Millbrook and MIRA, where it is safe and practice is carried out

under the supervision and responsible advice of an expert HPC co-driver.

At the proving grounds we treat all the roads as normal two-way highways, even though they are one-way. The roads have vertical bends, where the car goes light or

heavy over dips or crests. There are open
bends, as well as blind, acute deviations and
gradual curves, negative off cambers and
super elevations, all in all a great test of your
skill to drive safely and smoothly.

You will not be able to go to a proving
ground under your own steam. These
places are highly professional, designed
for the research and development of
motor vehicle technology, and there are
insurance implications. The instructor has
to be approved by the proving ground
management staff and the general public are
not normally admitted.

Be certain that before you drive any car at
a proving ground that it is prepared properly,
particularly as you may be travelling at the
maximum speed of your car on the high-
speed banking at Millbrook. The tyres need
to be fit for purpose and at the correct
recommended pressures, brake pads must

*In the 1960s the British School of Motoring's
High Performance Course used Brands Hatch for
safe tuition 'past the limit'. Here the track is
being used to simulate a two-way road.*

have sufficient depth and heat range, and
not be glazed and polished with slow
town driving.

For skid practice, the large parade-ground
areas at proving grounds provide the ideal
place to experiment safely. Not to loon
around in an undisciplined way, but to circle
the car around a constant radius white
circle at varying speeds. You may spin – in
fact if you don't, you are not trying to drive
fast enough. The exercise has to be very
measured, to judge cause and effect. The
constant radius circle will enable you to see
the effect that your car's acceleration and
braking has on the pitch (tip and tilt) of the
car and how it tracks around the circle.

**149**

*The Brands Hatch skidpan facility*
*in service during the 1960s.*

It is also essential to do this training on a Z-shaped track which has two sharp bends to the left and two to the right, with a large run-off area for safety. All this training is done at the limit.

These exercises have to be under the supervision of an expert coach, who is able to demonstrate to you the handling of your car, explain with a commentary what is occurring and show you expertly how to master the techniques yourself. It is really essential to have this training with your car to be competent, particularly before you go anywhere near a track day with a powerful, rear-wheel drive high-performance car.

On the proving ground you will gain confidence in the anti-lock braking system (ABS). You will see the effect of stopping in an emergency while cornering hard on the skid circle, to see how well the car stays on the circle line and pulls up with stability and no skidding.

Remember that electronic stability control (ESC) is switchable on certain cars, to enable you to gain slightly more traction and wheelspin to drive up a hill in slippery conditions – but you will not be covered by your insurance company, if you switch it off on the highway and crash! In the safe environment of the proving ground steering circle, you will be able to turn it off, to see the dramatic difference. On most supercars, the ESC has various settings; the circle is the ideal place to see the result of each setting, on different road surfaces, in safety.

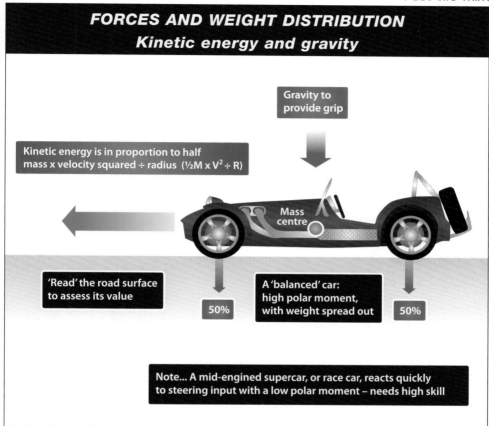

# FORCES AND WEIGHT DISTRIBUTION
## Kinetic energy and gravity

Gravity to provide grip

Kinetic energy is in proportion to half mass x velocity squared ÷ radius ($\frac{1}{2}$M x V$^2$ ÷ R)

Mass centre

'Read' the road surface to assess its value

50%

A 'balanced' car: high polar moment, with weight spread out

50%

Note... A mid-engined supercar, or race car, reacts quickly to steering input with a low polar moment – needs high skill

## Understanding the problem

Let us now look, in simplicity, at the problems involved when circling on a constant radius. Apart from the influence of power, brakes and steering, there are only two forces acting upon the centre of the weight of the car:

⊘ Gravity. In dips and crests, the car will go light and heavy, varying the grip of the tyres. Cars do not hold the road when they leave the ground and fly!

⊘ Kinetic energy, which is created by motion, which is proportional to velocity squared multiplied by the mass of your car, divided by the radius of the curve.

Kinetic energy creates momentum and is the force that is trying to take you straight ahead when you want to take a curved path. The centre of the car's mass is 18ins (45cm) or so from the road surface and kinetic energy is opposed by the grip of the tyres on the road; this causes the car to roll. Because we are sitting in the car, kinetic energy wants to take us straight ahead. We feel it as a sideways force called centrifugal force, but it is in fact the desire of our body wanting to go straight on that we feel, not a force at right angles to our side.

If the centre of the mass is towards the middle of the car, as in a mid-engineered supercar or racing car, it is said to have a low

**151**

# THE STEERING CIRCLE, MILLBROOK
## A diagram of the proving-ground facility

Steering pad has constant radius of 33 metres and constant road surface grip of 8mu. This illustration presumes no aerodynamic aids for downforce or speed

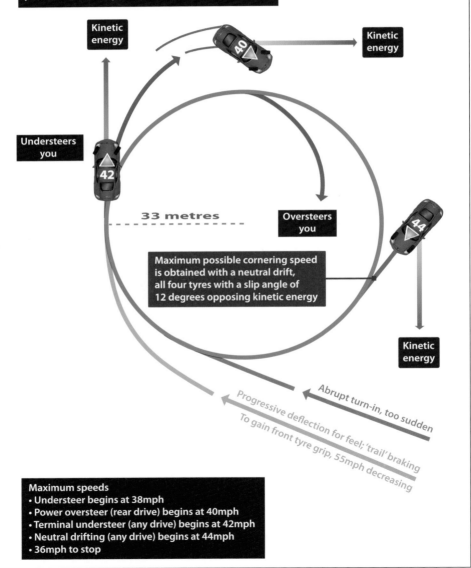

Kinetic energy

Kinetic energy

Understeers you

33 metres

Oversteers you

Maximum possible cornering speed is obtained with a neutral drift, all four tyres with a slip angle of 12 degrees opposing kinetic energy

Kinetic energy

Abrupt turn-in, too sudden

Progressive deflection for feel; 'trail' braking

To gain front tyre grip, 55mph decreasing

Maximum speeds
• Understeer begins at 38mph
• Power oversteer (rear drive) begins at 40mph
• Terminal understeer (any drive) begins at 42mph
• Neutral drifting (any drive) begins at 44mph
• 36mph to stop

# THE HANDLING COURSE, MILLBROOK
## A diagram of the proving-ground facility

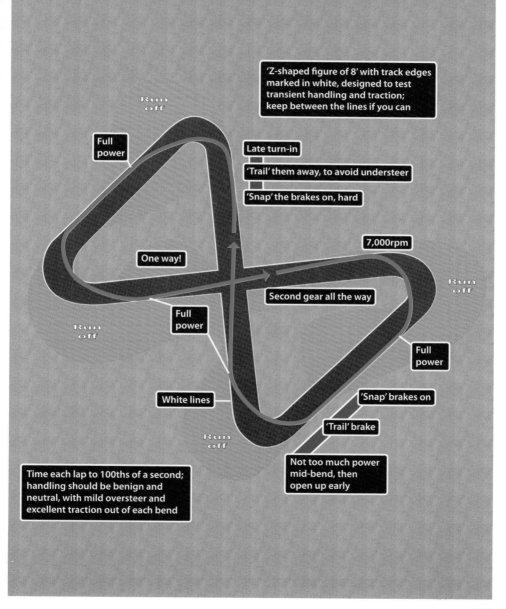

'Z-shaped figure of 8' with track edges marked in white, designed to test transient handling and traction; keep between the lines if you can

Run off

Full power

Late turn-in

'Trail' them away, to avoid understeer

'Snap' the brakes on, hard

One way!

7,000rpm

Run off

Second gear all the way

Full power

Run off

Full power

White lines

'Snap' brakes on

'Trail' brake

Run off

Not too much power mid-bend, then open up early

Time each lap to 100ths of a second; handling should be benign and neutral, with mild oversteer and excellent traction out of each bend

**153**

## VOICE OF EXPERIENCE

### Millbrook proving ground

Only after the preliminary exercises on the constant-radius circle and Z-shaped track is one competent to drive on the remaining areas of the Millbrook proving ground. Here, they have simulated all of the worst hazards they could find in Europe, all within five square miles or so. It is far better than any airfield, as there are more types of bend. The car will be light and heavy over dips and crests, some blind, some open, as on a typical mountain road. There is so much variation as the road sweeps over gradients; uphill, down dale, cresting, dipping, tightening, expanding, there is every kind of bend you can think of and more. Some are banked and super elevated, others negative, off camber, with changing width, presenting every kind of challenge and problem, to both car and driver. It is so natural, needing good hands and feel for the car.

polar moment of inertia. This means it will change direction quickly in response to the power and steering. This demands greater skill from the driver.

If the weight of the car is spread out, say with the engine at the front and a heavy transaxle unit at the back, it will have a high polar moment of inertia and will respond slowly to a change of direction. It will pitch more slowly as well, and this is by far the best drive layout for a rear-wheel drive road car. My Super Seven has this layout, with me, the final drive and the fuel at the back, and the engine at the front.

With front-wheel drive, the weight of the transmission is combined with the engine at the front of the car, giving it a shuttlecock stability which makes it stable and wanting to go straight on. Because the engine is over the driven wheels, it also has slightly improved traction, although rearward pitch will cause less front grip.

A rear-engined car will have superb traction for acceleration, but may be less stable in crosswinds and if it does spin, all that rear weight will make it rotate more readily.

Four-wheel-drive vehicles give the best traction of all, but will not give more roadholding when cornering if the car ploughs straight on. It will only give more roadholding if the tail slides, under control, as in rallying on special stages. Then, you can use power to exit the corner faster.

As you circle around the constant radius white line at an ever increasing speed, the kinetic energy will dramatically build up in proportion to the square of the speed increase, acting upon the mass of the car. Tyre grip will first cause the car to roll, then as speed increases the grip of the tyres will be exceeded and the car will begin to slide.

If the car slides first of all with its front tyres, it will steer a wider path than you expect it to follow, and steer a wide line, outside the circle. This is understeer. Practically all road cars do this on a dry road surface. It is safe, because it is relatively easy to correct with front-, four- or rear-wheel drive. You simply remove the cause, speed. Ease off the accelerator progressively, the car will slow down, and without altering the steering angle the car will return to the white line again. There is a tendency to apply a greater steering angle as you increase speed. Don't. The maximum slip angle to gain the best grip from the front tyres is 6-12 degrees. Full lock will just wear out the tyres.

As you increase speed, try not to complicate matters by changing the steering angle. Put on slightly more steering lock, up to a maximum of 12 degrees of slip angle, then vary speed gradually with power and notice the effect. More speed, more understeer; less speed, less understeer.

With a rear engine, the car will not oversteer on a dry surface, as long as you are not brutal with the power. As you progressively increase speed, it will gradually understeer more. Let's say the front slip angle is six degrees and you suddenly lift off the power. The car's pitch will change the instant you lift off. You must take off that front slip angle, because as the car pitches and tips towards the front, the front tyre contact patch will increase in size and provide more grip. If you do not remove the understeer, the increased front grip will cause the car to rotate around its axis and try to spin. This is termed lift-off oversteer, which is driver induced, not car induced, so always ease off the power gradually.

On ice or snow, as you gradually increase speed around the circle, the rear tyres may start to lose grip first and the car will steer a tighter path than you wish to take. This is oversteer. Eventually the car will rotate and spin across the inside of the white line circle, but only if you do nothing to correct it. Oversteer can be caused by harsh acceleration or excessive speed. Remove the cause instantly by lifting off the power and correcting, by keeping the front wheels pointing down the path you wish to follow. As the car recovers from the slide, re-correct by pointing the front wheels where you want

to go again. (Do not turn into the skid! You may go off line and, on the highway, hit an oncoming vehicle or obstruction.) Correcting oversteer requires intensive practice on different surfaces.

On a constant radius circle, the speed difference between where the tyres will start to slide and where the tyres break away completely is surprisingly small – only within the speed envelope of 4mph, say between 38 and 42mph on a dry, even, flat concrete surface, with standard production car tyres on a 33ft constant radius.

Running soft-compound competition tyres on my Super Seven, I can circle around 10mph faster in the dry and stop in a far shorter distance. This is roadholding, which is the grip a car has on the road surface, and it should be distinguished from handling,

*Oversteer may steer you on a tighter path than you expect to follow, without correction.*

# FORCES WHEN CORNERING 1
## Plan view

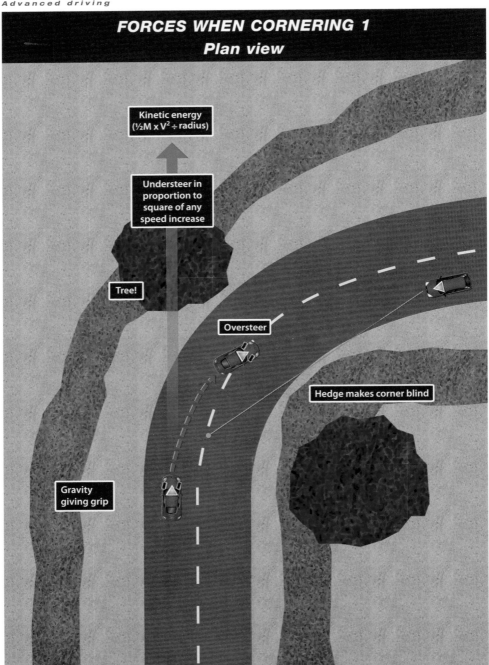

Kinetic energy
($\frac{1}{2}M \times V^2 \div$ radius)

Understeer in proportion to square of any speed increase

Tree!

Oversteer

Hedge makes corner blind

Gravity giving grip

# FORCES WHEN CORNERING 2
## *Perspective view*

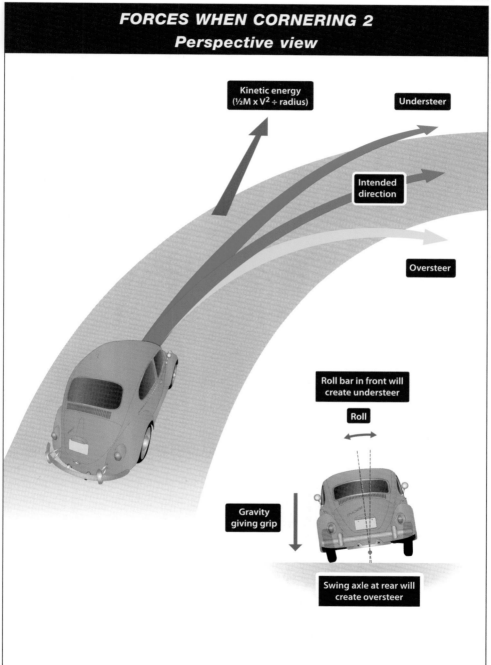

Kinetic energy
($\frac{1}{2}$M x V$^2$ ÷ radius)

Understeer

Intended direction

Oversteer

Roll bar in front will create understeer

Roll

Gravity giving grip

Swing axle at rear will create oversteer

*Understeer, which steers you on a wider path than you expect to follow, is safe and easily removed by reducing speed.*

which is the ease with which you can control the car around a bend.

You can alter the grip of the tyres front to rear, by altering the pitch (tip and tilt) front to rear, to load and grow a tyre contact patch to give greater grip, and, conversely, reduce grip with skilful and delicate use of acceleration or braking. The skilled can trade off the grip of tyres, one against the other. This is called tyre grip trade-off!

Let's take the maximum grip of a tyre at 100 per cent north or south in braking or acceleration – sideways grip is east and

west of the tyre. A good driver will trace the outer rim of the traction oval (it's oval because of the shape of the tyre contact patch) by blending steering deflection with easing away of braking on entry to the corner (trail braking) or, on a dry surface, blending progressively increasing power as the steering angle is straightened at the corner exit.

Cars handle differently on wet or slippery surfaces. At the proving ground, the skid circle will have lanes of differing grip around the circle. A dry surface will have a grip value, or coefficient of friction, of 0.8mu. The same surface when wet has a grip value of 0.6mu, only two-tenths less, but snow has only 0.2mu and ice may have as little as 0.001mu!

*This dramatic view of my much-loved Miller Minor on a race track serves to illustrate tyre slip and drift angles: slip angle is the angle between where the wheels are pointing and where the tyres are taking you; drift angle is the angle between where the wheels are pointing and where the car is taking you.*

An early Porsche 911 will understeer in the dry. It may understeer, first of all, in the wet. But on snow or ice it will slide at the rear straight away. The reason? No grip means no roll, so no roll stiffness. Running across the car, between the front suspension, there is a roll bar. When the surface is dry there is more grip, so the car

rolls more when driven at speed around a bend. It understeers, in proportion to the square of the increase in speed. The driver panics, lifts off quickly, forgets to remove the slip-angle understeer, the tyre contact patch grows, the front tyres grip, and the 911 swivels around into oversteer and spins. This is not car induced, this is driver induced. To my knowledge, this has never been said before and has never been explained by journalists.

These roads are one-way on the proving ground, but we treat them as two-way, with an occasional vehicle to pass. Because each road is a circuit you can get to know it like your favourite road and practise over and over, lap after lap. You can experiment

# TYRE/GRIP TRADE-OFF
## *Dry and wet surfaces*

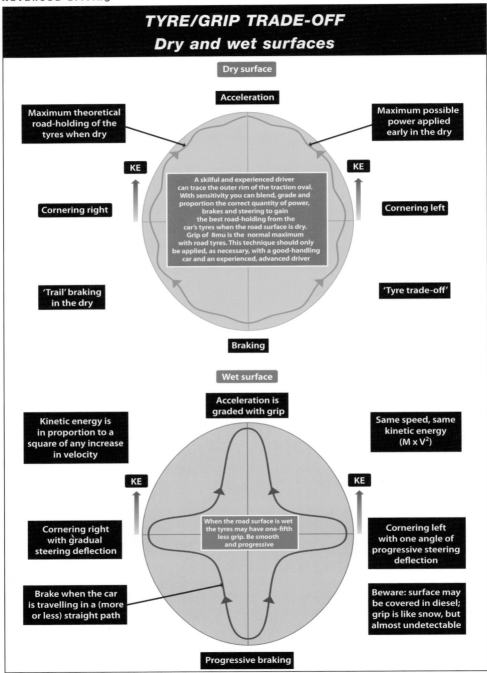

Dry surface

Acceleration

Maximum theoretical road-holding of the tyres when dry

Maximum possible power applied early in the dry

KE

KE

Cornering right

Cornering left

A skilful and experienced driver can trace the outer rim of the traction oval. With sensitivity you can blend, grade and proportion the correct quantity of power, brakes and steering to gain the best road-holding from the car's tyres when the road surface is dry. Grip of 8mu is the normal maximum with road tyres. This technique should only be applied, as necessary, with a good-handling car and an experienced, advanced driver

'Trail' braking in the dry

'Tyre trade-off'

Braking

Wet surface

Acceleration is graded with grip

Kinetic energy is in proportion to a square of any increase in velocity

Same speed, same kinetic energy $(M \times V^2)$

KE

KE

Cornering right with gradual steering deflection

When the road surface is wet the tyres may have one-fifth less grip. Be smooth and progressive

Cornering left with one angle of progressive steering deflection

Brake when the car is travelling in a (more or less) straight path

Beware: surface may be covered in diesel; grip is like snow, but almost undetectable

Progressive braking

and try different techniques, getting it right, or slightly wrong and analyse the difference. There is no question of using racing techniques: if you crash, you are not invited back!

## Controlling skids

Having learned how the car responds on the limit at the proving ground, the driver now needs to apply this knowledge to how to control a skid should one occur while driving on the road.

Skidding is the loss of control caused when the grip of the tyres becomes less than the forces acting on the mass of the car. The main cause of skidding is excessive speed by the tyro driver. Other elements of bad driving that can lead to skidding are sudden steering, irrespective of speed, harsh braking and fierce acceleration. It can also be caused by not matching engine speed to gear and road speed when changing down.

The smoothest control of speed under slippery conditions is obtained with highly skilled acceleration and gearbox sense, which of course, will control the speed of the engine, through the most appropriate gear, to the tyres. Braking, if done at all, and alterations to the steering, must be made with delicacy and progression, so that adhesion to the road is not lost.

Hours of practice are required on proving ground circles and alternate double Z-shaped bends marked with white lines and lots of run-off area, on all surfaces from a simulation of ice, with negligible grip, to a dry road. It will take years of practice until you acquire unconscious competence, and even then you will undoubtedly treat every vehicle with respect, until you can master every surface safely. Remember skidding is being out of control – I am not talking about rear-drive powersliding, which is under control, in the hands of an expert and strictly off the public road.

Skidding is caused by the driver using:
- Excessive speed (mass times velocity squared), which is the major cause.
- Sudden or excessive braking, if no ABS is fitted. Even then, stopping distance has to be assessed precisely to pull up safely.
- Harsh acceleration.
- Sudden, sharp or coarse steering deflection, in relation to a speed that is not in itself excessive.

Most small road cars are front-wheel drive. In most road conditions they will understeer, sliding with the front wheels and steering a wider path than you intend to. Uncorrected, they will go off in a straight line, towards the direction of kinetic energy. The cause is excessive speed or acceleration: remove the cause by lifting off the power and try to slow down. Avoid putting on more and more steering angle. It will not help, except in gravel or deep snow when the wheels will build up a wedge to slow the car down.

It is possible to rectify severe understeer by locking the rear wheels with the handbrake, to cause the tail to slide – a manoeuvre that needs plenty of room and hours of practice, only on the skid circle.

An exception is a sporty hatchback that has roll stiffness at the rear. As you deflect the car into a bend at speed, the rear roll stiffness will cause the outside rear tyre to slide first, oversteering the car on a steering path tighter than you expect and ultimately going off towards the inside of the bend.

To correct an oversteering front-wheel-drive car you should keep the front wheels pointing down the path you wish to follow and use more power to pull the front of the car forwards with acceleration.

The shuttlecock stability of the front-wheel drive car, with its stable understeer, makes front-wheel drive the safer option. It is also cheaper to make and gives more passenger space in a small car. I personally dislike front-wheel drive cars; they are generally safe, stable and boring! Not that it matters for gentle road driving, because unless road

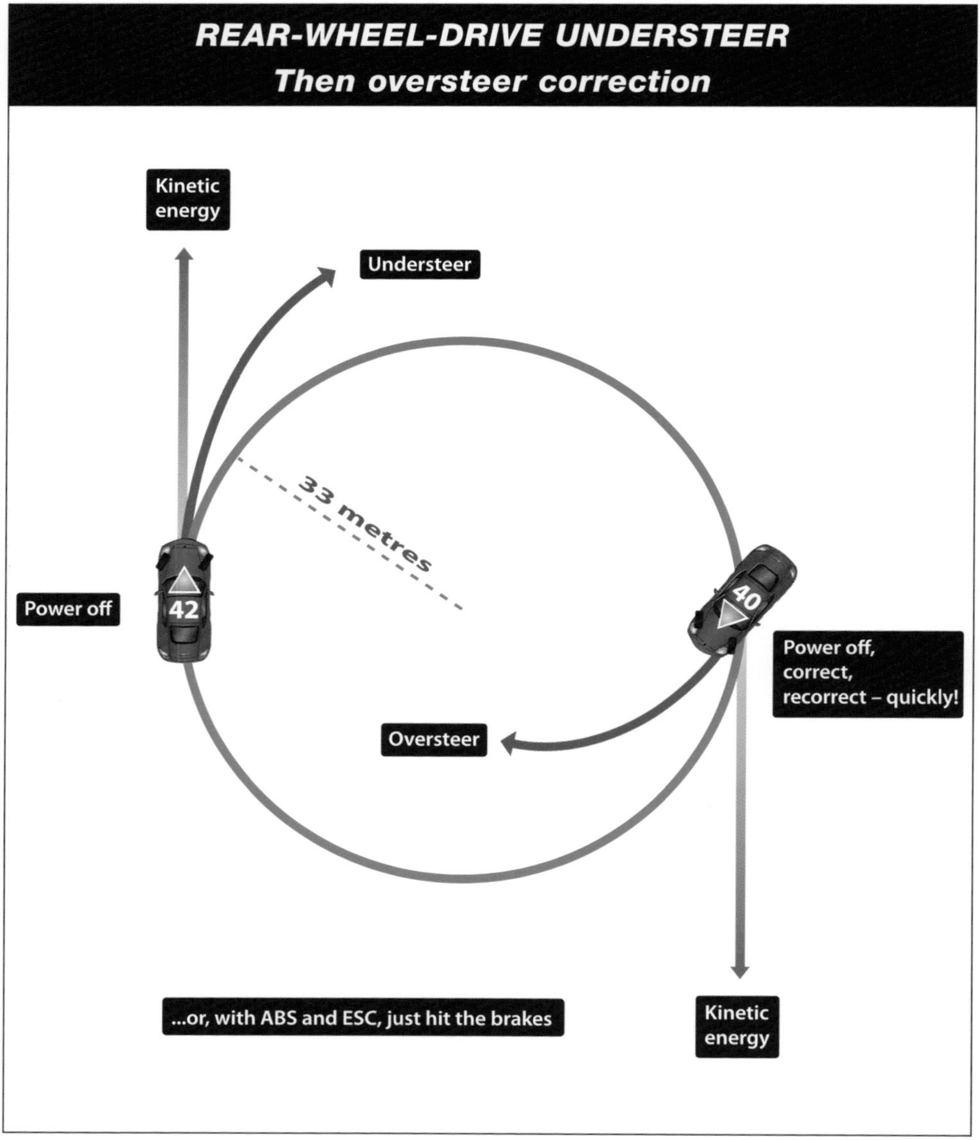

# REAR-WHEEL-DRIVE UNDERSTEER
## Then oversteer correction

Kinetic energy

Understeer

33 metres

Power off

42

40

Power off, correct, recorrect – quickly!

Oversteer

...or, with ABS and ESC, just hit the brakes

Kinetic energy

conditions are very slippery it makes little difference whether the drive is to the front or rear.

I dislike aggressive drivers of four-wheel drive cars in snow, who think their four-wheel drive will enable them to go around a

corner faster, or stop more quickly.

Four-wheel drive rally cars will corner more quickly if the car has a neutral handling characteristic: that is, all four tyres have an equal slip angle and all together point into the turn, opposing kinetic energy equally, to

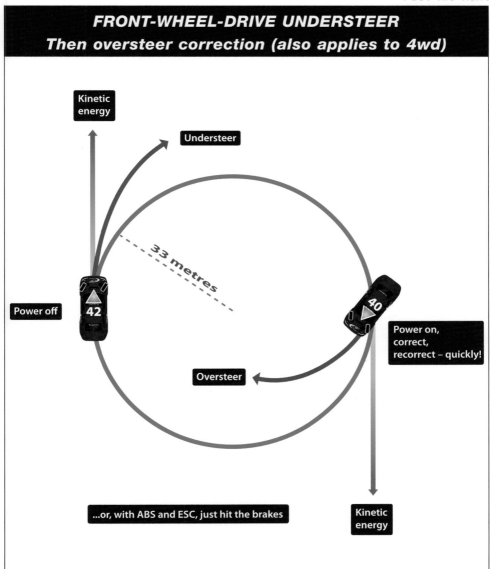

# FRONT-WHEEL-DRIVE UNDERSTEER
## Then oversteer correction (also applies to 4wd)

Kinetic energy

Understeer

33 metres

Power off

42

40

Power on, correct, recorrect – quickly!

Oversteer

...or, with ABS and ESC, just hit the brakes

Kinetic energy

help to take you around the bend. If the car understeers, four-wheel drive will not help as you have only two tyres opposing kinetic energy to take you around the corner.

What four-wheel drive does do is give excellent traction, to accelerate, to take you up hills in snow and help prevent you from getting stuck. This gives the inexperienced the impression that you can go around corners faster. Remember, there are still those four little contact patches trying to oppose kinetic energy – and, if only two are

**163**

# ACCIDENT AVOIDANCE WITHOUT ABS
## How to brake and steer

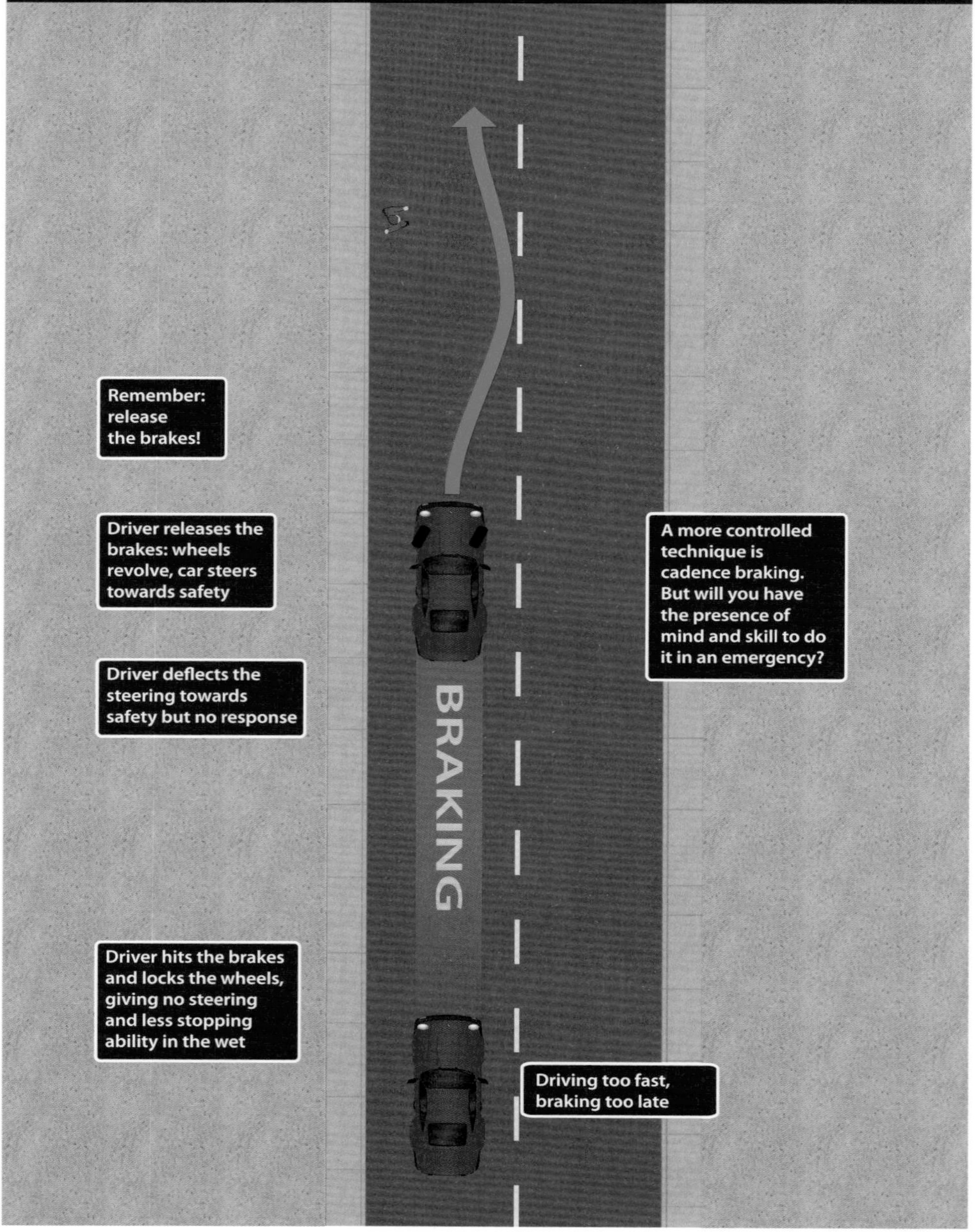

Remember: release the brakes!

Driver releases the brakes: wheels revolve, car steers towards safety

Driver deflects the steering towards safety but no response

A more controlled technique is cadence braking. But will you have the presence of mind and skill to do it in an emergency?

BRAKING

Driver hits the brakes and locks the wheels, giving no steering and less stopping ability in the wet

Driving too fast, braking too late

working for you in understeer, four-wheel drive grips no better than two-wheel drive.

To correct slides with four-wheel drive, remove the cause of understeer by lifting off the power, and for oversteer put on more power. In both cases, keep the front wheels pointing down the path you wish to follow. Do not go off line and steer too much, into potential danger. To recover, re-correct the steering as the car will invariably straighten up very quickly.

To summarise:

## Rear-wheel-drive skids

Understeer will slide the front wheels and steer a wider line than you wish to follow. To correct it:

- ➲ Remove the cause by lifting off the power.
- ➲ Don't apply too much steering, just point the front wheels where you wish to go. Then re-correct. And take off the steering angle you put on, quickly. Otherwise the car will snap into a skid in the other direction.

Oversteer will slide the rear wheels and steer a tighter line than you wish to follow. To correct it:

- ➲ Remove the cause by lifting off the power, instantly.
- ➲ Keep the front wheels pointing down the path you wish to follow, correct then re-correct, that is recover the steering you have put on, by straightening up again, quickly. Otherwise the car will snap into a skid in the other direction.

## Front-wheel-drive skids

Understeer will slide the front wheels and steer a wider line than you wish to follow. To correct it:

- ➲ Remove the cause by lifting off the power.
- ➲ Don't apply too much steering, just point the front wheels where you wish to go, then re-correct and take off the steering angle you put on, quickly.

Oversteer will slide the rear wheels and steer a tighter line than you wish to follow. To correct it:

- ➲ Use more power to pull the front back into line (I repeat, only on the skid circle, in which case skid practice is essential).
- ➲ Keep the front wheels pointing down the path you wish to follow, correct, then re-correct and take off the steering angle you put on, quickly.

## Four-wheel drive

For both understeer and oversteer, use the same correction techniques as for front-wheel drive.

## Electronic assistance

Anti-lock braking (ABS) and skid control (ESC) have evolved remarkably in recent years. ESC is tuned to every type and make of car, for every road surface condition. When understeering, it will automatically apply ABS to the inside back brake to try to stabilise the car. If the car oversteers, the sensors will recognise the condition and apply the outside front brake with the ABS system, to try to correct the car.

If a car fitted with ABS skids, whether it is front-, rear- or four-wheel drive, understeering or oversteering, bang on the brakes fast and steer where you wish to go. Overcome the prejudice of not braking in a skid. Nowadays, you do brake with ABS, the instant that the car skids out of control. It will save many lives if drivers will react to skids by braking hard and fast. All instructors please take note!

Despite this extraordinary technology, nature will win in the end. ABS does not make you invincible. Remember, a tree will kill – a tree doesn't move out of the way.

When an emergency occurs, brake hard to activate the ABS and steer towards safety. Try to avoid looking at the object you are likely to hit, look away and steer with the ABS firmly applied. If the impact is inevitable, a moment beforehand, take your foot off the

# CADENCE BRAKING (WITHOUT ABS)
## On/off variation of brake pedal pressure to retain grip and steering

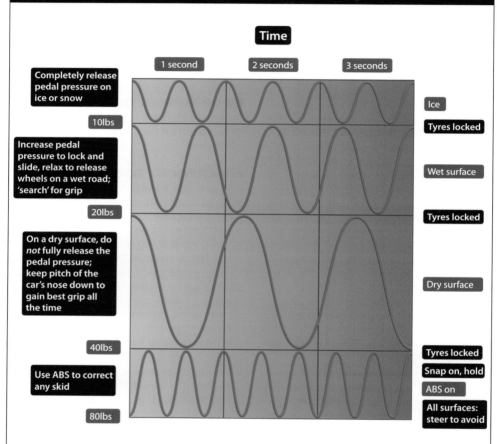

Time

| 1 second | 2 seconds | 3 seconds |

Completely release pedal pressure on ice or snow

10lbs

Increase pedal pressure to lock and slide, relax to release wheels on a wet road; 'search' for grip

20lbs

On a dry surface, do *not* fully release the pedal pressure; keep pitch of the car's nose down to gain best grip all the time

40lbs

Use ABS to correct any skid

80lbs

Ice

Tyres locked

Wet surface

Tyres locked

Dry surface

Tyres locked

Snap on, hold

ABS on

All surfaces: steer to avoid

Cadence (varied-pressure) braking is fluctuation of braking pressure to gain the best grip and stopping efficiency of the tyre, which occurs just before all four tyres begin to lock up and slide. On ice you will have to release *all* of the brake pressure, but on a dry or wet surface you release *only enough* pressure to enable the wheels to rotate again. Brake hard and steadily with ABS, as the best efficiency is achieved electronically. No driver, however skilled and composed, will be as efficient. You will be able to steer with cadence braking and ABS.

brake (otherwise the pedal will break your ankle) release the steering wheel and avoid crossing your arms over the wheel (or when the airbag explodes it will break your arms). Take the aircraft crash position, hands behind your head, to help to avoid whiplash.

Brake assist technology senses if you snap on the brakes quickly, boosts the brake system and produces extra pressure. This is because research has found that, in the first instance, when the situation demands that speed needs to be killed quickly, drivers do not brake hard enough.

Some expensive cars have Pre-Safe technology. If the car starts to skid and the ESC is activated along with violent braking, the system will take up the slack in the seat belts and tension them in preparation for the impending impact. It will also shut the windows or sunroof, lower the front passenger seat to the floor to get the

vulnerable head away from the roof and, if the car is a soft top, it will explode a roll over bar, to try to protect you.

Post-Safe activates once you have crashed. It will unlock the doors and a laser will display on the A and B posts to inform the fire crews where they can cut the roof off to save your life.

Ultimately, prevention is better than cure. It is better to develop your roadcraft to be able to anticipate and plan your driving far ahead, with detailed observation. Apply the driving plan decisively and deliberately, to always be in the right place in the road, at the right, safe and appropriate speed, in the right gear for the speed. Then there will never be a need for limit handling skills, or electronic aids, to help save your life.

*Heavy braking, with ABS activated, pitches the car forwards.*

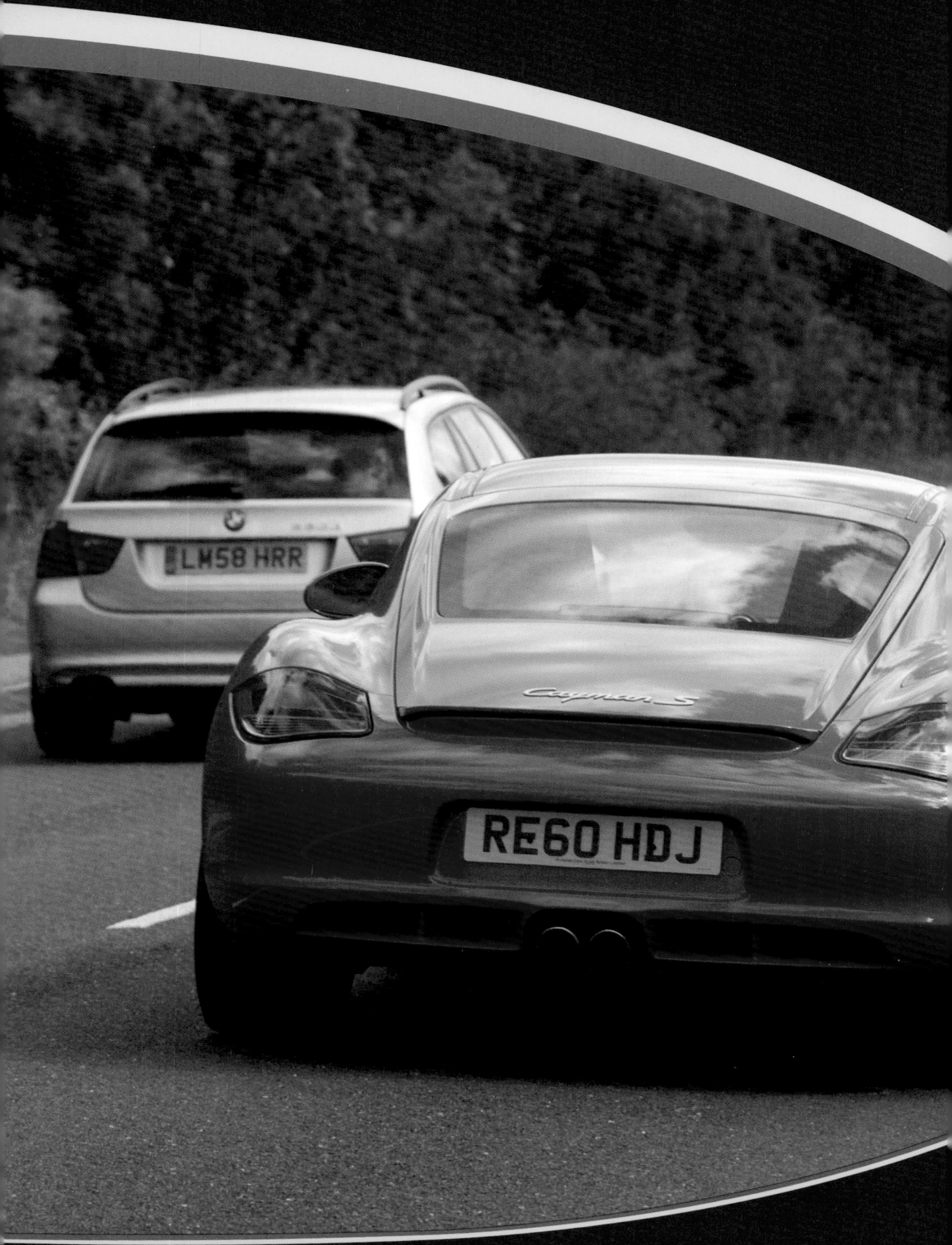
LM58 HRR
Cayman S
RE60 HDJ

# 10 Making progress

*Making progress by unobtrusive overtaking –*
*a powerful car makes driving so effortless, easy and safe.*

Unobtrusive progress is the hallmark of the advanced driver; the bad driver is the one you will notice. The kind of advanced driver I admire is one who can average 50mph on white-signed roads, with stops, in a red Ferrari, from Lands End to John O'Groats, without being seen to drive in an extraordinary way.

Progress that is beyond the reproach of others is difficult to achieve on two-way roads in the UK. You certainly have to behave well and understand other people very well indeed. As long as overtaking is done safely and is effective in shortening journey time, I don't see why we should feel guilty in doing so at the appropriate time, speed and place.

I try to drive at a different pace and style in France, different again in Italy and I enjoy it, more so than in the UK. People here tend to be cynical and jealous. I find, however, that I am received well in the Super Seven, less so in my red BMW (an E30 318is).

## VOICE OF EXPERIENCE

### A bad taxi driver

I once experienced a ride in a minicab that was very bad, uncomfortable and frightening. I asked him why he drove so aggressively, and his warped reasoning was to intimidate the driver in front to go faster, or simply to get out of his way, and to prevent another driver filling the space in front of him. He gave me a dramatic display of the attitude that we too often have to put up with on the road. I told him to stop, got out and gave him a piece of my mind. Not that it would do any good I suppose, even if I did threaten to report him to the local authority, which I regret I did not. Future passengers probably would not either.

## Making use of power

A powerful car makes driving so effortless, easy and safe. There is no need to use all of the power, all of the time, just the correct degree of acceleration for the situation, no more, no less. The ordinary driver does not appreciate the overtaking ability of a high-performance car. That is to be sympathised with. You must not breed any apprehension in others.

When demonstrated by an advanced driver, high performance is so effortless, taking all the frustration and danger away from motoring. For instance, a Porsche 911 Turbo encompasses that vital 40 to 60mph in a mere 1.2 seconds, when using full power in second gear! From 50 to 70mph in third takes only 1.7 seconds.

The 911 has a power-to-weight ratio of 319bhp per ton and costs over £100,000. My own Super Seven HPC is relatively inexpensive and has 450bhp per ton. It possesses the same 40 to 60mph and 50 to 70mph acceleration times, in first and second gear! This is one of the many reasons why I choose to own it, for this safe overtaking quality. Used with skill, care, consideration and responsibility, a reserve of performance like this can be safe for myself and convenient for others.

It is far more effective on single carriageways to shorten your journey time by taking the first, completely safe and convenient opportunity to pass, than it is to travel at high speed then sit behind a slow lorry and miss many safe opportunities to make further progress. Many drivers do this. They drive by mood instead of purpose, with highs and lows in concentration. They have difficulty in assessing speed and distance – hence accidents and frustrated hold-ups in crocodile queues. Following too closely, unable to see ahead properly, they sometimes try to stop others who can overtake from overtaking them, by tailgating. Selfish behaviour like that is an offence. I must admit however, it doesn't bother the driver of a Seven. You can leave this inconsiderate behaviour behind, safely.

Main roads of primary importance, called primary routes, designed and maintained by the Highways Agency, do not, in my view, provide enjoyable motoring. On single

*A good London taxi driver knows how to keep flowing through traffic.*

carriageways overtaking is often discouraged or prevented: long curves and restricted visibility; one gentle curve followed by another, mile after mile; traffic islands and hatching. All this is designed to keep you behind the slowest road user. Lay-bys are provided, but are not used by the drivers of slow vehicles – they should be! In Canada it is an offence not to move over if there are more than three vehicles following. Other countries often have more slow lanes provided for lorries than is ever the case in the UK.

With a powerful car, it is so necessary for you to be calm and calculating, deliberate and decisive. Using measured acceleration sense, you can slide by with power in reserve, picking your way past to the safe long gaps. In the crowded parts of urban England, the value of passing, to diminish what is perhaps only a short journey, is of less value. It is safer and more sensible to wait for a dual carriageway or motorway for crocodile queues to be broken up, than to leapfrog from one car to the next, which is a sure way to make yourself unpopular. On the other hand, the flat plains of rural eastern England are like parts of continental Europe. This will condition drivers to overtake with greater skill, as in countries where journeys are longer, and passing becomes necessary to make reasonable progress and headway through light, spasmodic traffic.

## Planning once more

The first thing to remember about progressive motoring is to plan your route before you start. There is no point in overtaking if you then take the wrong turning; you are just a menace, and a laughing stock if you have to do it all again. Give yourself sufficient time to complete your journey and pace it well. There is more to learn about pacing and how long a journey is going to take than about many elements of motoring.

Forward planning starts before your journey begins, and being correct in predicting

**171**

# THE RULE OF THE TRIANGLE 1
## *Safety, view, stability*

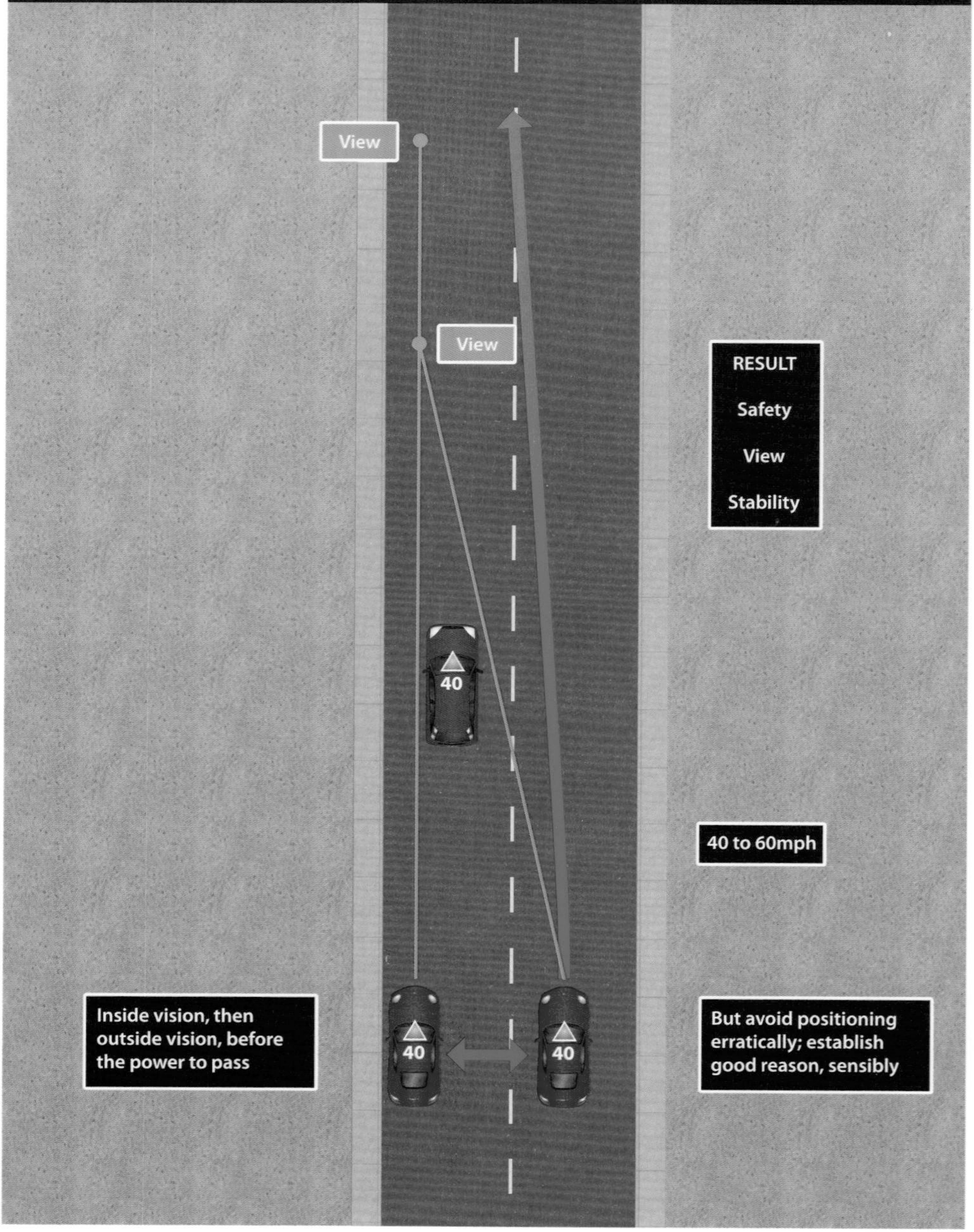

View

View

**RESULT**

Safety

View

Stability

40

40 to 60mph

40

40

Inside vision, then outside vision, before the power to pass

But avoid positioning erratically; establish good reason, sensibly

journey times is a hallmark of the most experienced advanced driver. In the UK there is so much roadwork obstruction. In Europe, average speeds are much higher, as they divert traffic for roadworks, or better still, complete the work at night. It is best to try to find out where they are before you start. Pay attention to your map craft before you begin, and program your sat-nav for the variety of roads across country, on non-primary A- and B-roads between small towns and villages. Meanwhile, let's enjoy what relatively free motoring we have and drive across country.

I avoid primary routes: they have removed all the joy from motoring, by discouraging and preventing overtaking on single carriageways, even to pass an obstruction like a 40mph speed-restricted LGV. It is one restriction after another: frequent island refuges, cross-hatching and blind long-radius curves. These curves are engineered to give a maximum length of sight line of 700 feet or 213 metres – not sufficient to slip by safely with the average car. One gentle curve after another, then a gentle crest, another curve and so on – enough to make you give up any thought of overtaking! So give up, don't fight to get by, wait for the next dual carriageway. It's far better to choose the non-primary A- or B-class roads and develop your roadcraft skills and enjoy motoring.

To enjoy a journey, set off early before the majority of people get out of bed. Only use motorways occasionally, if you have a long journey to complete, to bypass towns and busy industrial areas. Watch your speed carefully, and blend in to the pace of any traffic. Be discreet. Flow along. In town, drive slowly. It is not going to influence your journey time to rush, and a sense of speed is vital for safety.

If the town is strange to you, you will need to have your route confirmed with traffic signs and they may be visually concealed, behind buildings or other signs. Remember your map-planning and strip route as minor routes may not be signed clearly at all. Then try to keep the route secret, because the unskilled are more likely to crash on country roads!

If a journey through the urban sprawl is a regular occurrence, planning your route in your mind is essential. Local knowledge is your greatest asset; where the hold-ups occur and how the pace of the traffic is affected at different times of the day. Remember, highway engineers can alter the timing of traffic lights to control the pace of traffic. Try to listen to the local traffic information for likely problems and know your patch well. Investigate the alternative routes when you have time. You may have to twist and turn to avoid traffic, but choose a path that is as straight and as quiet as possible. But avoid rat-running, which the local authority will try to prevent, if they can, with one-way streets, no right turns and speed humps.

Flow along at an easy pace and give yourself time to look and see all there is to see at junctions; as they say, 'think bike'. The most vulnerable time is when you have lost your way, so stop safely, switch off your engine and set your sat-nav. Plan your driving path well ahead and avoid changing lane without good reason. In heavy traffic, the true meaning of lane discipline is self-discipline. Avoid weaving through traffic, swapping from one lane to the next, and stealing a march on the rest. It is unpopular, likely to be an offence, and is a sign of irresponsible behaviour, as well as a lack of anticipation and forward planning.

If lane markings allow, select the empty lane at traffic lights, or the lane of least resistance. Assess the likely progress of drivers you choose to stop behind. Do not use a lane that is marked for a right or left turn only, when you wish to go straight on – this is a minor traffic offence. The road on the other side of the junction often narrows and there will not be sufficient room if other drivers object to your bad behaviour and set off with venom. If we all behave badly collectively, we will suffer more than we do now, so do not goad others to behave badly.

Stop a metre or so behind the stop line at traffic lights, so that you do not disturb pedestrians or provoke other drivers to rush, and remember, do not move forward until the green light shows. Look right and left for 'red light gamblers', particularly at night or at busy controlled junctions.

It is most important to show a good example to others. If you drive a high-performance car, everyone watches you. They may be envious and only too ready to witness an indiscretion. There are people about with mischievous minds, so try to be beyond any reasonable reproach.

For most folk, everyday driving is in heavy traffic in town and on motorways, on roads they know very well. Only the lucky few drive in the country. So the standard of town and motorway driving, although highly controlled and regulated, ought to be high; sadly, in my view, it is not. The more of us there are and the closer we are together, the worse behaviour becomes. It is in the area of lane discipline and separation distance that many drivers need education, particularly in town, or where the road is not marked with white lines.

A driver with lane sense will not require road markings, merely judgement of space, all-round awareness and anticipation. It takes experience of driving to make progress through traffic without causing any problems to others. One must drive with care and consideration; be deliberate, decisive, enterprising and skilful. Use space to accelerate firmly, blending with the traffic flow when changing lanes.

A good London taxi driver will often keep flowing through the thickest traffic. Watch how he creates an extra lane when space will allow, anticipating traffic movement, filtering across, changing lane gradually, using other traffic to shield him, as he gives a thank you wave. Learn from him, as it is often best to accelerate firmly, along the traffic, to blend in and select your lane later, rather than cut across and stop traffic by intimidation, like some drivers attempt to do in this situation. It's a dangerous game and disruptive too.

Roundabouts, like circulatory systems, are only one-way streets that bend, so passing rules on them are the same, with passing permitted on either side. Nearside overtaking on a roundabout is not an offence, although it can be not sensible on occasion – a signal must be given and timed perfectly. Be particularly careful of the cut-in of the semi-trailer of an articulated LGV, when it bends around. If it is a box van, nearside or offside observation is not so easy, if nigh impossible on roundabouts.

Mirrors do not work when an artic is turning. A low sports car is mincemeat to an LGV at a roundabout, or on dual carriageways and motorways, especially if the LGV is foreign and left-hand drive. I doubt if the driver would know if his semi-trailer ran over a little sports car; he probably wouldn't even feel it! Never pass a moving LGV on the nearside with a low sports car, and think twice about passing on the offside on roundabouts; hang back!

To flow through traffic, like a London cab driver, plan ahead over the roofs of cars, using anticipation to be early. Don't drive on the brakes and follow others too closely. Instead, be remote and avoid getting involved with the bad driving of others – give yourself room to work. Quite the worst kind of driver I meet in a city is the one who is influenced by the bad behaviour of others and fights with them, with intimidation, by incessantly pushing forwards, following closely when there is no opportunity to make any further progress, surviving only by stamping on the brakes!

Firm acceleration can be used to advantage to fit in with traffic decisively when it is safe, reasonable and clear. A good example is when trying to fit into a traffic stream moving along without a break: accelerate

# THE RULE OF THE TRIANGLE 2
## *Explained in detail*

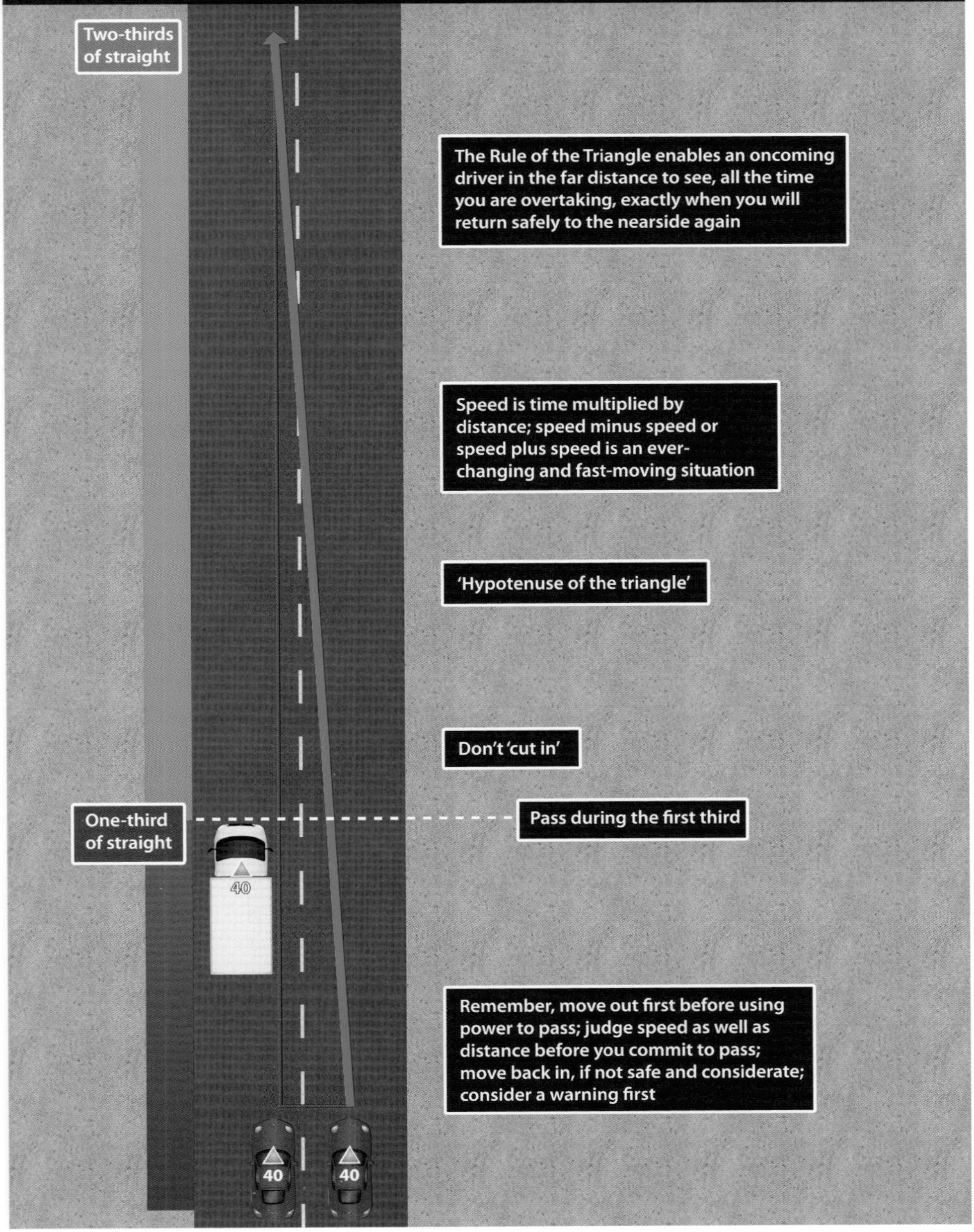

**Two-thirds of straight**

The Rule of the Triangle enables an oncoming driver in the far distance to see, all the time you are overtaking, exactly when you will return safely to the nearside again

Speed is time multiplied by distance; speed minus speed or speed plus speed is an ever-changing and fast-moving situation

'Hypotenuse of the triangle'

Don't 'cut in'

**One-third of straight**

Pass during the first third

Remember, move out first before using power to pass; judge speed as well as distance before you commit to pass; move back in, if not safe and considerate; consider a warning first

40

40 40

**175**

firmly to run alongside a safe gap, and ask with a signal 'please may I fit in?' Wait for evidence of a reaction first; obviously, don't force your lane change. Many drivers stop at right angles to the traffic and wait when turning left, holding up traffic behind. Instead, turn, accelerate and blend in once traffic speed is equal.

When joining a busy roundabout solid with traffic waiting on the approach, the left-hand lane is often more progressive, as traffic in this lane is shielded and blends in to the roundabout better. Take the most progressive lane for your direction and help to keep traffic moving. A frequent accident happens on the approach to a roundabout in the left-hand lane when there is a safe gap but the driver in front hesitates and stops. Look ahead, as well as to the right, and drive with care and attention.

Communicate with other drivers early. Don't be afraid to ask. Signal at least four seconds before a lane change, to give other drivers time to react: ask 'may I?' and wait to see evidence of reaction first. Furthermore, teach yourself the self-discipline to signal before you change lane. When you have received the co-operation of the other driver, who has priority, cancel the signal as your right wheels cross the lane line. Don't signal late and barge in, as most do! And don't rely on your door mirror: give a life-saver shoulder check, using side vision quickly, left or right, then blend in at a tangent.

Some drivers think that the only danger when turning left into a major road will come from the right; so they only look right when turning left. If it is clear from the right, a dangerous driver who cannot be bothered to wait may overtake a line of stationary traffic on approach to a blind minor junction on his right and hit the emerging vehicle – sadly, this common mistake is often fatal.

Cross-hatching down the centre of the road on single carriageways causes confusion to many. If the lines at the edge of the hatching are parallel and continuous, it is an offence to cross into that area except in an emergency. If the edge lines are broken, it is not an offence to drive on these hatched areas, but the result of doing so could be in certain circumstances. The advice in the *Highway Code* will be used against you if you cause a disturbance to anyone turning at a later junction protected by these white diagonal markings. The cross-hatching is not much use to protect the vulnerable right-turning vehicle if we all use it and drive on these areas without thought. So keep off the hatching if your presence is likely to cause a problem to turning traffic.

If you are turning right yourself, hatching is there for your protection, but it is only white paint! Drive over it if you need to clear fast traffic behind you. You must not however, if you cause disturbance to any vehicle opposing, that wishes to turn in front, or behind you, where the hatching is covering more than one turning. With fast traffic travelling along a single carriageway primary route, the turning lane within the hatched area frequently does not give sufficient room to slow down in this lane. A double line system is also often placed on the edge to stop you encroaching onto the hatching as you approach your turn. The idea is to slow the vehicles behind you; so, fit in with dispatch. Try not to slow traffic and cause obstruction to following drivers.

I sympathise with drivers of LGV artic semi-trailers. They must not leave the back of the trailer causing obstruction to nearside passing traffic, so they should line up early and use hatching on approach to a right turn, if legal, and position out of the way before braking. Carry out the same principle of sensible driving yourself.

One time not to use hatching to overtake is on the approach to a crossroads or junction on the right. You may be in conflict with the overtaken vehicle. Nor should you use it at the end of a dual carriageway; better to overtake at the beginning. Be early, not late.

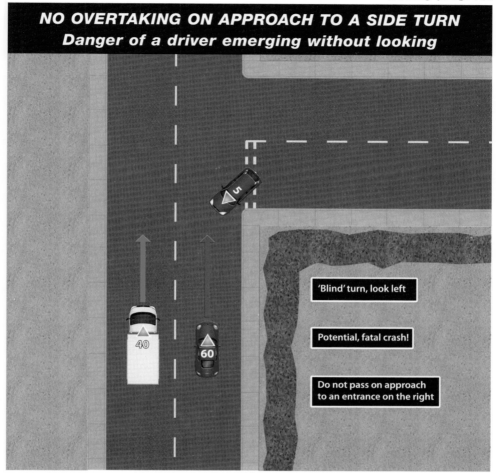

**NO OVERTAKING ON APPROACH TO A SIDE TURN**
*Danger of a driver emerging without looking*

'Blind' turn, look left

Potential, fatal crash!

Do not pass on approach
to an entrance on the right

# Overtaking

On single carriageways, it is overtaking technique that invariably requires radical re-thinking. The natural method of passing is to follow too closely, change down and swoop out with power applied from behind, steering and signalling at the same time, giving no time for others to react. This is not the safe way – in fact it is potentially dangerous.

If the separation gap in front is already dangerously close, then power from behind will close the gap further. Disastrous, if the driver ahead hits the brakes with a tyre-smoking stop! The overtaker only thinks of approaching traffic and loops around instantly committed to pass, without a clear view or warning to others. If people gave a moment's thought to this, they would see how potentially lethal this method of passing is.

Although it is the method used by the majority of drivers, power from behind is not the safe way to overtake in the light of more experience – just as in sport, the natural way of swiping a ball is not the correct technique

**177**

that will be demonstrated to you by your coach. In the first instance, you have to be taught with instruction, then coached on the finer points. Later, you may develop your own style, but the basic principles remain the same. The technique used may seem difficult for you to master at first, but later practice will confirm the benefits.

Small car driving seems to dictate overtaking with power from behind, to cut down the time spent on the other half of the road. But, if the danger is concealed when you commit yourself to the overtake, while still in a road position almost directly behind the vehicle ahead, a hazard may be exposed too late for you to do anything about it. Following closely, looking along the offside, a warning sign may be missed for a junction on the left. A driver may emerge and drive across the bows of the overtaken vehicle, and impact the overtaking driver. Potentially even worse perhaps, is the overtaking driver not noticing a blind entrance on the right of a fairly narrow two-way road and overtaking on the approach to it. The emerging driver will not think of looking left. They think the only danger will come from their right. Fatal!

On single carriageways, overtaking is relatively easy. It is the preparation for it that is difficult. It starts as soon as the vehicle ahead is sighted. The many questions to ask yourself are:

- Is this particular overtake going to be effective? In other words, is the pass going to be of value to shorten your journey time? Or are you approaching a town in the next couple of miles, for example, or a dual carriageway?
- Is the driver ahead likely to co-operate? Do they know you are there? What are they thinking about and what are they about to do? Is there comfortable room for everyone involved?
- Is there a safe gap to go for?
- What is the future situation most likely to be when you arrive at the vehicle ahead? Is there any junction or entrance – is a

bend or crest going to limit your view? Are there any warning signs? They may be obscured by vegetation. Is there a double line system, with get-back arrows in view?

All these questions, and others, should cross your mind as you time the close on the vehicle ahead. Don't charge or commit yourself from too far back. Instead, time your approach with constant long-range anticipation and judgement of speed and distance, applied with deceleration sense. Arrive at the right time.

Meanwhile, if it is evident that your forward planning informs you that there is no opportunity to overtake, or reason to pass, I see no point in following the vehicle ahead at less than a reasonably safe following distance, of one yard per mph of your speed. Keeping enough separation distance from the vehicle in front is vital to give you room to work and time to react. To be sure, use the two-second rule: count 'one and two' while waiting for a surface change or other marker to reach you from the vehicle in front. If you don't wish to pass, the gap is there for someone who does.

To leave a short gap, as many do, to try to stop others behind from passing, is an offence. If you, say 'Well, if I drop back, someone will fill the gap,' then, 'You are done, sir!' may well be a police officer's reply, as it is a traffic offence to admit driving without care and consideration.

In some countries, more sensible than ours, it is an offence to have more than three vehicles following behind you. To cause a following driver to carry out an unnecessary overtake on a two-way road is driving without consideration. There must be a sound reason to drive unnaturally slowly, as there must be to drive at very high speed. We all have a responsibility towards other road users.

It is driving without consideration for LGV drivers with a 40mph speed limit on single carriageways, or caravan and van drivers

# ACCELERATION SENSE WHEN OVERTAKING
## Pass in the first third of the straight

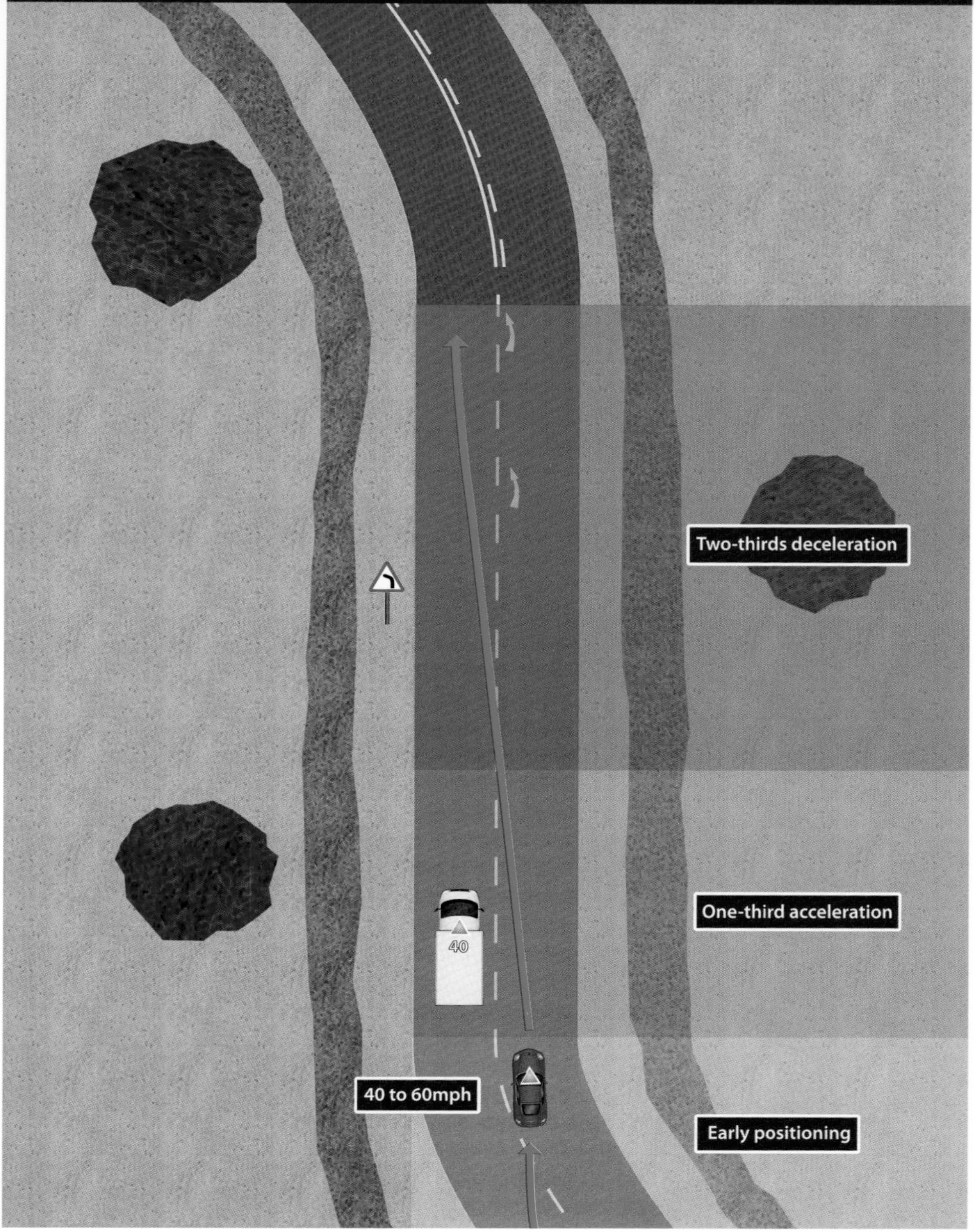

Two-thirds deceleration

One-third acceleration

40 to 60mph

Early positioning

**179**

*Overtaking triangle 1. Timing 'the close' in preparation for an overtaking manoeuvre.*

with a 50mph limit, not to pull over into a convenient lay-by to let following traffic pass.

According to research by the Transport Research Laboratory (TRL), we are safer driving behind the slowest vehicle in a long crocodile queue of tailgating traffic – pottering along towards the inevitable accident because the impact when it comes will be less serious. In my view, it is misguided to treat the population on the road as children, browbeaten and defeated. Realistic training is needed to develop our skill. We need to be inspired to improve, not restricted.

Try to avoid being the second vehicle in a queue for any longer than necessary. Overtake at the first completely safe opportunity. Be out and gone, as soon as possible, or otherwise hang well back.

There are three good reasons for the hang-back position:

- ➲ Safety to react in good time to a sudden stop.
- ➲ View is much improved, as your attention should be far into the distance. If you find yourself looking at the back of the vehicle ahead, ask yourself if it is because you are following too closely. Look down the nearside as well as the offside.
- ➲ Stability is much improved, if you have to alter course for any reason, such as a pothole or debris. The steering deflection in response to any hazard can be gradual.

## Seeing to overtake

You can see much better if you drop back while you look for an overtaking opportunity. The larger the vehicle ahead, the further back you must follow to be able to see, using a left-hand view along left-hand curves, looking underneath over crests, and

occasionally over roof tops. Where there are following cars, a view through the rear window and windscreen can be used to your advantage. Be constantly aware of what is going on behind you.

An extended safety line position will give you as long a view as possible on straight roads. Position as much as you can safely, using all of your half of the road. Ease away for oncoming traffic, but at other times, if possible, move up to the centre line, to see along the straight into the far distance, with an occasional mirror check to watch the situation behind.

Don't spend a moment not knowing what is happening in front of the vehicle ahead. Vary your position to see, gently. Don't weave about. If you spend a second at 40mph blind, you travel 66ft (20m) without knowing what is happening ahead. So drop back and use inside or outside vision to see and plan far ahead.

Through left-hand bends, the extended

*Overtaking triangle 2. Position out to maximise view for assessment before using power to pass.*

safety line position will occasionally give the longest view down the nearside. Your following distance may be too close if you have to hug the kerb to see. Use this inside vision until there is evidence that the bend is ending, then convert to an offside view, with mirror check, without closing up or committing yourself to pass; wait and see the complete situation first.

Through right-hand bends, the nearside position should be held until the view around the bend begins to lengthen. Power is graded so that no commitment to the pass occurs until a complete clear view is obtained. Then, acceleration becomes firmer as the road is seen to be clear. The steering angle needs little, if any change, to carry on into the overtaking position.

Early planning is essential, with a mirror check, to know in good time which view

**181**

*Overtaking triangle 3. Only use power to pass if it is 100 per cent safe to overtake, and take a gradual course back to the nearside.*

is required next, so that a gradual change of position can be achieved. You may then notice the opportunity approaching in plenty of time. This is fairly easy to see and plan on a straight road, but most roads in the country are not.

It may be reasonable to suppose that over the next brow, a straight section of road can be expected alongside the line of trees that is visible. So check your mirror and change down in anticipation. Think of the situation behind. Is a fast car or motorbike following closely and being a bit pushy, or are they content to follow safely and watch you? It is no use chopping the signal on as you pull out, giving them no time to react. Signal, 'I am planning to pass', at least four seconds before pulling out if you think they may

intend to come past you. You can always cancel if you cannot pass. If they hang back, there is no need. This signal, if required, should be started while you time the close around the bend, to put you in an overtaking position as the straight begins and your view opens up.

After all, overtaking is best accomplished where the view is best, right at the start of the straight, not halfway along it when the view is only half as good – hence all this early preparation. If the overtake cannot be accomplished during the first third of a moderate straight, don't attempt it; wait for the next straight. Obvious perhaps, but how many late chargers do you see?

You most certainly do not wish to charge with full power from too far back; trying to make up ground and cover the long safe following distance you have left, before passing the vehicle ahead. So, before overtaking it is a practical necessity to sacrifice your hang-back position. To close up to an overtaking position, on a straight road with oncoming traffic, station your offside wheels just left of the warning or double line system, two or three car lengths back. Now, use the mirrors, and change down, to have the engine speed between maximum torque and maximum power; say 3,000 to 4,000rpm, to have the best reserve of power to overtake. Do not change gear alongside the vehicle you are overtaking. You cannot accelerate during a gear change, and you will only have one hand on the wheel. If the overtaken vehicle swerves while you are changing gear alongside, you will be in trouble. So plan to change up before or after passing.

With opposing traffic on a two-way single carriageway, this preparation should be timed to perfection, as the gap in the opposing traffic is approaching, or just after the last vehicle passes. If the situation in the ever-changing scene goes against you, drop back to the hang-back position and start the planning and preparation again – all done with acceleration sense, not braking. If you have missed an opportunity, have a look in the mirror to see the road behind that you could have used to pass! Experience teaches.

Here is the approach:

- Preparation, and then execution:
- Apply the driving plan – mirror – hang back to plan and see best, inside left-hand curves, offside vision through right-hand curves and along the straight – signal, only if necessary, four seconds before – time the close – shoulder check – 'think bike' – change down – mirror, cancel signal – position out, before the power to pass.
- Judge speed and distance – look for entrances, particularly on the right – look across the bow of the vehicle you're passing – consider a warning note – only then accelerate, down the hypotenuse, on a straight line past – mirror, 'thank you wave' up to the centre mirror.

I recommend the rule of the triangle technique when overtaking. Move out smoothly along the base of the triangle to obtain a clear view past the vehicle in front, without making any commitment to pass, and then accelerate down the hypotenuse to overtake.

Having completed the preparation to pass, deflect the steering smoothly and gradually to move to the position you need to be in to see across the front of the vehicle you want to overtake. You must not apply the power to commit you to overtake, yet. Go out to look, before committing yourself, completely out on the course to pass, right in the centre of the offside of the road, on an extended safety line position. Then you can judge perfectly well, the speed and distance to the next bend or other hazard ahead. You can judge the length of the long vehicle you are about to pass and be sure it is entirely safe and considerate to overtake.

The confirmation of the rule of the triangle is safety, view and stability (along with a constant awareness of the situation behind):

- Safety. With a road position clear of the vehicle to pass, you have time to assess speed and distance. There is no better signal than an obvious road position. A warning may be essential for safety.
- View. Best from an extended safety line position, before committing to pass on a straight road.
- Stability. Power is applied in a straight line.

Visibility is dramatically improved by taking the extended safety line position, in the centre of the offside of the road. Let me try to explain with an optical trick. Take a pencil and point it end-on to your eyes; then, place it slightly to your left side and notice how much easier it is to judge its length. You give yourself the same optical advantage when you position out on the extended safety line, on course to overtake.

Do not concern yourself that anyone is likely to fill the space you leave on your left. It is obvious what you are doing to any responsible person. Although you think that the mischievous may attempt to move up on your left, it has never happened to me in almost 50 years of applying this technique, and I do not reasonably expect it to.

I don't go out unless I am 95% sure I can overtake, but that 5% makes the manoeuvre 100% safe. If you do not accelerate, you have not overtaken, and you can move gently back in, if you have to.

Positioning out to see, before committing to overtake, gives the same optical advantage when judging gaps in a line of traffic. This is an overtaking situation I may attempt far more frequently with my Super Seven HPC, as I have so much control and power. It is very tiny, so it takes less space, and the Seven is received well by others, because they want to have a look at this nutcase in a silly little car! When I am in my BMW they may not be so kind and considerate.

I will often say to a driver who is hesitating before an overtake that is easily on and safe, 'Go out and look to see how it fits – but don't accelerate and commit yourself unless you are content that it is safe for you'. I will never say 'Go!' and encourage someone to pass. It's too close for 'No!' to be mistaken for 'Go!' Instead, I will only ever command, 'Do not overtake!' I may however say, 'Decide!'

You must not position out unnecessarily when you do not want to overtake, or swerve about. It gives a bad example to others and could make a timid driver ahead nervous. Be steady and have a good reason to position out to look and assess speed and distance.

There are many potential dangers to think about before you commit yourself to the overtake. Search for concealed entrances, particularly on B-roads, with the possibility of a driver emerging without seeing you overtaking. A driver in an entrance to your left may think they can turn across the bow of a slow lorry or tractor, without seeing you overtaking, loop around and hit you head on. I must emphasise that the driver who turns left out of a concealed driveway may think that the only source of danger will approach from the right and swing straight into the path of an overtaking driver. This situation causes most accidents when overtaking, as there is a tendency for the overtaking driver to consider only the possibility of approaching traffic, not the potential of someone emerging. It is not only obvious clearly-marked junctions that you have to think about. Go out first and give yourself time to look, judge and see properly, before you go. If you haven't time to position out before putting on the power to pass, don't overtake at all.

Don't zip in and out, looping around vehicles. The other side of the road is not no man's land, to be in and out of as quickly as possible. It is to be used to your advantage, if it is safe to do so. You are only committed to pass when accelerating alongside; take time and care before you do. When passing a lorry, look for an obstruction like a very slow vehicle, cyclist or slow-moving motorcyclist, just in front of it.

When you get out onto an extended safety line position, before you commit to passing, consider first of all if the driver you want to overtake is aware of your presence. Are they giving any clue that they know you are there? After all, the driver is a stranger you have never met. You cannot talk to each other. The driver must be aware of you to co-operate, and if it matters to have their attention, use the voice of the car and sound the horn. It is better to make a noise than to have an accident. How can you expect the vital co-operation of the driver ahead if they display no clue that they are aware of your intention to pass?

It seems a national trait of ours to expect drivers who are about to be overtaken to see a signal from the indicator, yet fail to give them a warning by sounding the horn.

## DO NOT TRUST A TAILGATER
### Overtaking the tailgater

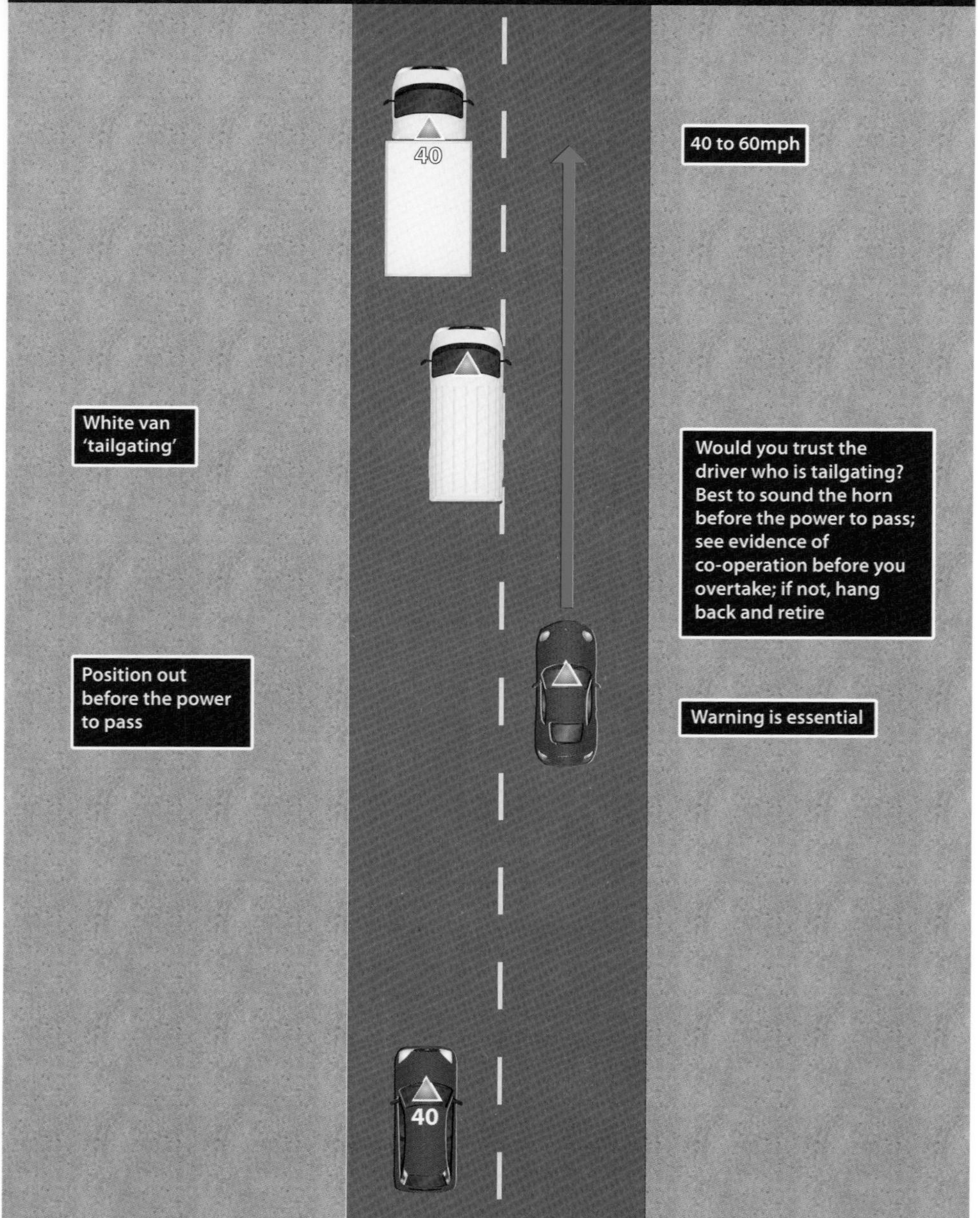

# DO NOT USE POWER FROM BEHIND
## *How not to overtake*

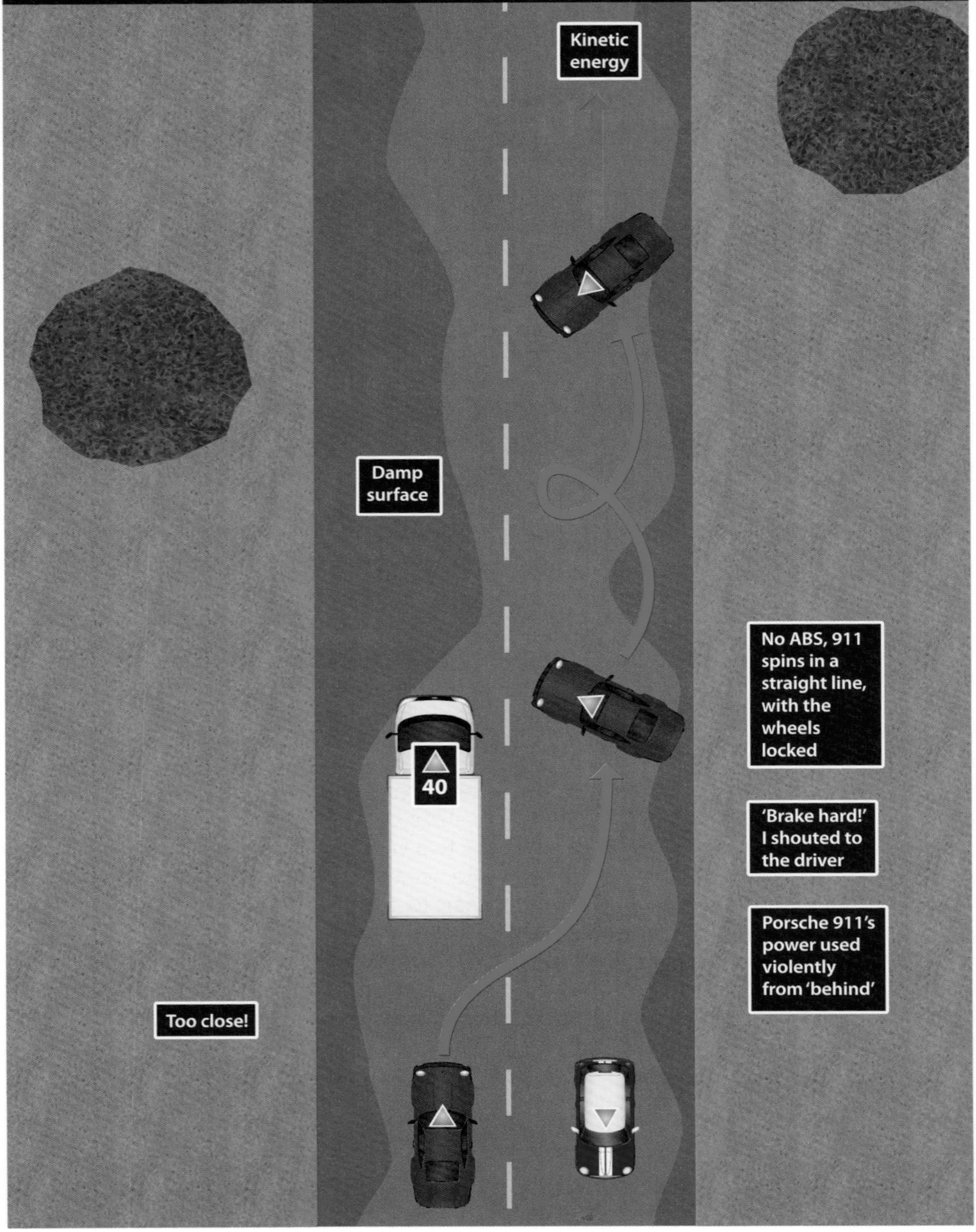

Kinetic energy

Damp surface

No ABS, 911 spins in a straight line, with the wheels locked

'Brake hard!' I shouted to the driver

Porsche 911's power used violently from 'behind'

Too close!

40

## VOICE OF EXPERIENCE

### How not to overtake

In the mid 1960s, HPC had an early Porsche 911 with a short wheelbase and skinny wheels and tyres. I loved it. My client and I had just met and he was a fairly press-on type who had never driven a 911 before. It was raining, and the country B-road was quite cambered, with occasional light traffic. Eventually, we came to pass a large goods vehicle. With forward planning, I could see that it was clear after the car approaching, and so was the mirror. My client changed down, swerved to the right, signalling at the same time and booted the power violently. At the time I was an inexperienced co-driver, and it caught me by surprise. The car fell over onto the negative camber on the offside and immediately span around!

Now, I never normally raise my voice in the car, but this was highly dangerous. I shouted at my client to brake hard. With no ABS when you lock the wheels, a car spinning and rotating with no outside influence will spin in a straight line, in the direction of the only force acting upon it, kinetic energy. With the wheels locked up, it span in a perfectly straight line. We rotated at least twice and it didn't touch a thing! The lorry driver stopped and so did an oncoming driver in the far distance. I asked my client if he was all right and he replied, 'Yes. I am sorry John. I won't go from behind again.'

I thanked both the lorry driver and the oncoming motorist for stopping to see if we were OK, and then, because my client was a bit shaken up, I drove off, with a salutary lesson well learned. I have never allowed anyone to overtake with power from behind again. I got on fine with my client after that and, with my instruction and coaching, he became a good driver as well as a long-established member of the High Performance Club. A modern 911, of course, is a very safe sports car with electronic aids for safe driving.

---

The indicator light is very difficult for a driver about to be overtaken to see in their mirror; it is far more effective, and safer, to use an audible warning and sound the horn before applying the power to pass.

Don't flash the headlamps if the audible warning is within earshot. Only use lights on a single carriageway if you are giving a warning at a great distance, and use them as a long light warning for at least four seconds. Don't flash them quickly, or they may be interpreted as a come on.

With a number of vehicles in a queue, showing no sign of wishing to pass, lights can be effective to attract attention. Be warned however, if they see a car with headlights on, it can breed aggression and they may close up to stop you from fitting in! So, only pass if it is safe. A warning is only an indication of presence, not commitment. Overtake one or two at a time, don't rush by too many at once, from far back. Pick your way through, with gentle acceleration sense, and supplement the single light warning with an occasional tap on the horn, if necessary, to a specific driver who is not paying attention.

Don't follow blindly behind a driver ahead who is already passing. It is obviously dangerous. You must be able to see far ahead and there must be a long gap to drive into. The driver ahead may hesitate and abandon a pass, so overtake the next vehicle only when the overtaking car in front is two vehicles or three gaps ahead of you. Remember, it is a voluntary action on your part to overtake a moving vehicle, you can always wait.

If confronted with a long queue, overtaking may not be effective to shorten your journey time. If you try, you may be unpopular and cause antagonistic behaviour. This may inspire a dangerous reaction.

## Correct technique

Stability of the car under acceleration when passing is only achieved with acceleration in a perfectly straight line, down the path

# WARNING WHEN OVERTAKING
## Use of main beam as four-second warning

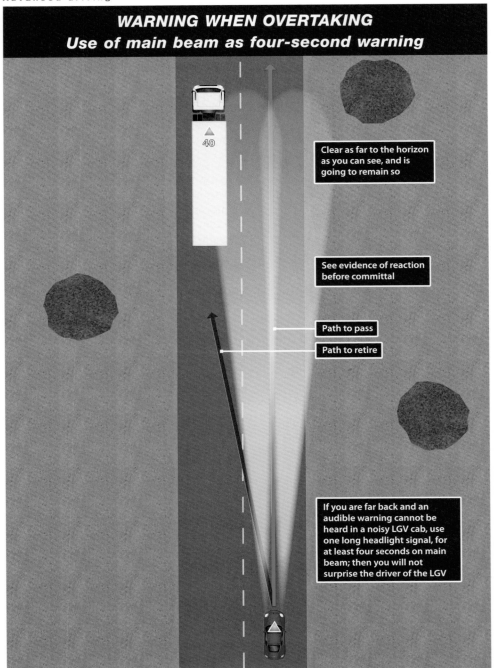

Clear as far to the horizon as you can see, and is going to remain so

See evidence of reaction before committal

Path to pass

Path to retire

If you are far back and an audible warning cannot be heard in a noisy LGV cab, use one long headlight signal, for at least four seconds on main beam; then you will not surprise the driver of the LGV

of kinetic energy. Boot a powerful car from behind a large vehicle, on a curving loop, while passing on a wet, steeply cambered road and your rear-wheel drive supercar (without ESC) will skid so fast you may be left wondering which way you are facing! So don't turn off the ESC. If you own a TVR or other fast sports car without ESC you may need advanced driver training to cope.

Always line the car up first. Then, and only then, grade acceleration to the degree you require, no more no less, particularly on a slippery surface. If you use power from behind, and the driver ahead lifts off the accelerator at the same time, or worse, applies the brakes hard, the gap ahead will snap shut instantly, giving you no time to react.

Selecting your course before the use of acceleration or speed is the correct application of the driving plan. By positioning out first, then accelerating down the hypotenuse in a straight line, an oncoming driver way ahead will see that, all the time you are committed to the act of passing, you are gently pointing the car back to your own side of the road, without cutting in. The approaching driver will be able to judge with greater confidence when you will return back to your nearside.

When overtaking it is important, if the situation demands, that all the power of the engine is used to pass quickly and safely. Don't be afraid to use the full travel of the accelerator, to change down to select the appropriate gear ratio between maximum torque and power, to make the engine sing, in order to gain the best from the car to pass quickly and safely. Many inexperienced drivers do not. They are afraid the car will be stressed too much if it makes a noise!

Engines make a noise, so what? A Ferrari and a Porsche make a lovely noise, like music to my ears! Drivers should go to a test bed during engine development. Engines are kept under full load, flat-out at 7,000rpm for three months! I can understand if they

wish to conserve fuel, but not in the middle of an overtake, surely. If you never use the full acceleration of the car, you never get to know how it accelerates. Your assessment of acceleration in relation to your judgement of the speed and distance needed to overtake is therefore faulty. If it is, training will help enormously. Then, hundreds of miles of experience of using power, with improved technique, will help you to drive progressively and safely.

Although the rule of the triangle is to steer out smoothly along the base and then accelerate down the hypotenuse, there is no requirement to carry out this movement of the car in two separate, distinct parts. One may co-ordinate the steering deflection with a light throttle, to flow into the extended safety line position, and then blend in progressive acceleration, once the view and stability are maximised.

Apply this technique with low-performance cars for reasons of visibility. It is so important to maximise your vision before you overtake. Speed is time multiplied by distance, so the time taken to position the car is time well spent, to judge speed, as well as distance. It is essential with all kinds of cars, but even more so with low-powered ones.

There are occasions when you have to select a course, well out to the offside, so that you do not cut in afterwards. With the full degree of acceleration applied you can be clear of the time exposed to danger very quickly, in a powerful car. When overtaking a large vehicle on a narrow B-road, you will have to steer a parallel course, but try not to shy away from the sheer size of a large lorry, to drive right over to the offside, too close to the ill-defined edge of the road into a gully, camber or gravel. Make this mistake and clip the roadside gravel or drop into a gully under full power and you could be in serious trouble. I notice that many drivers shy away like this. It is best to go down the middle of the offside, on the extended safety line position, leaving an equal margin of safety either side of your car between the lorry and the offside edge of the road.

When planning to pass a high-sided LGV, bear in mind that the driver will want to avoid overhanging trees and nearside sloping cambers and will occasionally drive towards, or even over, the crown of the road. So, position out onto the extended safety line position (not close behind, as many do) and wait. Wait, for the lorry driver to decide when it is safe and convenient for him to move over, to let you pass. If you sense, after some time of driving, that he is unaware of your presence, position out and give a medium or long warning note, but then pause, wait to see essential evidence of a reaction first of all, like a movement with the lorry wheels left of the centre line and a steady course, before you commit to overtaking. Then, a thank-you wave to the centre mirror, well down the road, when it will be seen.

A lorry driver can move over when there is another approaching vehicle and there is no reason why he should not take a road position left of a centre line when you wish to pass. But do ask first, with a reasonable request by road positioning and sounding the horn to communicate if necessary.

On a clear stretch of straight road, with long far views, and no offside entrances, select an extended safety line early on. Give a long light warning well back. It will give a clear indication of what you intend to do and will not surprise anyone. It will give the overtaken time to react to your intention and give you the best view to judge speed and distance. It is therefore a position of safety, which is clearly to everyone's advantage. The earlier you can take it with a long safe clear view the better.

However, do not commit yourself from too far back. Approach with caution. Look for evidence of a reaction first. Be sure the difference between your road speed and that of the overtaken is not too extreme. You must give yourself essential time to react.

There is a tendency for the inexperienced to forget about the hazard that follows an overtaking manoeuvre, and take the following bend too fast. Continue to plan, anticipate, judge speed and distance, and apply your forward planning with gearbox sense. Avoid changing up when the next hazard requires the same gear ratio to be used a short distance away.

To apply any technique, never be too pedantic. Every overtake is different, so be flexible and adapt. The expert will flow with a blend of control and co-ordination that is effortless, so that each overtake is beyond any reasonable reproach. Technique must be applied with mental attitude that balances progression and restraint, which is the result of many years of experience and practice.

On an occasion when you think you have missed an opportunity to overtake, look in your mirror when you get to the end of the straight and assess that long, clear road behind you. Learn from it! Next time, go out early, at the very start of a clear straight. With hindsight, experience teaches, with confidence and advanced technique.

## Overtaking on multi-lane roads

Overtaking on the dual carriageway or motorway, where there is no opposing fast-closing traffic, should be relatively easy, yet many situations occur where the potential danger is not anticipated. Often this is through lack of concentration, caused by boredom in the UK. Even though motorways are undoubtedly our safest roads, unnecessary crashes occur far too frequently. On the unrestricted German autobahns, lane discipline is far better. Drivers assess the value of what they see in the mirror and generally are far more realistic. At high speed, concentration has to be total. Safe following distances are monitored with cameras, which is a sensible use of them. De-restriction is, however, not sensible on unlit autobahns at night, in my view.

# OVERTAKING ON THE MOTORWAY
## Good practice explained

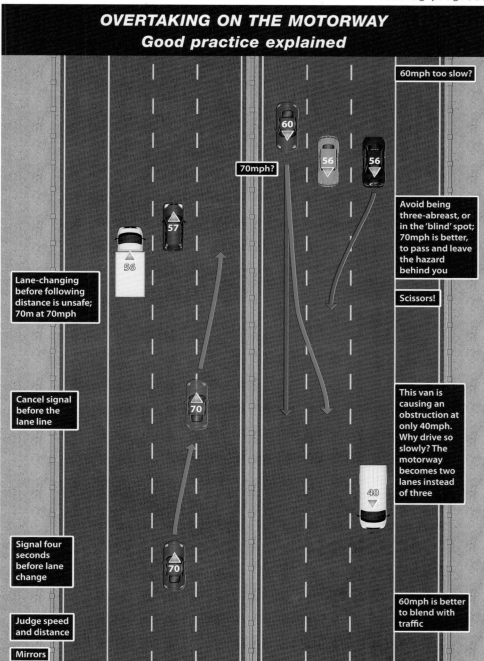

60mph too slow?

70mph?

Avoid being three-abreast, or in the 'blind' spot; 70mph is better, to pass and leave the hazard behind you

Scissors!

Lane-changing before following distance is unsafe; 70m at 70mph

Cancel signal before the lane line

This van is causing an obstruction at only 40mph. Why drive so slowly? The motorway becomes two lanes instead of three

Signal four seconds before lane change

Judge speed and distance

Mirrors

60mph is better to blend with traffic

**191**

# VOICE OF EXPERIENCE

## A compliment in Germany

I was driving down an autobahn in a Porsche 911 Turbo, which belonged to a client of mine. While using the full safe speed of the car without any element of danger or inconvenience to anyone, using only acceleration sense, not braking, to fit in with other traffic, I noticed another Porsche behind, but far back on the horizon. He did not close up when I came across slower traffic. This situation went on for some time. Eventually our exit signs came into view, so I started my signal very early, upon which the following Porsche closed up rapidly.

It was a police car. He pulled me over in a lay-by and asked me if my brake lights were working. We tested them and they were in good working order. 'You have a national speed limit in the UK. Where did you learn to drive like that?' he asked. We had a good chat and discussed the merits of the de-controlled autobahn for improving driving skill and the advantages of mirror assessment and lane discipline.

Germans are proud of their car industry and the high-performance cars and bikes they produce, and their driver education and training is far more realistic than that given in the UK. No information is kept quiet or withheld. All the help and assistance is given to you to use performance in the right place, safely. Then, if you do not, the heavy weight of the law will descend upon you.

The danger of social engineering on our motorways is tailgating, inspired by selfishness and the relatively slow speeds on UK motorways. Signalling with no time to react is seen all the time. Both are a sign of lack of education and discipline. Following distance cameras, to monitor speed and distance in relation to weather, are needed.

Overtaking on three-lane dual carriageways and motorways in roadworks can be influenced by the lane width, when the lanes narrow from 11ft wide (3.3m) to only 9ft (2.7m). This makes three-abreast motoring potentially dangerous, when you consider that large goods vehicles are 7ft 6ins wide (2.3m) and buses are 8ft (2.4m) wide. If one vehicle swerves in an emergency, there is no room to manoeuvre for anyone. In heavy traffic, it is impossible to avoid driving three abreast. In light traffic you may give it some thought. When passing, hang well back from both the vehicle you are following and the one on your left, if possible. Then, choose your time to pass decisively.

Heavy motorway traffic, which is progressing slowly in the two nearside lanes, will make a gentle left-hand curve completely blind, with a reduced sightline. Be sure your speed difference is small, say 20mph, to give essential time for you to react. Keep at least one yard per mph from the vehicle ahead. Moving from lane two to three, if it is clear over your shoulder, will still be relatively blind in the door mirror, because of the left curve behind. It may be best to wait for the straight, when you can see well behind in your mirrors. Think bike!

On busy motorways, the first part of the driving plan must be applied far in advance, with any necessary signal given with sufficient time for other drivers to react (at least four seconds). Make yourself time the signal before you change lane. Once evidence of reaction is seen then the signal can be cancelled, before the right wheels of your car cross the lane line. This will make you signal before you change your lane, not as you are doing it.

If you are travelling much faster than the vehicle ahead in your lane, then your course must be selected long before the following distance is less than safe. Just in case the driver in front of you slams on the brake in an emergency.

Some exotic supercars have very poor visibility to the rear, only marginally helped by door mirrors that must not be relied

upon. A flat mirror has a limited width
of view, but a convex mirror gives a false
perception of distance. It is essential to use
a shoulder check glance, using just your
peripheral vision. Avoid taking your eyes off
the road ahead for more than a quick life-
saver, for anything hiding in a blind spot.
Shoulder check joining motorways and for
each separate lane change. Use acceleration
in the acceleration lane to blend and fit,
don't gather speed from behind the vehicle
ahead, before changing lane, while you
turn and look behind. Many accidents at
the entry to motorways happen like this.
Be patient and wait for a gap behind in the
passing traffic; they have a priority not to be
disturbed.

Don't sweep across when joining the
motorway, from lane one to three. Instead,
after taking precautions, change lane
one lane at a time, with safety checks
beforehand. After passing, only return to the
nearside lane when the distance behind you
is safe for the driver following.

All of us should be aware that in the
UK there is no overtaking on the left

*Vans restrict the view through the curve*
*of this dual carriageway; concealed drivers*
*may be pulling out to pass.*

(undertaking) on motorways. Therefore, the
law may interpret that it is unreasonable
to expect someone to do so. A driver may
suddenly, at any moment, move over to the
left at speed.

However, in the crowded UK, the left-hand
lanes are often relatively free of traffic, with
drivers selfishly queuing up and tailgating
in the overtaking lane (with the warped
reasoning that, 'if I drop back, someone will
fill the gap', which is driving with an element
of danger and without consideration). Is the
cause of this behaviour anything to do with
the national speed limit? They use speed-
related separation cameras on unrestricted
autobahns in Germany, where lane discipline
and sensible use of the mirror is far better.

So what is meant by 'Do not overtake on
the left'? Well, when the speed of traffic is
very slow and queuing up, and the nearside
lanes are free of traffic, you may, if it is safe,
move up and fill the space. But you must

**193**

*In this view of the M25 the drivers – with one exception – are keeping a safe following distance and driving sensibly.*

take notice of the first vehicle you pass on their left and you must wait until the driver has re-passed you again before you move out into the overtaking lanes – otherwise you are overtaking on the left and that is an offence. In other words, you must not make any progress by passing on the left.

Undertaking at speed is reckless and rightly considered dangerous, as it is unexpected and unreasonable. Obstruction is also inconsiderate and if the lane on your left has a reasonably long gap for your safety you may be committing an offence if you do not move to your left into that lane. Two wrongs can produce a lethal situation.

Behaviour on our crowded speed-limited motorways is causing serious problems for us all. For the safety and convenience of

everyone, a safe following distance, plus a gentle change of speed when passing, up to 10 or 15mph is predictable. However, the speed limit on motorways and dual carriageways for cars and bikes is the same in lanes one, two and three. It sounds like a recipe for an explosion if one swerves! Does it make sense? If we all set off in heavy traffic and stay close to each other, we all become an accident waiting to happen, so it is better to spread out and try to create space around you.

If the vehicle you intend to pass in lane two is also closing upon someone else but is showing no recognition of this fact and giving you no signal, communication becomes important. So, if you receive no signal, communicate early. Don't rely upon a complete stranger, he may do the usual thing and pull out without warning, signalling at the same time, giving you no time to react. Don't flash the headlights, but use them for at least four seconds or until you see evidence of reaction. Be deliberate and decisive.

Look out for the influence of crosswinds in gales and bad weather, particularly on rear-engined cars. Gaps between the protection of banks or high bridges will cause a sudden gust. Caravans and high-sided box vans are most vulnerable, so pick them out and watch their progress. Lorries on motorways cut a bow wave, that draws and then pushes a car at speed, so anticipate it with a very mild steering correction and keep to the centre of your lane if you can.

Don't overreact if a tyre bursts while passing. If you sense instability with a gradual loss of tyre pressure, check your mirror, signal and kill your speed, if you can. But keep off the brakes if a tyre bursts. Instability may increase if you brake hard. Just concentrate upon steering with both hands until you are out of trouble. The minimum amount of evasive action is best, and a healthy control of your nerves is essential in any emergency. This is where electronic stability control (ESC) makes modern cars so safe, although the ESC may keep the car so stable that the inexperienced will try to keep going.

Primary route dual carriageways with intersections are potentially our most dangerous roads. Traffic will be crossing the path of cars doing 70mph. All slow traffic should display a yellow warning light on these fast roads, but still there may be pedestrians, cyclists or novices in cars or on motorbikes.

*Poor lane discipline and tailgating – intimidation witnessed on every journey. The road is damp too.*

# 11 Night driving

*On an unlit motorway at night you must be able to stop within the distance illuminated by your car's headlights on dipped beam.*

If you have a long journey to complete, you may decide to prepare the car the evening before and make an early start. By setting off at about 2am when there is very little traffic, progress will be excellent on country roads and the drive through the dawn, which is the best time of the day, should be one of the great joys of motoring.

A crystal clear windscreen, inside and out, is a must. Clean all the light lenses. Test the lights for operation, checking the reflection of the brake lights in a window (or get help to do this). It is essential to check headlights for adjustment both of the main beam, for range and spread of light, and for dip, that they reach to the left a little, but without dazzling oncoming traffic. To carry out this adjustment to the headlights drive to an unlit, quiet, straight country lane, put the hazard lights on, and with a screwdriver and torch to see, adjust the headlights precisely (although this may not be possible with some units).

Always carry a spare bulb kit, as a bulb can pop at anytime. If a police officer stops you for this mobile traffic offence, he cannot report you if you can change the bulb. It avoids the fine, points and the automatic breathalyser test. You should be able to detect if a bulb has gone – a walk around the car before you set off, with hazard lights on, is all that is required.

Many motorists do not like to drive at night. You will be fortunate if you do, and the most likely reason is that you have good eyesight and live in the countryside where you can gain lots of practice.

According to recent research, one in six drivers has defective eyesight, which is a large number of the 30 million car and motorcycle licence holders in the UK. Half of these have probably not had an eye test, while others simply do not wish to wear glasses. As 99% of the information we need to drive is obtained through our eyes, it is a horrendous statistic.

Pin-sharp eyesight is essential, and if you wear glasses don't forget to give them a good clean as well, although most drivers who wear glasses are meticulous.

## Lights and lighting

For many people who live in a large urban area, night driving is under powerful sodium street lighting, along routes and roads that are familiar. Headlights are mostly on dip, usually on a lit motorway or dual carriageway. In consequence, when driving on unlit country roads, they will not raise the headlights, because they are not used to doing it. It means they often drive slowly, cruising at 50mph.

Advances made in lighting technology have

*For many people night driving is mainly in urban areas under powerful sodium street lighting.*

been considerable in recent years. HID xenon headlights are 50% brighter, which on dip, approaching low down, are quite dazzling, especially for me when driving my Seven. Another source of dazzle is when stopping behind someone in traffic when the driver in front applies the brake lights. There is a tendency for the aggressive type of driver to drive around with fog lights on, in clear visibility. A stop by a traffic patrol officer (and a breathalyser) would cure the habit!

Rally cars used to have the most unbelievable barrage of lights, which seemed to turn night into day. As an amateur, I have been fortunate to compete in a few long-distance historic events and lighting of this kind had to be experienced to be believed. This extreme lighting carries extra responsibility, and any more than two extra lamps is now banned by the Motorsports Association for use on the public highway for road rallies.

When new, cars must conform to lighting regulations and have 55-watt headlight power. The range of visibility on dipped headlights on unlit roads should restrict our speed, which I suspect is the idea, but many drive too fast regardless. I would never walk down an unlit country road with no pavement at night. It is too dangerous. In my view the national speed limit does make

## VOICE OF EXPERIENCE

### Speed at night

I am personally in favour of the national speed limit for riders and car drivers on unlit roads at night, between the official time of dusk and dawn. We are required to tell the time of day for other restrictions, why not for the national speed limit? So in my own personal view, for approximately half of our 24 hours, the legislators have got it right.

But who am I to say? However, we must respect the law and tranquillity in our society is vital, but the national speed limit should, in my view, be seen to be sensible by the majority of the population, and be imposed for the sole reason of scientifically proven road safety, not for social engineering or any other unproven science.

sense on safety grounds during the night, on unlit roads.

However, the national speed limit will never be lifted unless motorcyclists and car drivers stop having crashes that seem to be caused, mostly at random, by a lack of concentration. We must drive actively and safely, not be disassociated from driving and passive in our minds, something that inappropriate slow speed encourages.

There is considerable skill required in timing, precisely, the use of the headlights between dip and main beam.

*Tough conditions at night in rain – dazzle from oncoming headlights.*

# USE OF HEADLIGHTS BEFORE OVERTAKING AT NIGHT
## *When overtaking on a two-way road*

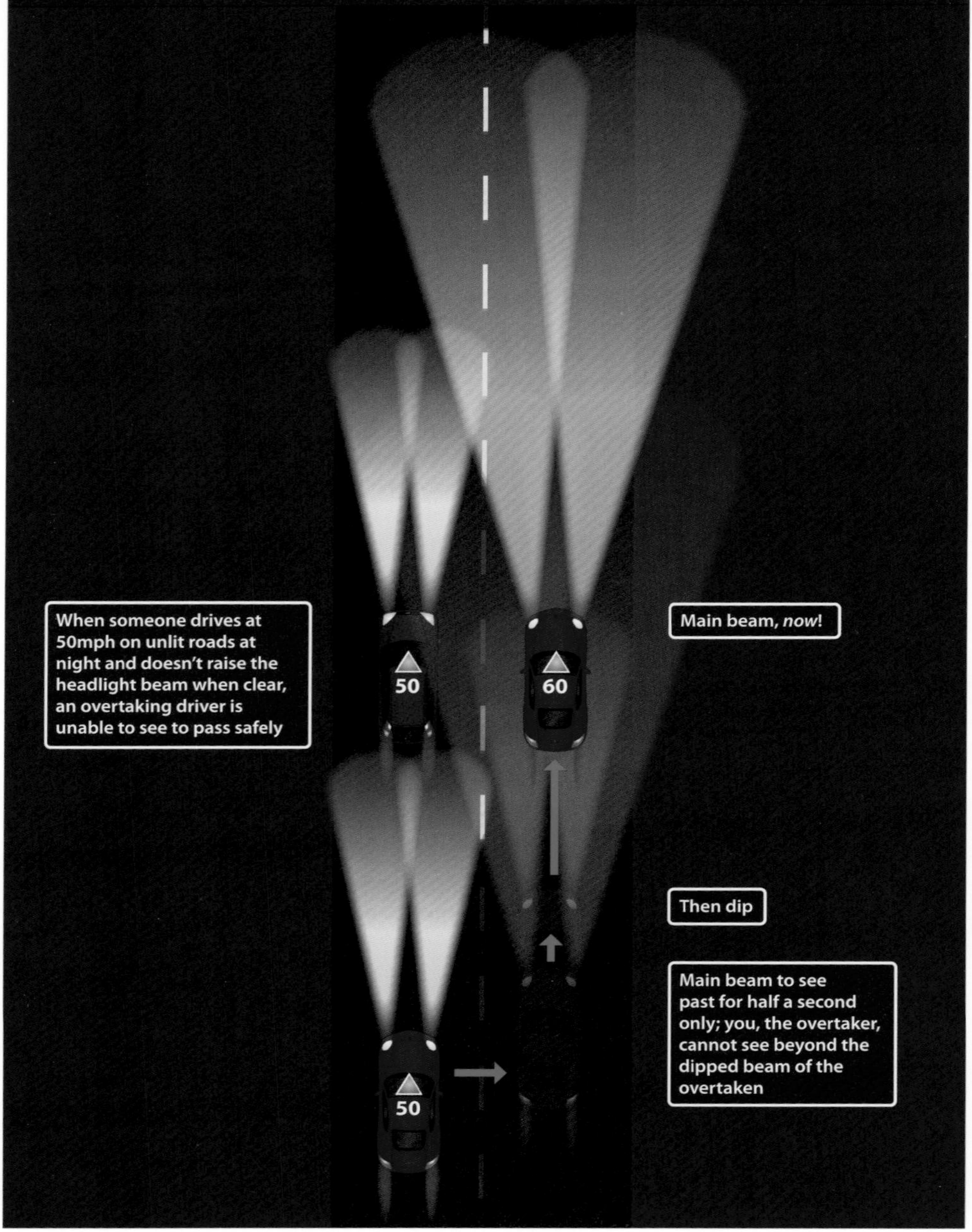

When someone drives at 50mph on unlit roads at night and doesn't raise the headlight beam when clear, an overtaking driver is unable to see to pass safely

Main beam, *now!*

Then dip

Main beam to see past for half a second only; you, the overtaker, cannot see beyond the dipped beam of the overtaken

# Main and dipped beams

On long, straight, level roads, plan far ahead, to even beyond the range of the main beam, to gather as much information as you can and store it in your mind in case you have to reduce your forward vision by dipping your lights.

When a car approaches on the horizon, dip a second after they appear, to show them that you have gone onto dip, and lift off the power, so that you can pull up and stop within the distance you can now see. Cast your eyes to the nearside and, if you can avoid it, try not to look at the approaching headlights; this may affect your night vision. If you are dazzled because the oncoming driver doesn't dip their lights, you may have to brake, to a standstill if necessary. Don't retaliate, except perhaps a very quick flash to remind them to go to dip. If no one else is approaching, go back to main beam the very split second they have passed. You need to see the best you can at the earliest possible moment. Most return to main beam too late.

Don't travel at high speed on two-way roads, or you will have to lose too much road speed to be safe on dipped beam. You will be rowing the variation in pace with the acceleration and brakes; instead, try to flow along using acceleration sense and avoid unnecessary braking.

On unlit roads in the country, lazy or inexperienced drivers, who drive mostly in lit urban areas, drive on dipped headlights all the time, at 50mph. To pass them is difficult, as you can only see as far ahead as they can, on dipped beam. The answer is to search for a view. At the beginning of a long straight, without gaining speed, move gently out onto an extended safety line position and briefly go to main beam to see sufficiently, then quickly back to dip. This will also serve as a warning. If it is safe, overtake and return back to main beam when alongside, to see as early as possible, without causing dazzle in their door mirror.

Around left-hand curves and over brows, dip early, before the opposing driver appears in view, particularly for a lorry driver who sits up high. Low down in my Seven, dazzle is a real problem too. Dip even at a hairpin to the right; it is expected, even though the angle of your lights away from the bend means oncoming drivers won't be dazzled. Dip for cyclists and pedestrians in the countryside. Be polite.

In hilly country, you can see in the far distance how a driver will light the way. If you are well back, they will display to you the configuration of the countryside and how it twists and turns, rises and falls, with the occasional flash of brake lights for the exceptional hazard. If the driver is good and makes reasonable headway, it will be best to follow.

# Night-time hazards

A flash can be used at a deserted crossroads, or when emerging from a T-junction in the countryside. Flash before overtaking on unlit two-way roads; but don't call someone out on dual carriageways or junctions. You may be responsible if an accident occurs. Main beam is a visual warning of approach only.

Assessment of approach speed to bends at night tends to be late, with insufficient time left to carry out the driving plan. This causes bends to be taken in the wrong gear on occasion, particularly if the lights are on dip during assessment.

Judgement of speed and distance prior to overtaking is also difficult. Road positioning may help you. Positioning over a warning line into a blind left-hand bend in daytime is dangerous and inconsiderate; at night on unlit roads it is most likely to be safe, and will give a far longer and earlier view into the bend. Any approaching car will be seen long before it appears in view – not so in daylight.

The rule of the triangle prior to passing is of great value to judge speed and distance on unlit roads in the dark. Be aware of old cars with dim lights, or tractors with

## AVOID BLINDING ONCOMING DRIVERS
### But be prepared to be blinded...

Dip early to try to avoid 'blinding' the oncoming driver; but you may be 'blinded' by the headlights of a fast-approaching driver who dips too late

Crest: link vision to speed and grip, to be able to stop

two headlights close together – they will appear further away than they are. Any road engineering tricks and traps can be far more deceptive and dangerous at night. So, watch out, particularly if it is misty or raining. In these conditions, speed must be kept down to give you and others plenty of time to react.

Pedestrians and cyclists tend to keep their heads down when it is raining hard. They may hear you and judge your distance, but not your speed. Dipped headlights must always be used in built-up areas, particularly in these conditions, to be seen between parked cars. Light pollution is now becoming a problem with shop fronts brightly lit. Some people even miss red traffic lights! Slow right down in the early morning and check right, left, and right, even if the traffic light is green. In the evening be the first to switch on dipped headlights and the last to turn them off in the morning. Know the lighting-up times. Years ago, I could never persuade drivers to turn dipped headlights on – now, I have to tell drivers to turn them off, when lights are unnecessary. Fashions change!

At the end of a night drive, think of your neighbours and arrive home quietly. Don't rev up before switching off, or slam the doors!

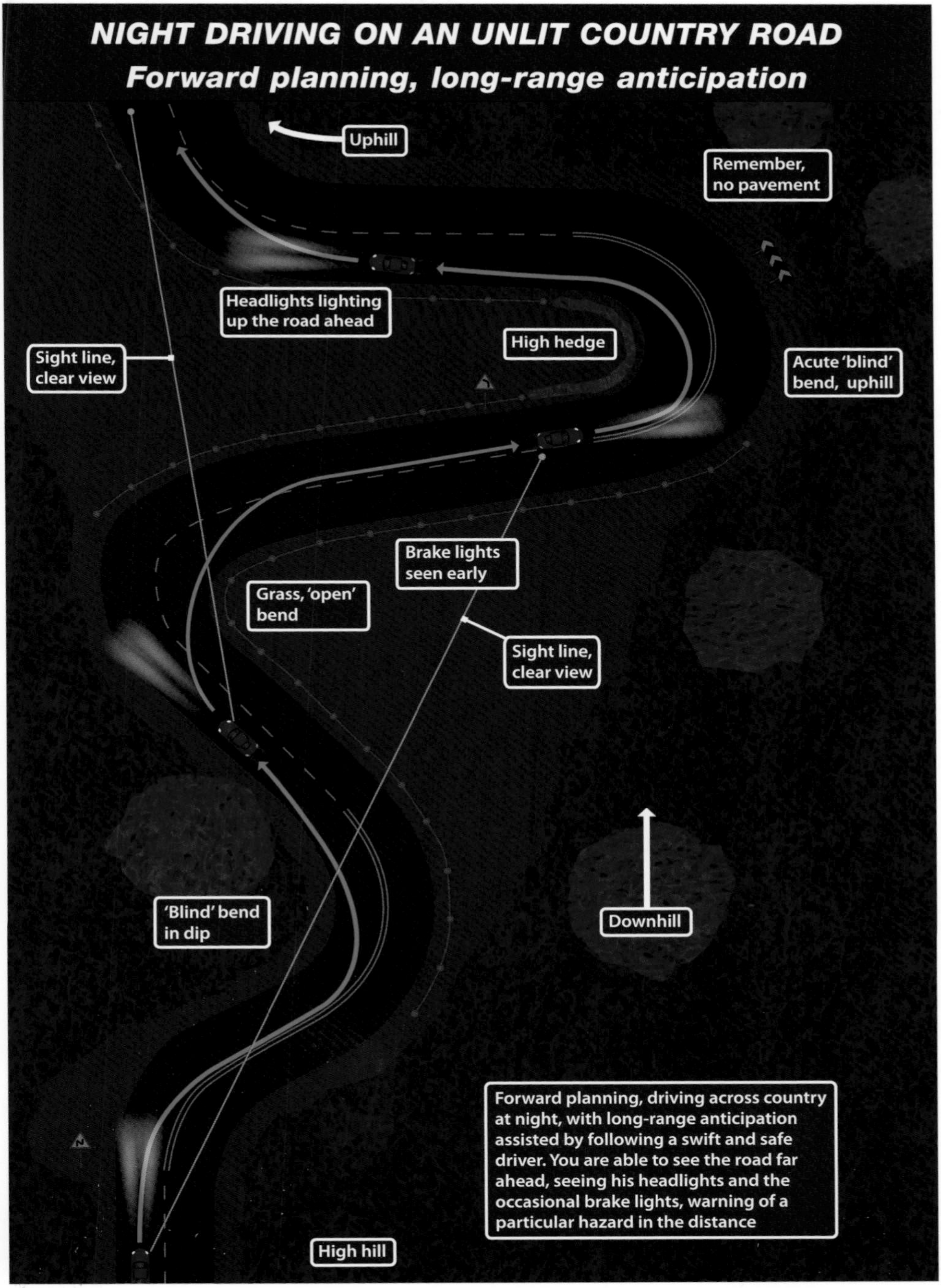

# NIGHT DRIVING ON AN UNLIT COUNTRY ROAD
## Forward planning, long-range anticipation

Uphill

Remember, no pavement

Headlights lighting up the road ahead

High hedge

Sight line, clear view

Acute 'blind' bend, uphill

Brake lights seen early

Grass, 'open' bend

Sight line, clear view

'Blind' bend in dip

Downhill

Forward planning, driving across country at night, with long-range anticipation assisted by following a swift and safe driver. You are able to see the road far ahead, seeing his headlights and the occasional brake lights, warning of a particular hazard in the distance

High hill

# 12 Bad weather

*The potential for danger ahead is self-evident...*

Fog is the motorists' worst enemy and when it arrives no sensible driver can travel quickly with safety on public roads. It is the great leveller, like safety cameras: no matter what skill you may have, it brings everyone down to the same level – only the reckless will drive fast in fog.

I have experienced the great smogs in London before the Clean Air Act, when you couldn't even see your feet, and once when walking in the country, I got lost in a field of cows! Thankfully, my sharp-witted dog found our way back home. Vintage cars have split windscreens, and not having the glass in front of your eyes was a help. But mostly, I hate fog because it plays tricks on the mind. It causes disorientation and can cause people to drive faster than they realise. Even 10mph is too fast on occasion.

A fixed stare at tail-lights ahead in the fog cuts side vision and removes the peripheral reference points which help locate objects in perspective. In fog you should glance at your speedometer frequently, keep your distance and link vision to speed and grip. In fact, my candid advice to anyone thinking of driving in fog is: don't!

*Fog on the motorway – very careful judgement of speed and distance required at all times.*

## Coping with fog

If you must drive, start by preparing yourself and your car as best you can. Wear comfortable clothing and clean your glasses if you wear them. Clean the windscreen inside to get rid of that haze (caused by the plastic dash emitting vapours) and give the outside glass a wipe with an alcohol-based liquid to make it crystal clear. Wipe all signal and light lenses clean. Top up the washer bottle and ensure your heater is working properly to clear the windscreen.

Ensure that your fog lights are working. Fog lights should be adjusted. I like them mounted low, with a spot lamp on the offside, picking out the left-hand kerb as far ahead as possible. The other lamp should have a wide, flat-topped beam, spreading light low under the fog, across the road. I prefer white fog lights and quartz iodine headlights with a sharp cut-off on dip, as they combine to penetrate low and deep and cut light reflection from the fog. Only use fog lights when vision is less than 100 metres (328 feet).

When driving in fog you should change your focal point frequently. Scan and move your eyes around the scene, searching for views that help you gain some perspective. It is difficult to locate your road position without being able to see road markings or, on country roads, without any markings at all. It is possible to experience real fear if you lose your bearings on a strange road in dense fog, just as you might be concerned if the light went out in a strange room. You bang into furniture while you fish around for

# USE OF LIGHTS IN FOG
## Fog is the great 'leveller'

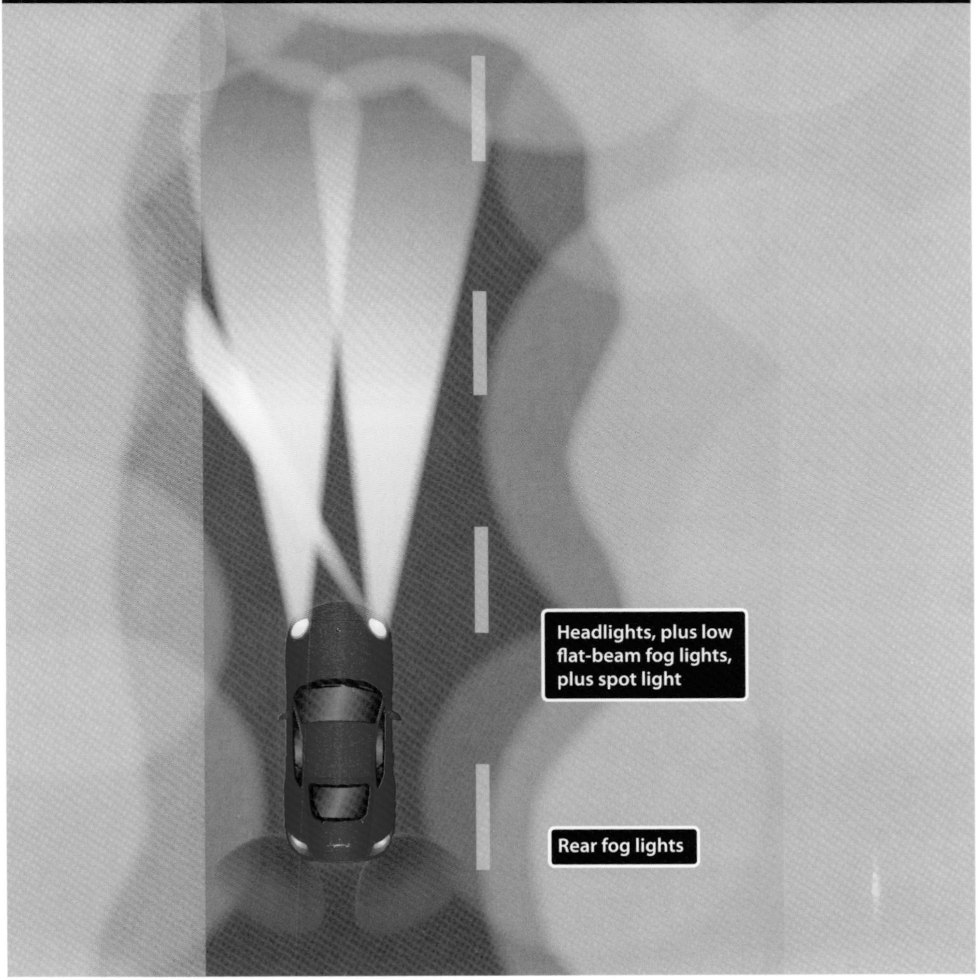

Headlights, plus low flat-beam fog lights, plus spot light

Rear fog lights

the light. In the car, you should crawl along and keep visual contact with the nearside edge of the road. Don't mistake a centre line for a lane line, or drive too close to it, as an oncoming vehicle could be straddling it. The edge line, if continuous, means the road is extra hazardous; if broken, less so.

In fog on motorways, you really need to know the locations of different coloured reflective studs along the motorway:

- ⊃ Red is between the hard shoulder and the carriageway.
- ⊃ White is between lanes.
- ⊃ Amber is between the right-hand edge and the central reservation.
- ⊃ Green is at a slip-road entrance or exit.

*Fog on a country road – only occasional traffic, few reference points to help judge distance.*

following drivers, listen for approaching traffic and turn squarely, quickly and decisively.

The density of fog changes often, from light mist to a wall of thick fog. Many multiple crashes have occurred through drivers not observing the obvious bank of fog ahead and slowing down in time. Go to the nearside lane when possible. In emergencies, switch on your hazard lights. It is terrifying to be passed by high-speed traffic in fog, with the drivers falsely convincing themselves that because it is a motorway it will be okay. Driving at an inappropriate speed, because others are doing the same, is not sensible – it is total madness. Matrix signs flashing a fog warning must only be switched on when vision is less than 100 metres, surely? Fog was the reason that the Government gave for introducing the 70mph speed limit – 70mph in fog! Many try. Now it only gives the inexperienced an incentive to use the speed limit as a target.

Mandatory safe following distances and temporary speed limits, I believe, should be introduced for both contraflows and driving in fog. Tailgating, a lack of concentration, signalling with no time to react, not signalling – these kinds of errors, not speed, are the causes of motorway accidents.

The golden rule is always travel at a safe following distance from the vehicle ahead. When visibility is clear, leave at least one yard per mph from the vehicle in front. Double that in the wet, quadruple it on ice, link vision to speed and grip and always be able to pull up and stop well within the distance seen to be clear.

## Winter roads

In winter, meticulous preparation is essential. Check your tyre pressures, including the spare. Carry tools and jump leads. Take a folding shovel and strap it down (I was hit by one once when rallying!). Have a large warm jacket and stout boots in case you break down. Check your mobile phone is charged.

To further confuse you in times of stress, green and yellow studs are placed at contraflow systems and roadworks. The same applies on dual carriageways. Your greatest asset is going to be local knowledge, but because you know the road, don't get impatient with someone who does not, or is fearful, or lost. You will see less, if you pass.

Don't hang on to the tail-lights of the driver in front; they may take a different route, go off the road or crash! Wind down your side window slightly, turn down a noisy fan and switch off the radio. Quieten down any passengers and listen at junctions. If you must turn right, do so at a light-controlled junction, where drivers expect crossing traffic. Always signal, position your vehicle early, wind down your side window, sound the horn, rest your foot on the brake if stationary to give extra light to warn

Consider fitting winter snow tyres if you live in hill-country. They really are fantastic and well worth the expenditure. They enable you to stop from 20mph on ice 40ft (12m) sooner, and 30ft (9m) sooner on snow. Tyres with studs damage the road surface and are, in consequence, illegal in this country. I do not like snow chains myself, but if you carry them, know how to fit them, by practising in the garage. If you prefer them to winter snow tyres, buy the best. Carry polarised sunglasses for low winter sun and keep winter gloves in the boot. A plastic window scraper is essential. Don't forget a high-visibility jacket and candles. Candles? Yes candles! Why? Read the 'Voice of Experience' panel and you'll see why.

We have dealt with skidding in the previous chapter, but seeing it written in a book is one thing; practising in your own car, in a safe environment with an expert instructor is quite another. We have carried out this safety training on the High Performance Course for many years. I strongly recommend this skill development, particularly if you have a powerful rear-wheel-drive high-performance car, without electronic safety aids like ABS and ESC, before winter arrives.

However, to recap: remove the cause instantly of any loss of control: speed, power or brakes.

Without ABS. Do not panic brake and lock up the tyres. This gives the impression of acceleration. Unless the road surface is completely dry, you will not stop quickly and there will be no steering control to correct any skid. With a rear-wheel-drive car, just lift off the power instantly the car skids and begins to slide out of control, and keep the front wheels pointing in the direction of safety and where you wish to go. Do not overreact and steer off the road or into oncoming traffic! Then, re-correct the steering, quickly, and point the steering wheel where you wish to go. For a front-wheel skid in a front-wheel-drive or four-wheel-drive car (understeer), the same

*Risk of aquaplaning occurs, even at relatively low speed.*

control is required. For a rear-wheel skid in a front-wheel-drive or four-wheel-drive car (oversteer), use more power to pull the car into line again – a tricky technique.

With ABS. Simple! Instantly react to the brakes and steer where you wish to go. Few instructors will tell you that: it is pure prejudice, and it costs lives! Ask the senior engineers who develop these systems and they will tell you: hit the brakes under all surface conditions. I know. I have tried many motor cars with anti-lock brakes, under every condition, for nearly 50 years, from a Jensen Interceptor of 1964! Experience teaches, so snap use of ABS, in an emergency, will save lives. It requires only practice to confirm the safety of ABS and ESC for yourself, but make sure you are off the public highway when you do so.

Vision is essential. All glass must be clear

*A typical dual carriageway after snow – lane one is negotiable with care, lane two is better avoided.*

before you drive off and kept clean when you drive, period. Warm, dry air is best when adjusting the heater. When you walk to the car and nearly slip on the ice, it's obvious that the car lock may be frozen, so warm the key gently. Don't damage the wipers and blow the motor by switching them on and don't pull them off a frozen screen either, as you will rip the blades.

You may be nice and warm in your cosy modern car with ABS, ESC and four-wheel drive, but if the roads have not been treated, they are still lethal. If only the main roads have been treated, back roads will be icy, so be warned. Local authorities are so keen to warn people about everything else, yet fail to

warn people about ice on minor roads. Does that make sense?

Aquaplaning may occur when the tyre tread depth is less than 3mm. The tyre floats across standing water, giving no grip and pulling the car to one side. Don't brake and don't apply any steering angle at all, because the tyres are off the road surface. If you do apply steering, then when the tyre touches the road again it will veer violently towards your pointed steering angle. The answer is, avoid the water! When you see it, slow right down and if there is oncoming traffic wait until you can drive around it. The advice for floods is the same. Stop and try to assess how deep it is. That's not easy to do, so it is best to avoid it and take another route. If it is shallow, go slowly; engage a low gear, slip the clutch and keep the engine speed high.

# VOICE OF EXPERIENCE

## A flying Finn

I was once asked by the British School of Motoring to go to Belgium to give training for an international chemical company with staff from all over Europe. It turned out to be one of the worst winters of the 1970s with snow up to four feet deep. Now, in Belgium at that time, there was no driving test and zero motoring education and accidents were legion. If it snowed, the motor insurance industry would not insure, unless the company had a good record. This company did, as they were safety conscious. However, garages in Belgium are under the houses with a steeply sloped exit ramp. Most of the candidates for training could not make the exit and gave a polite phone call to that effect, so I extended my breakfast and read the paper.

However, this day was different. Spot on time, someone asked 'Mr Lyon?' He was from Finland, but spoke very good English. He was an enormous fellow, I guess about 35 years of age and had a real presence, with piercing eyes and high intelligence. I said, 'It's very bad weather today and I intend to drive to the Ardennes Forest.'

'No problem,' he replied; that turned out to be his favourite expression. We examined his car, which to my surprise was a large, rear-drive, 3-litre BMW. I had a look in the boot to see what extra equipment he carried. There was the usual tow-rope, heavy clothing and a folding shovel, but also a box. I asked what was inside. 'Candles.'

'Why do you need candles'? I asked. 'Well, if we get stuck, we cannot use the engine and heater, as we would get gassed in the deep snow, so we light a candle to stop us freezing.'

'Okay,' I replied, and thought that it was going to be an interesting day. We set off sideways, which we seemed to do all day.

The snow was bad, and the roads deserted. As we progressed into the countryside, conditions became worse and I was astonished by his skill. He had some very good snow tyres fitted, but no studs, and if there was a snowdrift, he charged it, with on-off cadence throttle control. He forced his way through. At one time we came to complete white-out conditions and I suggested we should turn back. 'No problem,' was his reply. I had total faith in this remarkable driver, and I asked him when he had learnt to drive like this. 'When I was eight years old.'

'EIGHT?'

'Yes, you see we lived on a farm, far from the nearest town, so my parents taught us to drive on frozen lakes, in case of emergencies.'

The weather cleared and we could see for miles, with beautiful scenery and clear skies. We flowed along at high speed, with fantastic car control. He asked if I would like to drive and I readily took the wheel. The tyres were fantastic and I really enjoyed myself. Eventually, we came across a chap driving a snow-plough. I stopped, waved him down and in my best, broken French I asked him where the nearest restaurant was. 'You crazy!' he exclaimed, 'Go stay in the next village.'

'It's okay. He is Finnish,' I replied. We settled down in this very good restaurant and had an excellent meal in front of a roaring fire, intending to stay overnight, as the snow outside was now falling horizontally outside.

'You know, John? I think we go home. I have a busy day tomorrow.'

'What?' I answered. 'Yes, it's no problem.'

We got back at about 9pm. I was so impressed that I recommended his driving to the committee of HPC for our highest award of skill, HPC Gold! The chaotic incompetence of UK drivers on snow is pathetic by comparison.

Lorry drivers and 4x4 drivers, slow down! Test your brakes afterwards, with a light application of your left foot.

During windy weather, don't overreact to crosswinds. Try not to veer violently, just anticipate the draw and bow wave from large goods vehicles. Keep away from cyclists, they are entitled to wobble.

A cyclist's wobbling distance was called 'Parker's distance' after Lord Justice Parker – it should be 6ft (1.8m), allowing sufficient room for them to topple over. If you can't give them a 6ft clearance then wait behind until you can. It is a voluntary action to overtake anything moving, you can always wait behind and pass later.

# ACCIDENT AVOIDANCE
## *Leaving the road can be better than hitting head-on*

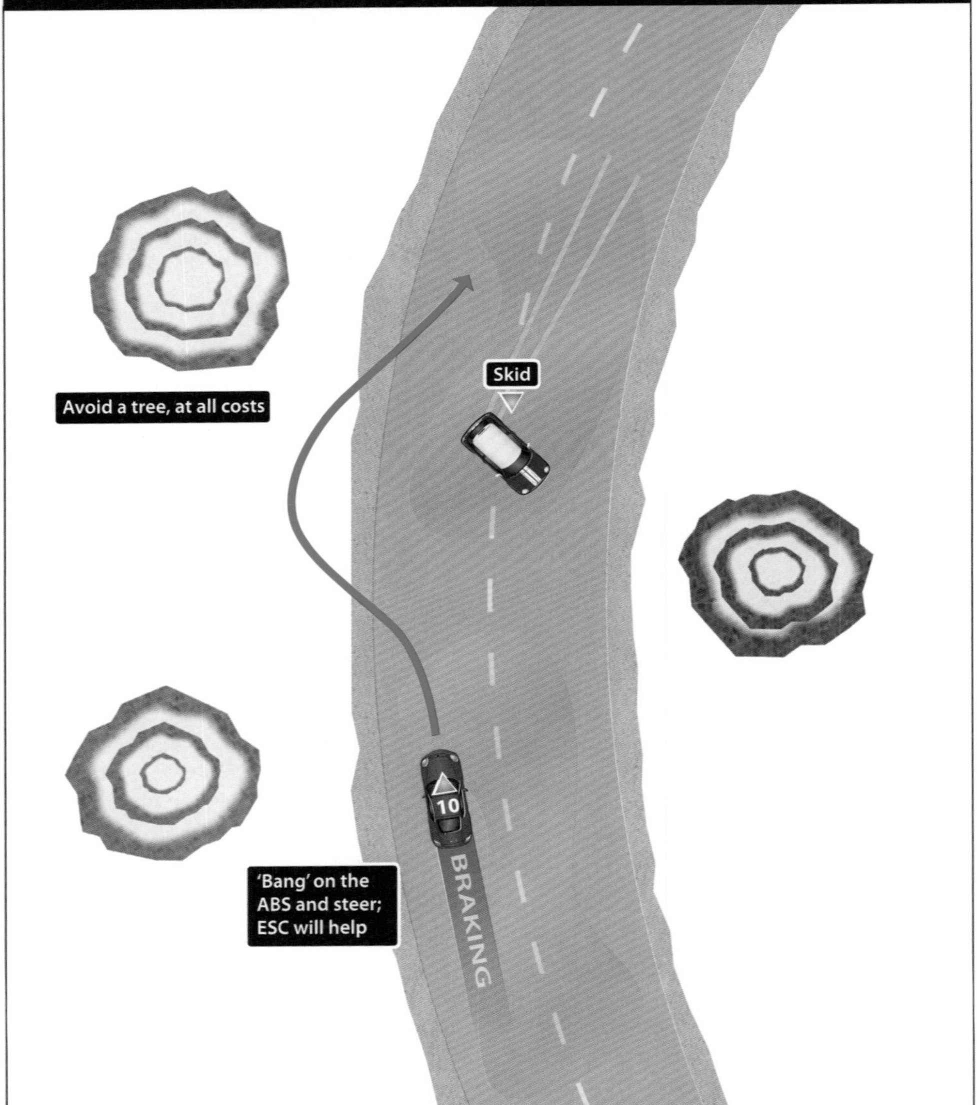

Avoid a tree, at all costs

Skid

'Bang' on the ABS and steer; ESC will help

BRAKING

10

# VOICE OF EXPERIENCE

## ABS and over-confidence

I was at Leith Hill in Surrey with a client in his Saab. It was fitted with ABS, and in consequence the driver was over-confident. We came to what I knew was a steep descent. I told my client to stop, well back from the hill and gave him a briefing. 'You cannot stop as you go down, so stop at the top and look down to assess the situation.' As I was saying that, a van passed us at speed. There was no way he was safe. We edged up to the top and looked down. The van had lost control and hit a bank. I hopped out and called down, 'are you OK?'

'Yes,' was the reply but he lost control again. 'Stay there!' I called out. I made my way cautiously along the snow bank. 'May I drive? I am covered by insurance,' I said. Very gently, I cadence braked down the hill almost to the bottom. The van driver took the wheel and promptly lost it! I returned to my client in his Saab, asked for the wheel and, using the snow bank and better grip with ABS, we managed to descend very slowly to the bottom, where the client took over again, realising the difficulty. He tried other more gentle hills himself later, with rather more caution. Experience teaches, sometimes.

## Ice and snow

In this country, we seem to be seriously affected by snow during a bad winter, perhaps because snow does not occur all that frequently, and the local authorities have not invested in the expensive machinery required to deal with it. Motorists currently give central funding £48 billion a year in direct taxation, with an estimated £150 billion in indirect taxation, and they say they have no money? Only one-tenth of this revenue is spent on roads.

There is also the competence of the British motorist to deal with the winter to consider. Countries that have serious winters like Finland have appropriate driver training. In comparison, we are not very good in bad weather. The number of single vehicle crashes in ice and snow tell their own story.

When driving in snow, without snow tyres, set off in second gear, with delicate power, gently fluctuating the throttle on and off, as the best grip will be found just before the wheels spin. Rock the car backwards and forwards, until underway. Hills present the greatest challenge. Apply the driving plan with the correct position, speed and gear to take you all the way up. Don't follow someone. Wait until it is clear. Keep up momentum and try not to have to stop. You may not get going again and will have to go back and have another go. Downhill

is potentially dangerous. Prepare as best you can. Keep to a very low speed in a low gear and hold back your speed by cadence braking if necessary. If you drive in the mountains regularly in the winter, it is worth fitting narrow wheels and snow tyres; they are good in wet weather too.

On ice the most amazing experience is to drive on studded tyres. It is like driving on a wet road only with a more gentle and benign response. Snow tyres are also extremely good. On a Citroen 2CV, they are even better. You need soft suspension and narrow tyres. The stiff suspension and wide tyres of a supercar are hopeless on ice and snow. The slightest uphill gradient and you are stuck, wheels spinning, while a 2CV sails by!

When cornering in snow and ice, it is essential to approach at the correct slow speed, positioning to gain the best grip and margin of safety. In the right gear, be under control with delicate acceleration sense and be sure you are perfectly straight before using power at the exit. Stopping distances on ice will be ten times what they are in the dry, even with ABS.

Overtaking in snow, on two-way roads, is considered anti-social and dangerous in the UK. So don't upset other road users by doing it. Snow has at least twice the grip of ice, which has virtually no grip whatsoever. You cannot stand up on it! So drive very, very slowly and keep going if you can.

Black ice is very difficult to see, but will glint in the sunshine and moonlight. The tyres make no noise when running over ice and steering will be as light as a feather. Stability is possible, but only in a perfectly straight line. Any disturbance will upset the car, so you must use the most extreme sensitivity and delicacy with all the controls. Great smoothness, a sense of speed, acceleration and gearbox sense, keeping as high a gear as you can to avoid wheelspin, will be best. There is no substitute for experience and practice with your car.

## Using a 4x4

Watch out for an approaching driver or rider losing control. Look for an escape route. It is best to steer around rather than to apply the brakes and stop. If you do you will be a sitting duck! If you do slow, be sure you keep an eye on the mirror and go off the road if necessary, to avoid an impact on ice. If you are hit from behind, you will be propelled forward at half the impact speed, assuming vehicles of equal weight, and you don't know where you will end up.

Large 4x4 vehicles are very popular. I think people feel safer in them and are fed up with being bullied in the city environment, so choose to buy a large, high vehicle to avoid intimidation. In some ways, they are not very practical in town, being difficult to park and uneconomical, and they appear to be aggressive, which makes these drivers unpopular with other road users.

I used a 4x4 in the army and if I were to embark on an expenses-paid world trip, I would choose one. Advances made in electronics have given these vehicles amazing performance across loose surfaces, hills and floods, although they need experience and training to get the best out of them. Be warned, they are not infallible, particularly on tarmac at high speed, and even more so when going backwards at speed, being

unstable if you have to swerve when reversing. That's an unusual thing to do, I know, but security drivers be warned.

When driving a 4x4 on soft ground, use acceleration and gearbox sense to control the vehicle with the engine. Plan ahead and pace your driving well. There is no need to charge ahead at high speed, the vehicle will traverse slowly and steadily, negotiating rough terrain effortlessly. Many have thick anti-roll bars in the suspension, which cause them to rock from side to side, which is uncomfortable when sitting so high.

Keep your side windows up and get out and investigate on foot any hazard you are not sure about. Firstly, look down any deep, steep descent and form your strategy to negotiate it. Floods should not be attempted without careful thought, or without a snorkel intake to the engine. If one is not fitted, know the height of the intake above the ground. Do not cause a large bow wave. Take it gently.

When driving across country, you very occasionally have to use momentum to get you through. Only experience and lots of practice will tell you when. Use the differential locking device for very difficult conditions. It can lock the diff, front to rear and also across the axle at the rear (and on some vehicles on the front axle too) and give you proper four-wheel drive for extra traction. Do not use the diff locks when turning on firm ground. You will wind up the transmission because the wheels all have to rotate at the same speed. This can cause considerable strain to the transmission and potential breakages.

The electronics fitted to modern 4x4s are amazing. The descent speed regulator (DSR) will automatically keep the road speed to a crawl down hills. If you really get stuck, use the winch, if fitted. Link the wire to something stout, like a large tree trunk. Stand well back when outside the vehicle, at least 50 yards (45 metres) away. If the wire snaps and lets fly, it can kill you!

Off-road driving can be very enjoyable. It seems a shame to see these large and highly capable 4x4s used only for the school run. If you do, in my view you will look silly and open yourself to ridicule. With congestion charges, insurance, fuel consumption and dramatic depreciation, they can cost a considerable amount to maintain. Some might say, 'So what? I have earned my money with hard work and I will buy whatever vehicle I like!' But I don't see the point of trying to drive these vehicles economically, diesel engines or not.

*Parked cars line this street – how long would it take to stop if a child ran out from between them?*

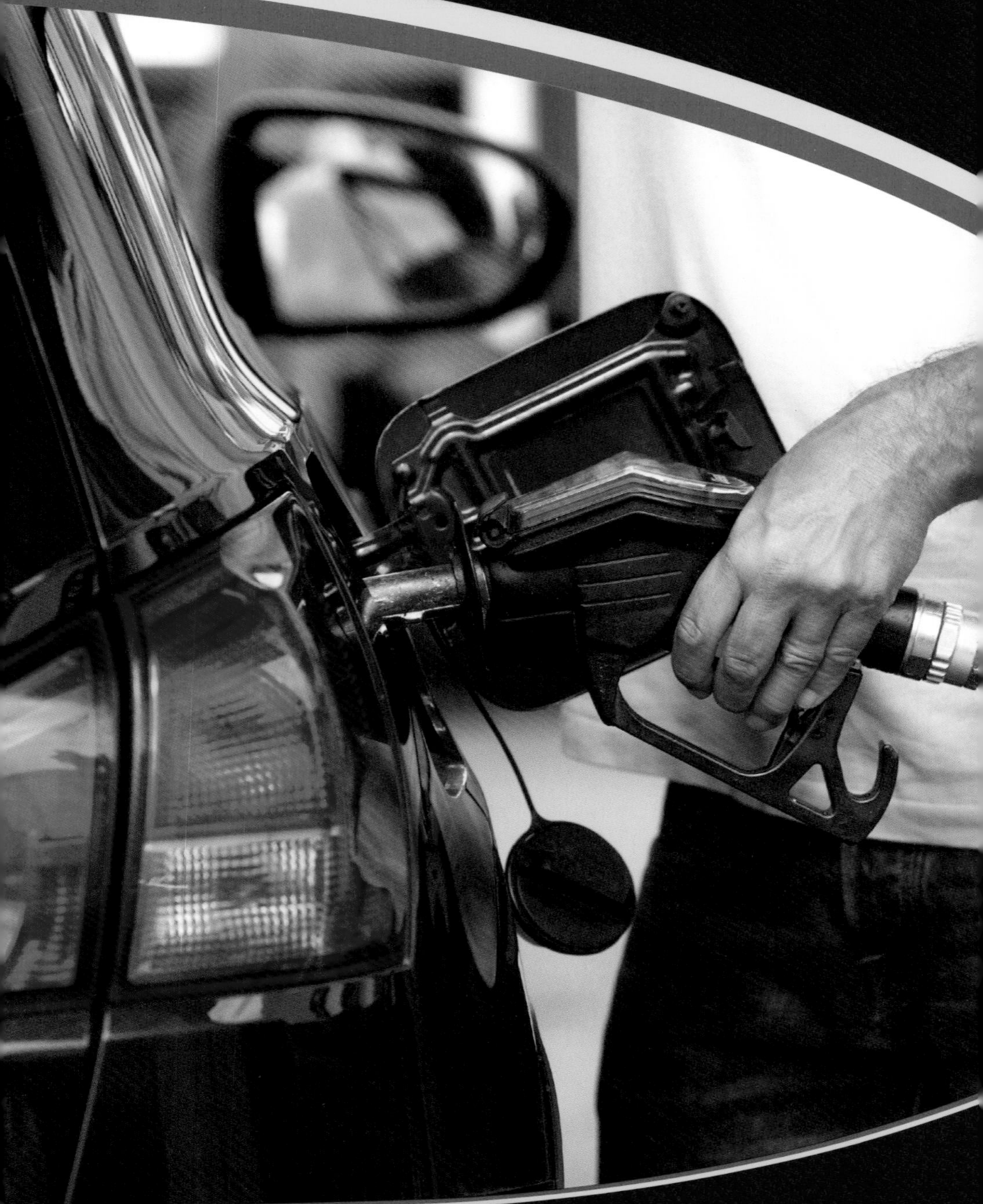

# 13 Economy driving

*Besides your choice of car, the major influence
on use of fuel is the way you drive.*

The majority of drivers are sensible and responsible and they drive slowly and safely. To drive economically, they use light acceleration and pick up pace gradually. There are times in everyone's life when driving for economy takes priority and matters more. When you are at university, out of work or retired and living on a pension then there is a need to save money, and acquire the skills to improve your driving to save fuel.

## Cars and fuel

No matter how well you may drive to reduce motoring costs, if you possess the wrong car, it defeats the object. No limousine, 4x4 or supercar is going to be as economical as a tiny city car. It is also important to tune the engine to be as economical as possible and service the car at the manufacturer's recommended intervals. Any car with under-inflated tyres, binding brakes and a smoky engine is not going to be as economical as it should be.

As an enthusiast, you may wish to service your own car, but cars today are becoming so complicated that unless you have a classic car, or a simple sports car like my Super Seven, it is impossible. If you do your own servicing, be sure you dispose of the consumables responsibly. Take them and the oil to the local recycling facility for professional disposal.

I don't drive the Seven economically, but then I don't use it very often, purely for competition and pleasure motoring. On the other hand, I drive my 1.8-litre BMW economically on the majority of occasions.

Neither of my cars has a catalytic converter, as both were made before they were required. These exhaust treatment systems remove 75% of carbon monoxide, nitrogen oxide and hydrocarbons (but not carbon dioxide), but for the first five miles (8km) or so at the start of your journey, they do not work sufficiently well to be of any value. As most trips in the car are less than five

miles, they may be of little value to the environment. They also do not work above 3,000rpm. Their advantage to enthusiasts is that manufacturers have spent millions, producing engines with almost racing car engine efficiency, with twin overhead camshafts, variable value timing, short stroke engines and sophisticated materials to overcome this exhaust blockage system.

Crash safety has made cars heavier and engines have had to become more powerful to produce the same acceleration, although this is so rarely used by the majority of drivers in the UK; a low-revving diesel engine is far more suitable for most.

Turbocharging has been a lifeline for the diesel engine, which has become much more powerful in consequence. Once on the move, advances in noise and vibration technology have made them so quiet and smooth that at motorway speeds you can hardly tell if it is running on diesel.

Diesel is horrible to handle when you fill up. Few bother with the gloves provided at fuel stations, which makes dermatitis a likely risk. On the other hand it is not commonly known that unleaded petrol fumes in repeated doses are carcinogenic as well as volatile, causing fire in crashes.

The Government has tried to control our consumption of fuel by progressively raising the tax on it, currently to 80p for each litre of unleaded, which is excessive. The rewards of motoring still make it worthwhile, for the flexibility to go anywhere you wish, at any time, and to establish your own identity with the choice of car you drive

Alternative forms of personal transport, by comparison, are inconvenient and uncomfortable. I do have a bicycle at home and I used it for short trips in summer weather. However, I do find it so uncomfortable in our cold climate and inclement weather, which in my youth did not seem to bother me at all! I have a motorcycle licence, but I am not a natural biker, born to ride. As we know, motorcycles

*For fuel economy, take as little luggage as you can! A laden roof rack can cause fuel consumption to increase by 25%..*

bring more risk, but they are economical.

I know it is not easy with a family, but take as little luggage as you can. The extra drag of a roof rack will cost 25% more fuel consumption for a given cruising speed, or 15% with a roof box, and when towing a caravan, or a race car, as much as 50% more fuel is consumed. Plan your route to be as straight and direct as possible. Country roads and hills will exhaust fuel more quickly and a route in town will cost both time and fuel.

An automatic transmission gives 10% worse fuel consumption, as does air conditioning, so switch it off in good dry weather. Keep a log of mileage and fuel used with servicing intervals and car costs.

Don't forget that new car depreciation is the most expensive cost involved with the running of a two-litre family car, at 25p per mile, as against fuel costs which are currently 16p per mile. In percentage terms, the cost of fuel is only 10% of the overall cost of running a car. The energy required to build a

new car far exceeds the energy used to run it. Best to drive your car into the ground, like I do.

## Economy techniques

Personally, I dread to think of the money I have wasted on my hobby of motoring and competition driving. It has been a major factor in my disposable income. Still, that is my choice. Apart from your choice of economical car, the major influence upon the fuel you use is your own driving. Everybody accidentally exceeds the speed limit on every journey at some time or another. If you say you do not, I suggest you are being economical with the truth!

So to drive economically:

- Keep to the speed limit and proportion the pace of your driving in relation to the prevailing speed restriction.
- Use light, small throttle openings with a maximum of 3,000rpm to let the catalytic converter work and to avoid unnecessary emissions.
- Change up early and use a high gear and the torque of the engine without straining and labouring it. Do not coast

by depressing the clutch too early or selecting neutral. This bad habit may catch you out on emerging into a major road or roundabout, causing you to miss a vital gear change and leaving you vulnerable and exposed. Try to miss out intermediate gears if you can and don't change down through the gearbox when stopping. Take one gear for one hazard. Switch off the engine if you stop for more than one minute.

⊘ Avoid overtaking on two-way roads, except for an exceptional obstruction that is moving along very slowly. Then, choose a very long view to avoid firm acceleration; but don't compromise safety.

⊘ Drive at the most economical cruising speed, which is 50mph in many small family cars. Understand that this can cause unnecessary obstruction. If it does, find a convenient lay-by to pull into to relieve the following traffic.

Some drivers act selfishly, just to conserve their own fuel cost. This selfishness can cause frustration, impatience and in consequence, actual danger to others. It is no use them criticising someone else's reckless driving, if selfishness is the root cause in the first place! We all have a responsibility towards each other, to blend the pace of our driving to the pace of the rest of the traffic and to drive with consideration towards each other.

The advanced skills of roadcraft will come to the fore when driving economically, but there are potential dangers in the high-gear, light-throttle cruising style. A lack of concentration is a major cause of road crashes and serious errors. A disassociated passive state of driving contributes towards it. It is far better to be active and safe.

The major controlling influence in the variation in speed is the driver's control of the accelerator. This control works both ways, for accelerating and decelerating. It is more effective to control and vary road speed in a low gear, at an engine speed of at least

2,500rpm. So, when road conditions require a high engine speed and the correct gear to safely vary road speed, the appropriate gear ratio should be selected, at the right time.

An example is on country roads, to vary road speed for a series of bends, gradients and overtaking, when safety takes precedence over economy. So country roads are not the best ones on which to conserve fuel. Primary routes and motorways are more suitable, but try to blend and fit in to the general pace of traffic. Avoid causing any obstruction and always endeavour to drive with a spirit of consideration to everyone.

Your own fuel saving and road safety is increased by forward planning, long-range anticipation and hazard perception, and acting correctly and sensibly upon what you see. Total concentration, constantly scanning all around the road scene, is essential to pick out the most important potential danger. Recognise each hazard early and act upon it. Avoid unnecessary braking, or worse, heavy braking, leading to excessive fuel consumption. Keep a good safe following distance and avoid stopping unnecessarily. Arrive as the hazard has opened out, or has disappeared.

Finally, if you park, don't be a nosey parker. Reversing into a parking space is safer, because of the improved view, and it's more economical to manoeuvre when the engine is warm than when it is cold.

In the future, I believe we will be driving hydrogen-electric powered vehicles. Be warned that these cars are very quiet, so pedestrians and cyclists watch out. A warning tap of the horn may be essential to attract their attention, but how many drivers will bother? They say this technology will save the planet, but will it save lives? As long as I can, I will choose to drive my Super Seven HPC at the weekend only, and overtake safely. Thank goodness we live in a country where we can choose what we drive, as long as we have a social conscience and drive safely.

# RETIRING TO A LAY-BY WHEN TOWING
## To allow following traffic to pass

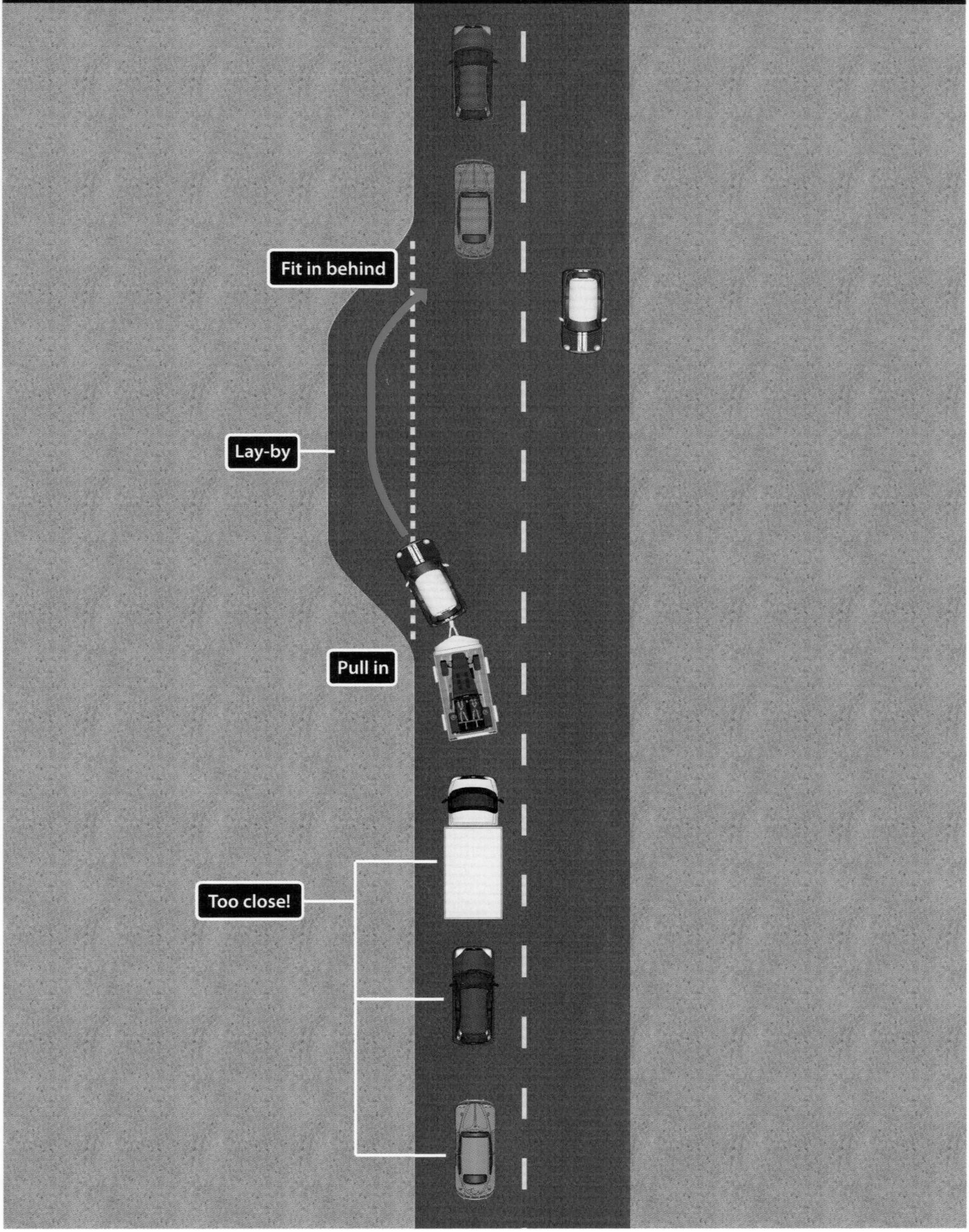

Fit in behind

Lay-by

Pull in

Too close!

# 14 Track driving

*A picture of concentration: racing my Super Seven HPC at Spa-Francorchamps.*

Let's look at an aspect of advanced driving that many drivers are intrigued with, but that is a mystery to many. How good am I? There is only one way to find out, by competence in motorsport, not on the public road.

The late Tommy Wisdom was a most successful racing and rally driver. He came third in the Portuguese Grand Prix in 1951; competed 12 times at Le Mans, failing to finish only once and in 1950 setting the 1,500cc class record; in 1932 he won the Alpine trial, as well as winning his class five times and collecting two Alpine cups for penalty-free performances; he competed in 22 consecutive Monte Carlo rallies, finishing second on one occasion; and in his nine Mille Miglia races, he won the GT class three times.

Tommy became the chief executive of the British School of Motoring (BSM) in 1961 and inspired BSM to start the High Performance Course in 1962. The manager of the course and my predecessor, John Miles MBE, was also a rally driver. We called John the 'genial genius'. He seemed to be as fast as Fangio and was quite the best advanced driving coach I have witnessed.

I try to continue the HPC tradition of involvement in motorsport, having competed in 200 competitions, winning 96, with 33 fast laps and records – a win-to-start ratio of 48%. Small beer in comparison to Mr Wisdom's international record. He became

*A grid full of BSM High Performance Course cars at Brands Hatch in the 1960s – the HPC ran the very first track days in the UK.*

*Super Sevens racing, my championship-winning car with lights ablaze to pass.*

fed up with the British establishment's war against the motorist, and he even resigned from his golf club when they placed speed humps down the drive!

I don't think he would be a happy man today, with the profusion of speed limits and speed cameras. It is no wonder that there has been an explosion in the popularity of track days. Some would say this is a good thing, to get the boy racers off the public highway and let them release their speed happiness away from the rest of us. I do not agree.

I believe that track days develop cornering and overtaking techniques that are inappropriate and downright dangerous if applied on the public highway by those without roadcraft training. Witness the thousands of crashes when overtaking and loss of control in bends on country roads by male drivers aged 17 to 25. I think track days encourage misdirected overconfidence, leading to the belief that smooth handling is all there is to advanced driving.

The BSM High Performance Course ran the very first track days in the UK for both BMW and Porsche in the 1960s. Despite slick organisation and discipline, crashes occurred and cars were written off. When the car is not their own, track speed encourages the irresponsible to drive recklessly.

I will not sit alongside any driver I have not met before on a racetrack; it is too dangerous without safe limit handling first on a proving ground. Spinning and potentially crashing on a race circuit is obviously highly dangerous.

Furthermore, I do not advise anyone to take an unmodified production car onto a race circuit. It is a road car and is not developed for the extra pressures of high-speed race driving. The exception is a rear-engined Porsche with its dry sump and excellent brakes. Insurance is possible, but is expensive and it will ruin your record if you crash a valuable road-going Porsche on the track. My Super Seven HPC has the same dry sump and brakes, is equally fast on the circuit and is considerably less expensive to repair and maintain. It is also light on tyres.

As an enthusiast, you will want to have fun and enjoy your high-performance car by extending its performance and your own ability. The last thing you want to be told on the circuit is not to pass on curves and overtake only on the left along straights. On a clockwise circuit this requires having to move across the track frequently. Obstruction causes long M25-like queues to form behind the slowest, least experienced driver, who may be apprehensive, incompetent, or refuse to move over to the right, off line. According to the Jim Russell International Racing Drivers School (where I was an instructor), restricting overtaking on the right, on a clockwise circuit, is potentially dangerous for novices.

An aggressive individual can make track driving a stressful misery for inexperienced drivers who are trying to learn; dividing attention to the mirror at high speed can cause it all to go green with control lost very quickly. There is also a tendency to watch the driver in front and to follow while he drives off the track!

Both you and your road car are possibly not prepared, which is a potential disaster from the start. I personally see no point in potentially damaging yourself and your car, without a real objective, as you will not be allowed to take a lap time because you are not competing and it would invalidate both the organiser's and your own insurance for the day.

I know all this sounds negative, but experience teaches and I have to tell you. However, with enthusiasm you may not want to heed my advice and go along to a track day anyway. Best of luck; but first, some simple advice.

Apart from normal servicing, there are essential elements of car preparation to consider.

The standard braking system is designed for road use, even in supercars. The brakes may wilt after only three laps. Fit harder competition pads, front and rear, to avoid fade and brake failure. They may squeal and grumble at low speed.

Do not change the tyres or fit wide wheels, the suspension settings may be disturbed. Extra grip will cause oil to surge, so top up 1/8in (3cm) above the high mark on the dipstick. Oil will take a 70-degree angle in an engine sump with 1G of cornering or braking pressure, whereas 0.8G is the design maximum for road cars with ordinary road tyres. A race circuit surface dressing can create far more than 1G of grip.

Fit a full harness seat belt and consider getting a more supportive seat to hold you more securely when cornering. A roll-over bar is not required for track days, even in an open-top car. Even a fire extinguisher is not mandatory.

Make sure the mirrors give a wide view and are sufficient to see all around, to the rear and far behind.

Be sure you have the legal tyre tread depth and inspect them all before you go home. That means at least 1.6mm, three-quarters around and across any part of the tread. No deep cuts or bulges, on the inside too.

Do not modify the suspension; you may cause extraordinary problems and ruin the car's balance. Millions have been spent on a car's development to make it safe for you. I have never driven any modified road car that has been successful on the highway, without sufficient finance, development, time and expertise from a major manufacturer.

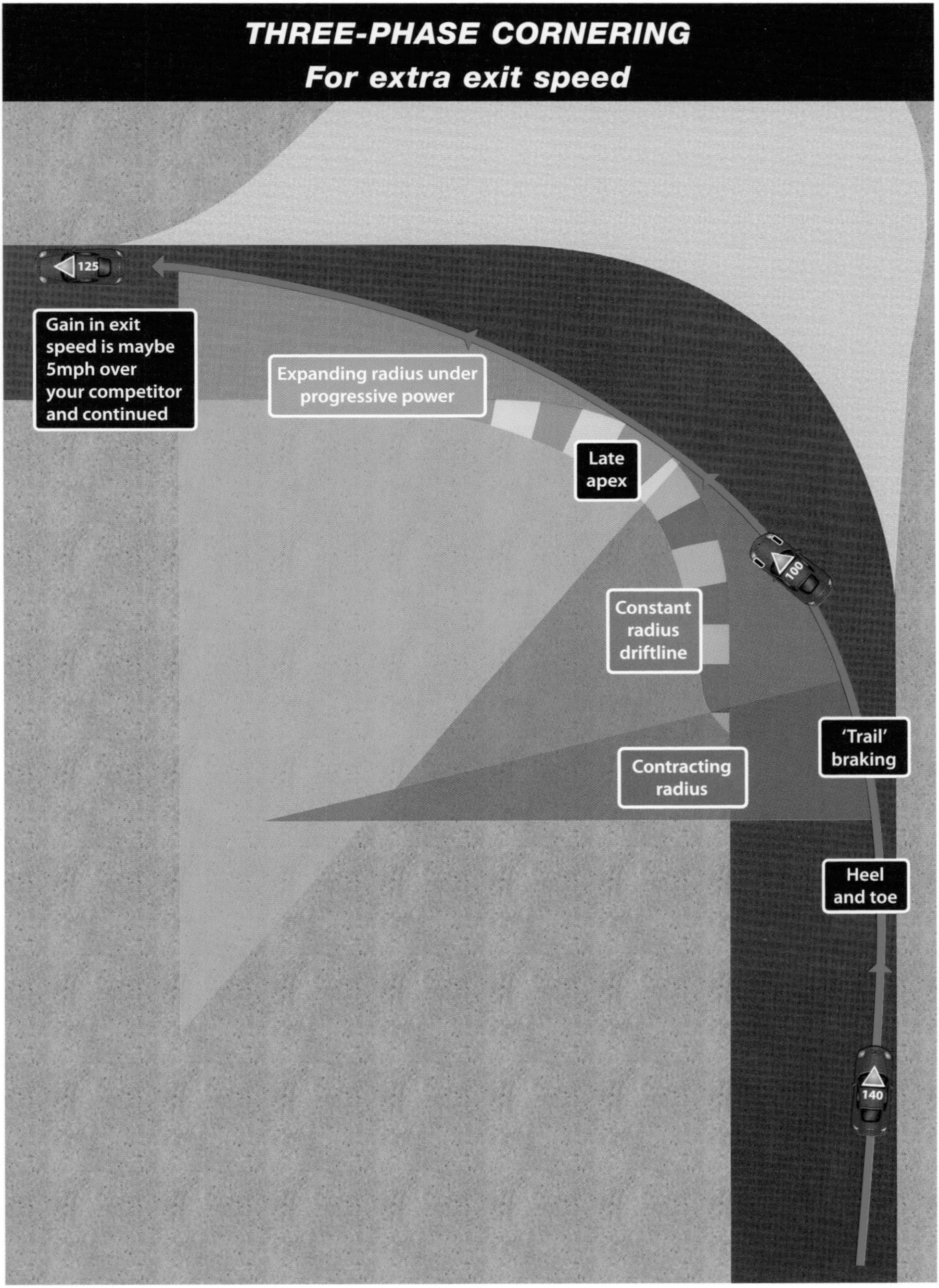

# THREE-PHASE CORNERING
## For extra exit speed

125

**Gain in exit speed is maybe 5mph over your competitor and continued**

**Expanding radius under progressive power**

**Late apex**

100

**Constant radius driftline**

**'Trail' braking**

**Contracting radius**

**Heel and toe**

140

# Hillclimbs and sprints

Instead of risking all on a track day, my advice is to begin with tarmac sprinting or hillclimbing, which has less potential to damage you, your bank balance or your expensive supercar. My advice is to join an RAC Motorsports Association Motor Club; after all, in the end, you want to enjoy yourself and develop your skill, by comparing your performance and by competing as safely as you can. Nothing else compares. I have had the misfortune to have suffered shunts when racing through mechanical failure in production cars, and without safety equipment I would not be here today. Don't go to a track day to mix with incompetent drivers, in road cars, who think they are the next world champion!

After joining an RAC Motorsports Club, you can then apply for a speed competition licence. You will receive the MSA *Blue Book*, which is the code of motorsport. Try www.msauk.org or telephone 01753 765000 and ask for a speed licence, if you start with sprinting or hillclimbing. You will not be required to take a medical examination and it is all quite straightforward. Don't be put off by the enormous amount of information in the *Blue Book*. It is for the benefit of everyone involved in the safe use of a car in motorsport. Read only what is appropriate for the branch of motorsport you have chosen. You will also be advised by friendly officials when you begin. If you start with sprinting or hillclimbing you will not have to take a one-day MSA approved race drivers' course to start with, that can come later.

Motorsport is a demanding, potentially dangerous and serious undertaking, with some highly-talented people involved. Never underestimate their abilities. It is not possible to dip your toes in without getting your feet wet! Enthusiasm is highly contagious and motorsport is probably the most enjoyable and satisfying sport to be involved with. So, what I am about to advise is in my experience the best, safest way.

First, do your homework. Decide which championship and class of competition you wish to run. Keep it simple: start with the standard classes of either sports or saloons, divided by engine capacity. With sprinting or hillclimbing it is you, your car and the circuit you are dealing with and finally, the other competitors on the time sheet, with whom to compare your performance.

If you are like me, it will take you time to develop the skill to drive quickly enough. Competition driving is as far removed from road driving as flying an aeroplane; so be patient and drive within your own improving ability and don't crash.

It is essential to choose the right car to compete with. If you can, choose something extraordinary that no one else has thought of and stand out from the crowd. Don't be part of the tribe. Choose rear-wheel drive if you can, it will teach you more about throttle control and handling. Aim to drive precisely, but with a little fire and brimstone to create a spectacle and become noticed as someone who has car control and winning potential.

Study the power to weight ratio, weight distribution and suspension design of your car, to assess how competitive it is likely to be. Most things in motorsport have been done before, so examine any history if you intend to compete with an old design.

Preparing a sports or saloon car for tarmac sprints or hillclimbing is simplicity itself for the standard classes:

- Have the car serviced, preferably by a company involved with motorsport. They will inform you of any weaknesses in the car.
- Consider whether to fit adjustable dampers and slightly harder brake pads, front and rear. Only fit tyres permitted from the 1A list of tyres in the *Blue Book*, for standard production classes.
- Identify the battery negative earth lead with yellow tape.
- Mark the direction of the ignition switch to 'off'.

# CADENCE THROTTLE USE
## *To maximise grip on race start*

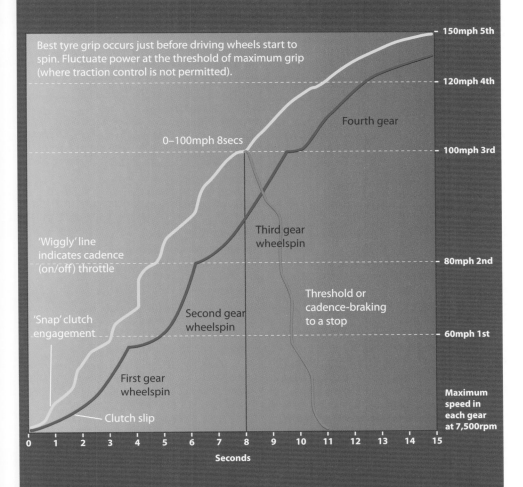

Best tyre grip occurs just before driving wheels start to spin. Fluctuate power at the threshold of maximum grip (where traction control is not permitted).

150mph 5th

120mph 4th

Fourth gear

100mph 3rd

0–100mph 8secs

Third gear wheelspin

80mph 2nd

'Wiggly' line indicates cadence (on/off) throttle

Threshold or cadence-braking to a stop

60mph 1st

'Snap' clutch engagement

Second gear wheelspin

First gear wheelspin

Maximum speed in each gear at 7,500rpm

Clutch slip

0  1  2  3  4  5  6  7  8  9  10  11  12  13  14  15

**Seconds**

**Illustration example is Caterham Super Seven HPC EVO: Vauxhall 2-litre engine (235bhp, 185lb/ft torque), Quaife straight-cut gearbox, Rocket ratios, 3.9:1 limited-slip differential, 13in wheels, weight 530kg**

**0–100mph 8secs; 100–0mph 3.1secs; 0–100–0mph 11.1secs**

## VOICE OF EXPERIENCE

### Sir Stirling and me

If you are humble and respectful, other competitors can be very friendly, giving you encouragement and helpful advice. Sir Stirling Moss tells the story of when he first started hillclimbing as a young man. He checked his time after a climb and found that another competitor had beaten it. So he wandered around the paddock in search of the faster driver and found it was a very elderly gentleman with thick bottle-bottom glasses. While watching him prepare for his next run, he was surprised to see him take them off and put on his plain racing goggles. After another immensely fast run, Stirling asked him politely, 'Excuse me sir? I noticed that you removed your glasses and yet your racing goggle lenses are uncorrected. How do you manage to see clearly and yet produce such a fast time?'

'Well, my boy,' he replied, 'I don't brake until I see the corner!'

⟳ Fit a matt black timing strut, with the height and area described in the *Blue Book*.

⟳ Mark the towing eye, front and rear, with a yellow arrow.

When you arrive at the venue, sign on first, go to the noise check, then have your car scrutineered, with competition numbers each side. If it is your first event, the scrutiniser will be lenient, but will not allow you to compromise your safety. Buy the best helmet you can afford and fireproof overalls, gloves, socks and welt-free race boots.

If you enter a sprint at an established racetrack you will start individually, for either one or two laps, with strictly no overtaking. Obstruction is highly unlikely, as the fastest will start first of all. It may be the first time you have used the full road width when starting to compete. If you can, walk around the circuit or hillclimb first of all and work out the geometrically perfect steering path from the edge, to the apex, to the far edge again. The geometric line may be not what you actually use, but is the start of your

thinking. Examine every detail, looking for every surface change, patch, bump and kerb, to decide whether to ride it or not. Gain a sense of position and space.

When you drive fast you will change the path you drive in the light of experience. Adapt. Be flexible. If the bend is of moderate severity and is followed by a long straight, it is best to sacrifice your approach line and speed by being slightly late when you turn in, to gain an expanding radius towards the apex and the exit, so you can apply power earlier. If the straight is long, 5mph gained in exit speed will continue all the way along the next straight, which is usually longer than the preceding bend. Reductions in lap time don't just come from cornering!

Long fast curves can have an apex area, where you hang on to it for a moment or two, before you release the car at the exit. The best circuits are hilly and are a far greater challenge for car and driver. Hillclimbs by definition are steep and demand early power application and traction out of corners. You may enjoy it so much you will want to race, but to enjoy yourself be attentive and dedicated from the beginning.

The secret of success in motorsport is plain hard work. Racing is like war. It is a question of logistics, finance, preparation, teamwork, knowledge, skill and tenacity from all in the team. Driving is only 25% in the equation of success. A healthy bank balance is essential, particularly when starting out. Like showbusiness, you are only as good as your last performance. A good performance might encourage someone to invest in you, but only if the team is gaining consistent results, with a smart, well turned-out car and presentation. Allocate 30% of your budget towards testing and development.

Sprinting, hillclimbing and rallying are rather more social than motor racing and, as I mentioned before, my advice before you start racing is to enter a sprint at one of the circuits you may be racing on later. It will

*Racing at night: this is me in a Jaguar E-type during an endurance race at Spa-Francorchamps.*

get you used to the pressure of competition. People are more helpful and friendly. They are primarily competing against the watch and only indirectly against you. If you are new to them, they tend to be inquisitive and ask questions. If you are not going to compete with them seriously, or for very long, you can be friendly in return and give them as much information as you wish. If you beat them however, they won't be so forthcoming, and neither will you!

Get used to starting and getting off the line. You may stall. Better to do that in a sprint than to do it in front of a field of aggressive racing drivers, or you will be asking for a rear-end shunt before you get started.

Hillclimbing is demanding and good fun. Usually the course is tight and twisting. You can examine your starting efficiency

with cadence throttle control, which is an essential skill to learn. They will post the time you take for the start during the first 60ft and your maximum speed at the end of the longest straight. Also, you can compare your overall time with your competitors at the end of each run. Hillclimbing is very exacting and it will teach you to acquire perfection to be fast. There is not much margin for error, so don't try to throw the car around, be neat and precise instead. The experience can be salutary, because the good old boys may not look like racing drivers, but most of them have been doing it for years and are very, very quick. It is a very specialised area of motorsport and demands its own skills.

Even if your objective is racing, you may

enjoy speed events so much that when you become middle-aged and sensible, you might well return to the sport. Prescot and Shelsley have a wonderful history of famous drivers and cars; you can compare your times with those in years gone by. These two venues in particular are lovely places and should be experienced by all competitors sometime in their lives. The atmosphere is almost English garden party, particularly at Vintage Sports Car Club (VSCC) events. There is plenty of time for socialising (once you have solved problems with the car of course), which is all part of the fun.

## VOICE OF EXPERIENCE

### First in everything

One of the best racing drivers I ever met was the late Bernard Unett. He was a real racer, tough, consistently driving on the lap record, lap after lap, never giving an inch.

Bernard was all about being first. He was first to arrive on the circuit in the morning, first to sign on, first into scrutineering, first into the assembly area. Then he would be first to gain pole, and first across the line. I did one race at Thruxton with Bernard as number two driver in the works Chrysler team and finished second.

He was a professional engineer and test driver, completing thousands of miles of flat-out driving, able to hone the works cars to perfection. So, as I do, take his example and try to be the first to arrive at the circuit and thereafter.

*My race at Thruxton as team-mate to Bernard Unett – who wanted to be first in everything.*

# THE NÜRBURGRING, GERMANY
## Start of a lap of the Nordschleife

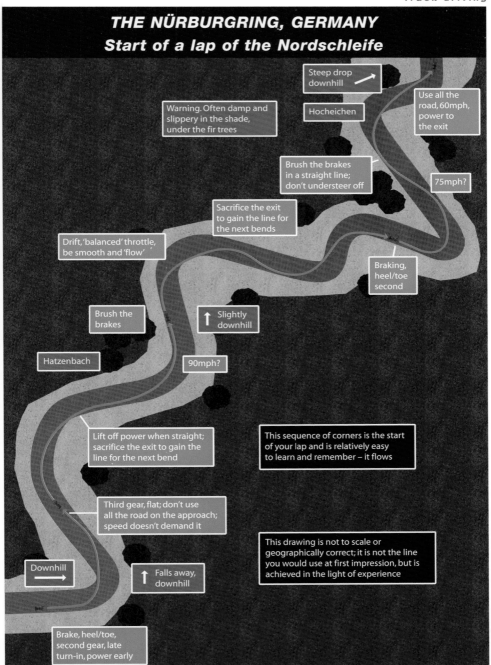

Steep drop downhill

Hocheichen

Use all the road, 60mph, power to the exit

Warning. Often damp and slippery in the shade, under the fir trees

Brush the brakes in a straight line; don't understeer off

75mph?

Sacrifice the exit to gain the line for the next bends

Drift, 'balanced' throttle, be smooth and 'flow'

Braking, heel/toe second

Brush the brakes

Slightly downhill

Hatzenbach

90mph?

Lift off power when straight; sacrifice the exit to gain the line for the next bend

This sequence of corners is the start of your lap and is relatively easy to learn and remember – it flows

Third gear, flat; don't use all the road on the approach; speed doesn't demand it

This drawing is not to scale or geographically correct; it is not the line you would use at first impression, but is achieved in the light of experience

Downhill

Falls away, downhill

Brake, heel/toe, second gear, late turn-in, power early

# SPA-FRANCORCHAMPS, BELGIUM
## *The line through Eau Rouge*

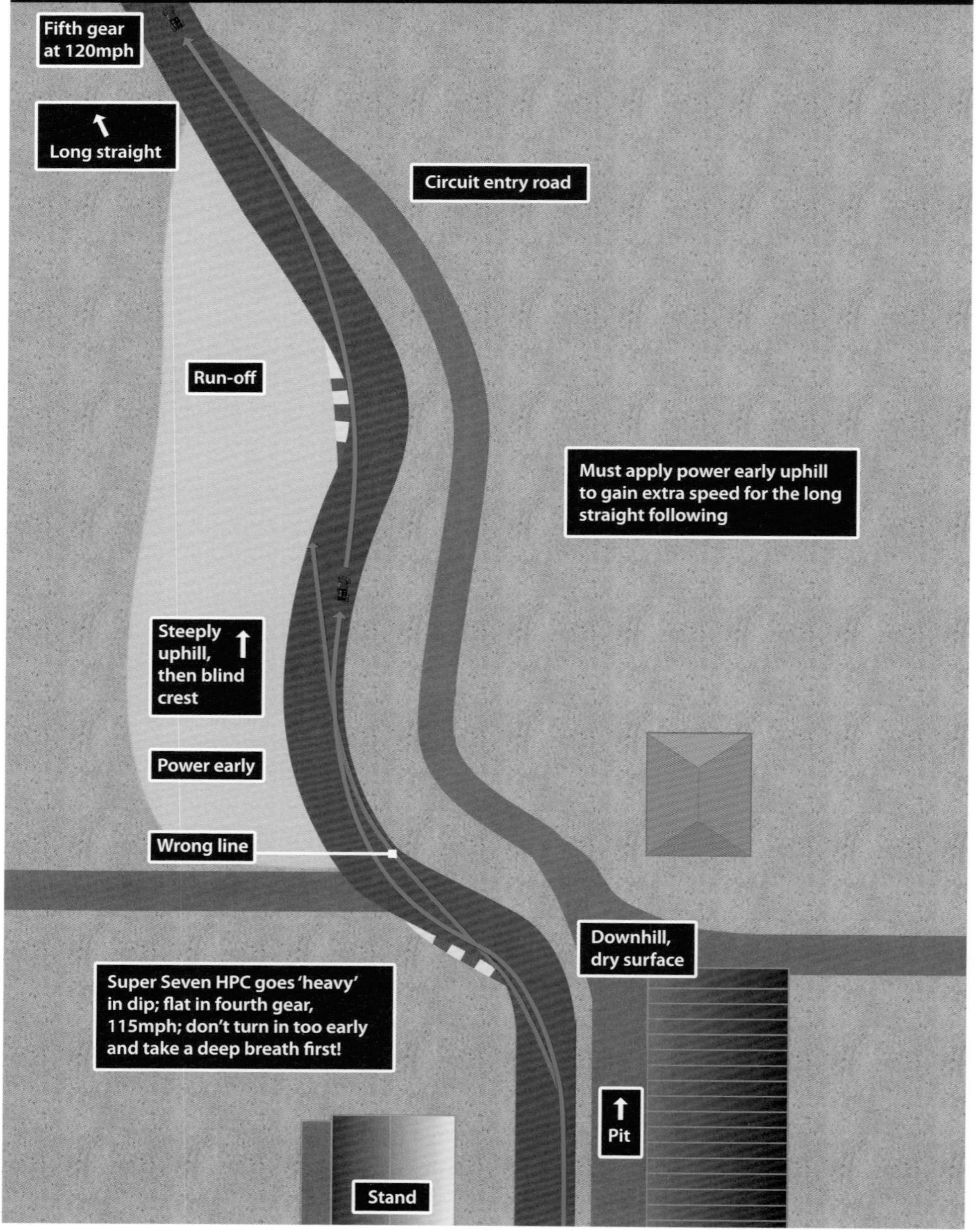

**Fifth gear at 120mph**

↑
**Long straight**

**Circuit entry road**

**Run-off**

**Must apply power early uphill to gain extra speed for the long straight following**

↑
**Steeply uphill, then blind crest**

**Power early**

**Wrong line**

**Downhill, dry surface**

**Super Seven HPC goes 'heavy' in dip; flat in fourth gear, 115mph; don't turn in too early and take a deep breath first!**

↑
**Pit**

**Stand**

# Club motor racing

Club motor racing with a historic or classic car is served best by either VSCC, the Historic Sports Car Club or the Classic and Sports Car Club. In addition, there are racing clubs where you will be able to gain the widest invitation to organised races run by other motorsport clubs. These are principally the British Automobile Racing Club (BARC) and British Racing & Sports Car Club (BRSCC). The 750 Motor Club members are also invited to most events in the UK and provide the widest range of racing classes for impecunious racing enthusiasts.

If you decide to compete in club motor racing, detailed preparation will be the secret of success. Firstly, do your homework and study the regulations. Can you modify your car, and by how much?

Developing your car to be competitive will take time and money – lots of it. You will need to take out as much unnecessary weight as you can and add a roll cage. Blueprinting by an engine builder can add as much as 25 per cent more power even with a standard engine. You will need to spend a lot of time testing with different suspension settings and tyres to find the most competitive set-up.

As opposed to having playful fun on track days, circuit test days are for serious race car testing. You will require a race driver's licence and be able to show you are competent to test at racing speeds. You must now apply for a Go Racing driver pack from the RAC Motorsports Association, complete an approved course at a race school registered with the Association of Racing Drivers Schools (ARDS) and take a medical. You will need to pass a written exam and a simple test of your basic knowledge of race procedure and overtaking.

The practical test can either be in a race saloon or your own car, which will be scrutineered to see if it is properly insured and prepared. The instructor will demonstrate with a commentary how to leave the pits, take a smooth line through the corners, use the mirrors sensibly, explain the overtaking rules and safe passing technique, even how to leave the circuit. You will then be required to emulate this, driving smoothly at a reasonable pace that blends with the traffic, passing safely, taking an efficient steering path and obeying any flag signals for ten laps or so.

Be sensible and it is easy. Just don't get in anyone's way, and try not to spin or frighten your examiner! In other words display that you are reasonably safe and competent to start racing. A few sprints and hillclimbs beforehand will help, but you must also display your ability to drive safely in traffic at speed. Track days may give you a false impression of your imagined ability. Be warned, racing could be a salutary experience. For your first six races, you will still be required to display a novice cross as a warning to others to look after you.

If you find your driving is not up to it, get hold of the best coach around. Get data logging fitted to your car and bring your coach along. In three laps he should be able to put a trace on your system which you can work towards. If he is not faster than you, give him the boot! On the other hand, he may be your greatest asset. There is usually more time to be found by improving the driver than in any part of the car's development, so coaching can be the best money you can spend.

As a racing coach myself, I cannot improve the driver if he is trying to fight a bad car – and often he doesn't know it is bad! Sort out the car, then the driver. It's an ongoing process. If you have any doubt about your own experience and ability, find the driving coach from the beginning. Your engineer may be able to work with him better than yourself. He will make the whole process quicker and more efficient, saving both money and development time. Your own ability will progress far more quickly, along with the car. Be sensible.

Don't let your own pride stand in the way.

Before the race starts, I like to sit in the car, but some drivers go walkabout to try to psych you out, by being over-friendly, or making snide remarks. Have none of it; stay in the car, concentrate and think of the circuit, the key corners where you can gain exit speed, or those that are near flat.

Tyres, brakes and engine oil are going to be cold, so for the first two practice laps, gradually warm them up, then if you have a clear lap on the third, go for it. If someone quicker goes past, then follow and slipstream them if you can. Work hard, get a sweat on and mean business. Examine your lap time or signal board each time around. Remember, there could be an incident and they may cut the practice period down, so go for a good time as early as you can. Note when practice is to finish and go for a quick time in the last few minutes. Don't mix it with the others: hang back for a lap then go for a time. Be hard, neat and quick. After the chequered flag at the end of practice, cool everything down, and keep off the brakes as much as you can.

If you end up on pole, no problem, all you have got to do is get a good start and drive on the lap record every lap and demoralise the opposition – easy! If not, or if you are in a lower class running mid-field, you may be in trouble. Most of the accidents in racing occur in the first corner, or at least the first couple of laps. Then, the race will settle down.

Having said that, most club races are only ten laps long and you may decide to 'tiger' to make up ground while everyone is being cautious and getting some heat into their tyres. Plan tactics. Go and watch how the starting lights work at early races, they are all slightly different. If it's a flag start, watch the starter; they each have a different style, a slow rise, quick fall, or a quick up and down to catch you out.

If accidents occur in the first corner, the carnage will usually end up on the outside of the circuit. So I have found it best to charge down the inside of other competitors; but others may have a similar idea. Go for space for the first corner or so, definitely do not take the ideal line, because some other racer will take advantage. Give them no chance, keep tight to the inside, if necessary. If they tailgate into a hairpin, back off then go for it and you can catch them out, forcing them to lift or a touch of brakes. This is racing, not a game of chess.

For the second or third lap, try to escape and create as much time and space behind as you can. Then pace the race and start to look after the car. Consistency is the objective, each lap time on or near the lap record is achieved like the timing of a metronome.

It sounds strange, but racing costs lap time. While you dice, others will catch you up and two will make four and worse – an accident is the likely result. This is where all that preparation pays dividends. Be clean, neat, fast and demoralise all of them. If you are forced to follow, it will be best to sacrifice the approach to a key corner, put the power on earlier than your competitor, catch up and slipstream to pass under braking. Feign, and then make one move, preferably down the inside of the next corner.

The driver who you intend to overtake is only allowed to make one change in defensive road position to try to block your pass. So, try to get him to make a wrong move. Be decisive, brake after he has applied his brakes, and be sure you lead into the corner, with at least your back wheel level with his seat, so that you can take your line. However, you have no right to cut in front unless you are clear. Reducing speed at the very limit of tyre performance, with trail braking, is an essential skill. Avoid 'flat-spotting' the inside tyre as it will vibrate and cause drag; less roll stiffness at the front is an asset here.

Club road racing is non-contact, but don't expect others to respect your shiny bodywork. Be hard but fair, and take no

prisoners. If you are nudged into a spin and the rotation is into the curve, keep your steering correction applied, stay off the brakes, throw the front around and let the car spin tightly. Each spin will then follow around the curve, and as you lose speed you can catch the car easily when you are pointing the right way.

If you want to spin in a straight line down the centre of the track, hit the brakes and lock up the tyres. Stay on the brakes as the car spins and only release them when you are stationary. As your direction is predictable, be sure you are pointing the right way and then scoot off, quickly. Better to have flats on the tyres than a bent car against the barrier! Not many racers, including some in F1, have these recovery skillls, and sadly many who race lack various essential skills and are frankly incompetent.

*A great photo of me at the wheel at Brands Hatch in the late 1960s. The Alfa is certainly on the limit but under complete control, even if the back wheels are off the ground!*

Before embarking on racing it is wise to practise on a skidpan at slow speed.

Weaving along the straight, or crowding in curves or bends and being eased off, is often witnessed despite this behaviour being an offence that warrants a black flag. So, be calm, calculating, deliberate and pass decisively. Race for every split second; never let up, wear them down. Go to war. Inflict your unrelenting will to win. Give the impression you are willing to do so at all costs; of course you are not, because you want to be safe, but you want to give the impression that you consider yourself to be immortal.

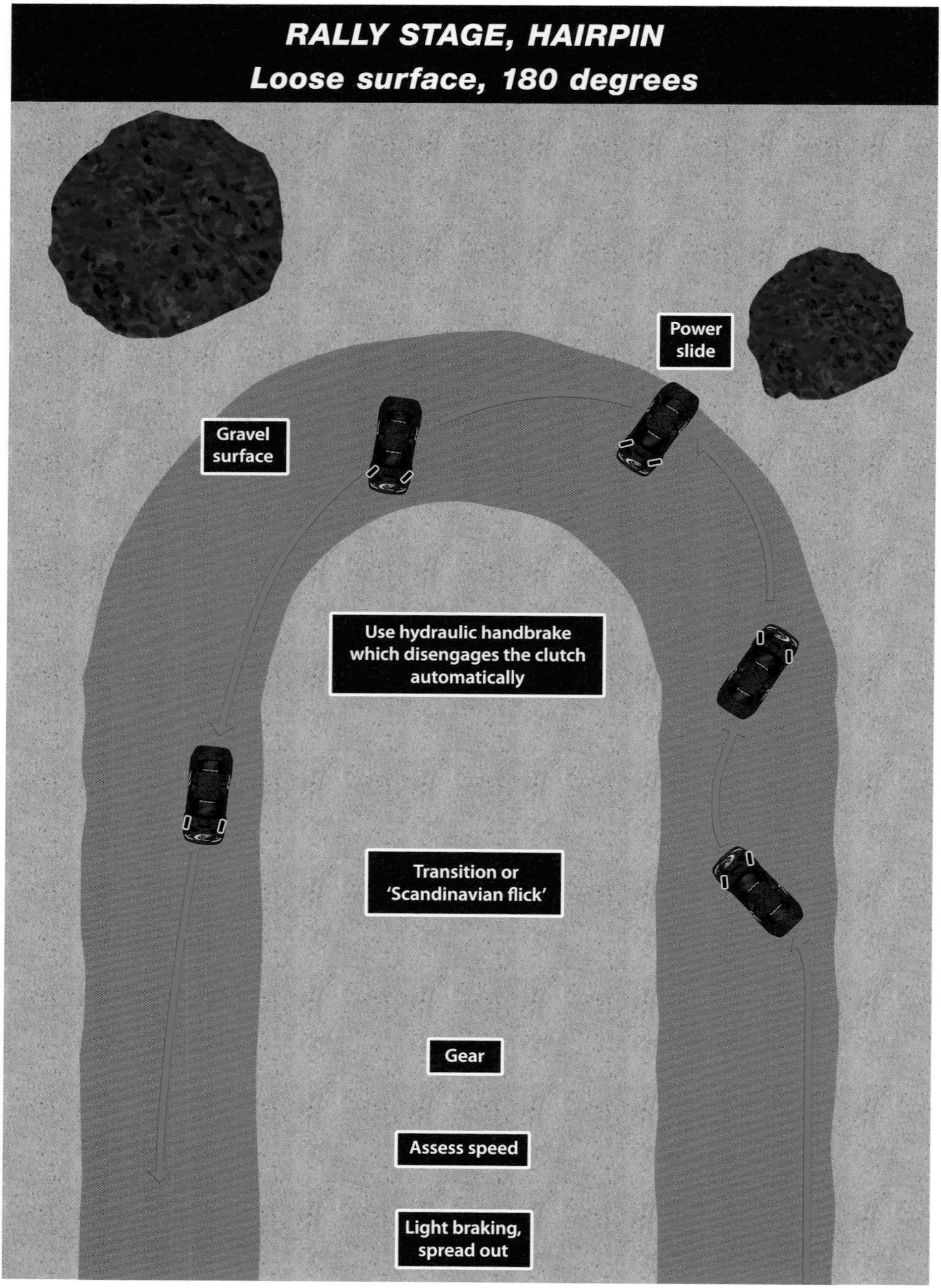

# RALLY STAGE, HAIRPIN
## Loose surface, 180 degrees

Power slide

Gravel surface

Use hydraulic handbrake which disengages the clutch automatically

Transition or 'Scandinavian flick'

Gear

Assess speed

Light braking, spread out

Championships are often won by dominating and winning in the early races. After that, the other competitors will improve, develop their cars and catch you up. So, initial testing is vital and then you must consistently aim to put yourself on the podium as frequently as possible.

## Rallying

Rallying is a whole different ball game to circuit racing. Car damage is appalling, and you need a complete garage facility with a bodyshop to keep you going. Your team has to be willing to work flat-out for 24 hours during the event with many late nights for a year or so beforehand. The dedication needed in rallying is amazing, before, during and even after the event. And again, you need to have a healthy budget to prepare the car fully.

Rallying is so car damaging it can be difficult for someone like myself who has mechanical car sympathy. Personally, I love rally driving and sideways is my style,

*The fabulous Lancia Stratos – I was fortunate to be a test driver for the Chequered Flag rally team.*

but unfortunately I have never had the facilities of a large garage and team to sustain the effort. When I was a lad I was a navigator on road rallies even before I could drive, experiencing many accidents. This was followed by a little rally driving to gain an international rally licence. I was very fortunate to be the test driver for the Chequered Flag Lancia Stratos Team, testing on both loose and tarmac stages.

The kit you require with your support team is extensive. You'll need a van and canopy, generator and lighting, portable welding kit, tools, spares and tyres. Only experience will dictate what the crew should take. They have to cart this lot at high speed to the next service area, set up in all weathers in some remote spot, without getting lost on the way. All in time for our hero to arrive with what remains of the rally car.

A rally car has to be developed specifically

**239**

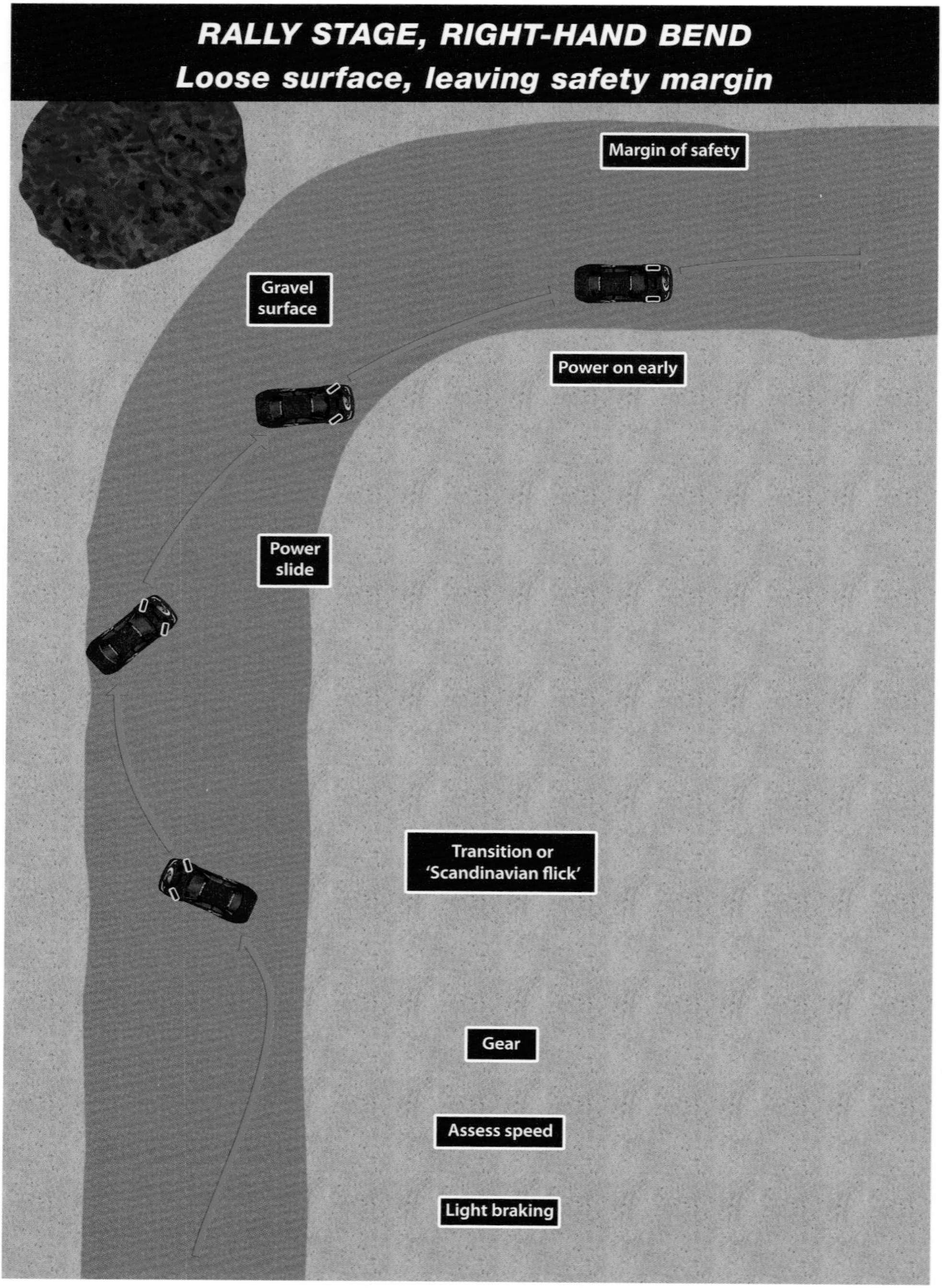

# RALLY STAGE, RIGHT-HAND BEND
## *Loose surface, leaving safety margin*

Margin of safety

Gravel surface

Power on early

Power slide

Transition or 'Scandinavian flick'

Gear

Assess speed

Light braking

for loose surfaces with a raised ride height. It needs a neutral balance that permits driver-induced final oversteer, and a relatively soft, long-travel suspension with a good ride to absorb the pounding you will receive in the car. A balanced pitch is necessary to fly and land well. Tyres wear out alarmingly quickly and make an enormous difference to performance on the different surfaces that you will experience.

You must develop the skill to powerslide a rear-wheel drive classic rally car on all road surfaces. Start by driving on a very slippery road surface at a relatively low speed. Turn the steering wheel, then brake the traction of the rear tyres by using sufficient power, or depress the clutch then sharply re-engage it, or use the hydraulic handbrake to momentarily break traction. Then put on the power to sustain the slide.

The steering path has to be curving, but keep the road speed to a pace a little too slow in relation to that car and surface, otherwise the car may understeer, due to too much speed. Now, this is where skill is required; you will have to use exactly the right amount of power to keep the tail at a yaw angle of 15 to 25 degrees. Too much power and the car will rotate and spin; too little and the car will recover and come back into line again. The front wheels must be pointing exactly down the path that you wish to travel. You correct then re-correct, to point the steering wheels where you wish to go. There is a co-ordinated blend between measured acceleration sense and power, with the steering angle to point you in the right direction and road speed controlled, all at the same time! If the slide is going too far into yaw you must back off the power, or quickly dab the brakes to kill speed; if the slide is beginning to recover, more power must be applied instantly. Surface changes must be accounted for, as well as camber and gradient.

Change of direction from a powerslide one way to the other is called transition.

This demands extended skill to back off the power to transfer weight, swing the tail by being slightly late in re-correction, and then use measured power to slide the other way. It needs confidence and practice to perfect the skill. But once acquired, like swimming or riding a bike, you never forget it. It is a skill that will make you safe on loose surfaces. When you sense you are out of control, you must know when to lift off the power. It is my confirmed opinion that you are never going to be a safe and competitive rally driver at high speed unless you can powerslide on poor surfaces.

Sliding with front-wheel drive or four-wheel drive needs a totally different technique, with most of the power going to the front wheels. Use more power to correct excessive yaw, which is the opposite technique to correcting rear-wheel drive oversteer. If the four-wheel drive has more power proportioned to the rear (as in a Porsche 911 4WD) then the car control technique is similar to rear-wheel drive, and is remarkably efficient. Modern works rally cars are neutral and are very easy to drive on the limit, with hardly any excessive steering angles to apply, and in consequence, they are very fast and safe.

Try to acquire a flowing style, using minimal steering inputs, without sharp edges. The greatest skill is acceleration sense to gain speed early and to control the car. Don't be hard on the brakes. The difference between the good and the very good is that the very good brake less. Know your car's limitations by spending weeks of testing to try to break it! Then, cure all the problems with preventative maintenance. Strengthen what you have to and lighten the rest.

Pace notes have to be honed and perfected with brevity. Plan far ahead and be sure the notes are read in sync with your forward planning, or ever so slightly before the hazard comes into view. Bends and surfaces must be graded on the notes. Use simple words or numbers to describe various hazards: flat right

# REVERSING A RACING CAR TRAILER
## Reversing technique when towing

Secure the load and be certain the hitch and lights are 100% secure and working before you set off

All-round observation is essential for the safety and convenience of other road users, including pedestrians. Don't complicate the technique; keep it simple in your mind, keep looking all around to be sure the road remains clear, front, rear and all around

Use minimum steering angles to correct. Use the car to reverse the trailer. Try not to think what the front wheels need to do

Watch the front of the car to be sure it does not cause obstruction to someone passing. Stop if anyone is approaching. Ask a friend to help and keep watch

Not too far

Only practice will enable you to master reversing. Try to reverse in a straight line to begin with

or left – slight – fast – square – long – back – open – tightens – hairpin – crest. Have codes and numbers to signify approximate distances. Any mistake or mistiming will mean a crash into the trees, or over a cliff! Professional trust on both sides of the car will enable you to blend together with your navigator to make an efficient team.

Be calm, calculating, deliberate and decisive. Don't fight the car – it costs time. Be smooth, concentrate on using the power early and shape your steering path to be straight as soon as you can, with plenty of margin for safety at the exit; in other words don't develop the habit of using the full width of the road as the corner finishes. Most accidents occur at the exit of the corner so choose a late apex every time.

Don't lose your way, or be late at control points; many rallies are lost by being late on the road. Concentrate all the way, even on quiet road sections – you're still rallying. Ask your co-driver to drive, particularly if you feel tired as the adrenalin subsides. Drive gently, and very quietly through villages, particularly at night, and keep to the spirit of the law. It's no excuse to say that you are an exception, just because you are driving on a rally. So what? It is still a public road. You will be eliminated if you commit a traffic offence.

In my view you have to have both skill and responsibility to be a safe rally driver, as thousands of enthusiasts will be watching. There is a profound and clear distinction between skidding and powersliding. Even though powersliding is under your control, at any moment it could become a skid out of control and it is therefore reckless to practise on a public road. Acquire the skill under expert coaching at a proving ground before you enter a rally. My advice is not to enter a rally unless you can powerslide safely, as rally driving requires a wide range of driving skills on all surface conditions.

Highly skilled roadcraft is also essential to drive safely and progressively between stages. As a seasoned race and rally driver you will

*In my Super Seven at Snetterton's 'bomb hole', demonstrating with a passenger at a track day.*

acquire years of experience of extreme car control at high speed. This enables you to be calm under the pressure of an emergency, and have handling skill in reserve to help you to avoid any accident situation.

I have found that long experience of competition driving is a great help for advanced motoring, as you lose any tendency towards inappropriate speed-happiness. You will avoid skidding like the plague. You become a balanced and mature advanced driver, relaxed and content with the world of people, cars and driving, knowing that next weekend you are going to enjoy the ultimate challenge to your motoring skills in competition with highly-skilled drivers. Only motorsport will help you to gain this sense of proportion.

Remember it is a sport. Enjoy yourself, have a laugh. Becoming so intensely involved with the world of motorsport, you have to guard against being carried away by it all. The highway is where you spend most of your motoring time and mileage, and you never finish learning. So, it is important to continue to develop your roadcraft skills.

As John Miles once said to me, 'There is nothing I enjoy more than driving quickly, but I never forget there is another day tomorrow.'

# 15 Advanced driving in the future

*As long as roads like this remain for enthusiastic drivers to enjoy, there will always be a future for advanced driving.*

**A**s a driving enthusiast I am concerned for our future, but I am also amazed by the science-based technology that is improving cars to make them safer and easier to drive. Undoubtedly our Government is going to ensure that the motor industry will face its responsibility to avoid waste and become less reliant upon fossil-based fuels. However, there is no need for motoring to become nothing more than boring transportation from A to B; competition and demand will see to that, with motorsport leading the way.

## Safety first

Apart from forcing green technology upon us, the Government can, and will, make motoring safer. Already accident statistics have improved – largely, I believe, due to improved secondary safety car design features such as seat belts, airbags, crumple zones and the electronics of ABS and ESC.

Primary safety, for avoiding the accident in the first place, is far more vital in my view. It is in this area that the Government can be of far greater influence. After all, it is the driver who must always accept responsibility for being in control of his or her own behaviour on the road. Currently, I believe motorists are giving the impression of being defeated by an oppressive motoring environment.

'Safe driving for life' (the DSA objective) has been proven during almost half a century of continuous operation of the High Performance Course. You could say that HPC has an almost unique record. Since my days at Hendon in the late 1960s, we have been grading all drivers who have taken training with HPC, based upon the system used at police driving schools. Let me explain.

Originally, police drivers attended a standard course of five weeks. The first week was spent in the classroom learning the mechanical theory needed to become a sympathetic driver; how engines, clutches, gearboxes, brakes and suspensions work. This was followed by 45 hours of training behind the wheel to achieve a grade of Class 5.

If you drove well, showing the promise to become a future traffic officer, you would be given extra training on vans and be classified as Class 4. After 18 months to two years of experience, you would be asked to return to the driving school to take a short, Class 3, intermediate course of two weeks and 25 hours' duration, to see if you had the mental and physical ability to drive both rapidly and safely.

Only when a vacancy occurred would you return to the driving school for the advanced course. It was of six weeks' duration, with 105 hours behind the wheel of (relatively) high-performance cars. If you gained more than 86% on your final drive you would be classified as a Police Class 1 driver. If you gained a lower mark, you would be Class 2. Three senior officers would sit in judgement of each student to check that their driving was beyond any reproach at speed.

I believe driver classification or grading should be reintroduced, not only in the police service, but also in the civilian motoring world, to raise the driving standard amongst all riders and drivers. It would undoubtedly be expensive, but less expensive than the ultimate price. The cost could be paid for in the private sector by raising the insurance premiums of less safe, accident-prone, inexperienced drivers.

## Better testing

The first step I would like to suggest is to improve the basic L-test run by the DSA, as 20 per cent of all fatal and serious injury accidents are caused in the first year by males aged between 17 and 25, in mostly single-vehicle crashes on country roads, particularly on unlit roads at night.

Here is what I would suggest to improve and extend the L-test for novices:

*Yours truly about to set off to provide advanced driving instruction in an HPC Triumph TR8 – the pupil is motoring journalist David Vivian.*

*Caterham branded its ultimate Super Seven the 'HPC' and required all customers to take the High Performance Course.*

⊘ Introduce a written exam on the *Highway Code* and the DSA book, *Driving*.

⊘ Improve hazard perception, to test observation, anticipation and forward planning. Not, as it is at present, mostly a test of reaction in staged scenarios.

⊘ Split the practical driving test into two sections. Part one, lasting one hour, should include not only town driving as at present but also country road driving with overtaking and making reasonable progress, negotiating bends and hills, and single and dual carriageways on primary routes.

⊘ Part two of the practical driving test, also one hour long, should encompass

motorway and night driving on unlit roads.

After passing the L-test, a further series of tests could grade drivers in five stages:

⊘ Grade 5. An advanced driving test (two hours) would include all the elements of the L-test, but to a higher standard of progress and safety, based on police driving technique. It would be conducted by the Institute of Advanced Motorists (IAM), the Royal Society for the Prevention of Accidents (RoSPA), the Driving Instructor Association (DIA), or the High Performance Course (HPC). Drivers would need to pass this test before attempting the next grade.

⊘ Grade 4. An equivalent to the RoSPA Gold test (three hours), encompassing all of the above, plus night driving on unlit

roads. It would be conducted by RoSPA, HPC, the DSA or the DIA. No more than four minor faults in driving would be acceptable to pass, before being permitted to acquire the next grade.

◉ Grade 3. Achieved after two and a half days of training with the BSM High Performance Course, visiting the proving grounds of Millbrook and MIRA to assess safe handling skills and potential safe use of speed, as well as assessing roadcraft on the public roads to and from these venues, with commentary. All driving technique would be based upon police driving methods for safety. This grade must be acquired before being considered for the next grade.

◉ Grade 2. Professional coaching under the supervision of an approved driving instructor who is police-trained – a serving or retired police driving instructor – at speeds appropriate in daylight on country roads, to assess the mental and physical ability to travel safely in excess of the national speed limit. The length of training to be given would be appropriate for each individual driver or rider. After this coaching, a driving test would be arranged with a qualified advanced police driver examiner, with the instructor in attendance, the test to be taken at the nearest police driving school.

◉ Grade 1. Awarded to swift and completely safe drivers who gain a pass mark of more than 86%, and have proven, after extensive coaching, to be among the best drivers in the world, capable of driving both fast and safely.

We produce the best racing drivers in the world on the circuits, so let's produce the safest drivers on British highways.

## Incentives for improvement

If drivers are not inspired to receive coaching, they will not take it, unless they are already enthusiasts for advanced driving or have high-performance cars and wish to use them safely on a proving ground or circuit. There seems to be an enormous demand for track days, which are in my view inappropriate and of limited value for improving driving on the public road.

To provide sufficient incentive to improve the standard of safe driving, I consider it essential to give Grade 1 drivers an exemption from the national speed limit between the official times of dawn till dusk, in good clear weather conditions. This will, I believe, raise driving standards and encourage lane discipline on motorways and the proper use of mirrors, as in Germany.

I have proven on the High Performance Course that there are motorists who do have the funds, time and skills to achieve HPC Gold or Grade 1. As a percentage of the overall motoring population this is tiny, about 0.001% of the 30 million car and motorcycle drivers. With the numbers involved, it should cause no significant increase in the 14 per cent of the UK's total $CO_2$ emissions currently caused by cars and motorcycles.

Driver grading would require an amendment to road traffic law, with regard to this speed limit exemption, for it to be recognised in the system by the Government, the police and the judiciary. You never know, but if the Government could see the sense of a national speed limit exemption for the elite of safe drivers who are Grade 1, the present national speed limit might be our greatest asset in providing an incentive to improve.

As in aviation, the answer to improving driving standards is education and training. Better driving means fewer accidents, which means more revenue. It would be self-funding through the insurance industry.

Driver grading would also give far greater flexibility for the judicial system to grade the severity of any traffic offence to fit the crime, and to proportion the remedial training required. It may encourage pride in driving, and encourage drivers and riders not to re-offend.

It also must be seen as desirable to have periodic training and testing every five years to maintain standards and reassess the driver grade acquired so far. This element should not only be mandatory, but backed by financial incentives from the insurance industry, reflecting the realistic increase in safety, skill and expertise that evolves with time and the experience of each road user.

High-performance cars, particularly in the supercar bracket, demand to be driven well, with a heavy weight of responsibility resting on the driver. Supercars will never disappear and performance will increase as time goes by, national speed limit or not. But does the driver match the performance of the car? Superbikes will also continue to be made and it is even more vital that the rider's responsibility and skill matches the motorcycle's ability.

The alternative is to stay as we are. Apart from fleet training, the DSA is mostly involved with training and testing inexperienced and novice drivers. There is no official advanced driver training for Approved Driving Instructors (ADIs), only voluntary testing to fleet standard, which, in my experience, is only equivalent to Grade 5.

The basic L-test is not providing sufficient incentive to the general public, or the driver training industry, to improve. The L-test forms the beginning of our motoring experience, but is that experience sufficiently wide, given the limited time element of the driving test? After turning right, overtaking a moving hazard on a two-way road is the second major cause of death or serious injury; is that situation properly covered by the L-test? What about night driving, motorways, skid control and taking bends and corners on country roads, where many single vehicle crashes occur to tyro male drivers? Is the L-test fit for purpose?

Grade 1 drivers (Gold Driving Club members) will need to be identified easily by other road users with a gold background to the number plate, an electronic chip in the windscreen of the car (behind the driving mirror), and Tracker. The driving licence would be identified visually and electronically for traffic patrol officers to inspect.

For the most serious of traffic offences, sentences, in my view, should be more severe than they are at present. It also seems to make no sense to give a licence back to an offender after a long ban without giving them remedial training. The problem, caused either by the wrong attitude, or bad habits like tailgating, will persist, possibly causing another crash. In the event of any blameworthy crash, a driver could be degraded to the basic level and points added, or a ban given, depending on the severity of any offence, including exceeding any posted speed limit.

Eventually, when it is considered that the public on the road will accept it, the European satellite Galileo will control our speed electronically. Meanwhile, if the authorities read this book, I hope they don't give me the same sort of treatment that was meted out to Galileo all those centuries ago.

I consider Great Britain to be no longer Great, but slowly falling asleep at the wheel. I am not nihilistic, but altruistic, and I suggest we wake up the 'Lyon' in Great Britain again. Let us show that we can drive both fast and safely at the right time and in the proper place, and make British motorists the great advanced drivers that they should be.

It is my sincere wish that you enjoy a lifetime of both swift and safe driving. I hope that *Advanced Driving* will help you to appreciate what is involved and that the hard work required does not put you off. Instead, let's try to further our enjoyment and skill in safe driving. I am sure that if you follow my advice, your contribution will be profound.

*Porsche Cayman S in its element, on a rewarding cross-country route in Rutland.*

# Index